LANDMARKS OF THE WORLD

LANDMARKS
OF THE WORLD

BILL PRICE

canary
press

This 2007 edition published by Canary Press,
an imprint of Omnipress Limited, UK.

ISBN 13: 978-0-95379-762-2

Printed and bound in Thailand

1 3 5 7 9 10 8 6 4 2

Design concept: Omnipress Limited
Cover design: Anthony Prudente on behalf of Omnipress Limited
Images: courtesy of Getty

INTRODUCTION

Like many words in the English language, the term 'landmark' can take on a number of different meanings. For the purpose of this book it is used to describe any feature, whether man-made or natural, that has acquired a special significance beyond its physical appearance, or its mere function.

Of course the choices in our final list are entirely subjective, but this book would be of no real use if I had just written about places I like. If I had come up with a set of my personal favourites alone I might have included my back garden, but although it is undoubtedly a landmark to me, if I was being honest, it isn't even a landmark in my street, never mind in the wider world. Most would agree that there is a core selection of locations that any list of greatest landmarks simply would not be complete without. The Grand Canyon, the Great Wall of China and the Leaning Tower of Pisa are just a few of these high-rollers, all of which

feature in the book. I have also included a large number of articles on lesser known landmarks which are certainly no less phenomenal. Who knows, they may even entice the reader to explore places like the exquisite Alhambra Palace in Spain or the labyrinthine streets of Mont-Saint-Michel for themselves.

In compiling this list of the greatest landmarks in the world, no rigorous selection criteria were applied other than all the places chosen had to be exceptional. It's true that many featured sites — like the magnificent Chartres Cathedral, or the Dome of the Rock — are extremely beautiful. These I have chosen not for their beauty alone, but for the haunting effect that beauty has had, and continues to have, on countless generations of visitors. These are special, often sacred places that are able to inspire a sense of awe in people regardless of culture or faith. Few things can alter the human spirit like witnessing first-hand the white-rush of Niagara Falls,

or basking in the coloured light from the stain glass window at Notre Dame.

One cannot help but notice certain recurring themes in these incredible structures. For example, both the Taj Mahal and the pyramids of Egypt were built for love and grief and as a mark of memorial. Other featured landmarks are bombastic symbols of wealth and influence. Some are ancient — like the Pantheon in Athens, and some are contemporary — like the Burj Al Arab in Dubai, but both these buildings share a strikingly similar raison d'etre — to communicate a message of growing cultural dominance to the rest of the world. One thing is for sure — while fashion, architecture, technology and even gods change — the sources of man's ambition and motivation have remained the same throughout time.

One thing that has become apparent to me during the course of writing this book is how extraordinary our world remains. I suppose I had become so used to the

horror stories surrounding its continued destruction that I had lost sight of the spectacular beauty that is still present. I am not for a moment suggesting that the many threats are not real. I know we have nothing to be complacent about, but I do think that we should occasionally celebrate what we still have, rather than continue to mourn all that has been lost and despair for the future. The Galapagos and the Serengeti. Lake Baikal and the Amazon. These for me are among the most wonderful places in the world. Having said that, if I had to pick one of all the landmarks in this book, I'd choose the Battlefield of the Somme, not because it is a natural wonder, certainly it is not, but because it holds important family associations for me. I am responding to it through my experience of life and, where someone else might see a collection of farmers' fields, I am looking at a landscape of memories.

CONTENTS

ALCATRAZ

In the 18th century, when California was still a Spanish colony, a small island in the middle of San Francisco bay was named La Isla de los Alcatraces, the Island of Gannets, no doubt because of the seabird colony which is still a feature of the island today. The name had been Anglicised to Alcatraz Island by the time California was annexed by the United States in 1850 and, as San Francisco was expanding rapidly during the Gold Rush, a lighthouse and fort, which included a military prison, were built on the island.

These days Alcatraz Island belongs to the National Park Service, as part of the Golden Gate Recreation Area. It is one of the most popular tourist attractions in the area, being only a short ferry ride from Fisherman's Wharf in San Francisco. Visitors can admire the views of San Francisco and the bay area, visit the oldest working lighthouse on the West Coast and walk around the ruins of the fort, but what they have really come to see is what has made the island infamous, the prison. Known worldwide as Alcatraz or 'The Rock', the military prison was converted into a federal prison in 1934. The Federal Bureau of Prisons selected the island as the site of a maximum security penitentiary to house prisoners who were considered to be incorrigible or too dangerous to be held within the existing prison system. Alcatraz, which is clearly visible from San Francisco, can be interpreted as the Federal Government's wish to demonstrate its commitment to tackling the rapidly increasing crime rate apparent in America in the late 1920s and early 30s. The Government was doing something about crime and being seen to be doing something.

The prisoners were held in separate cells and had to earn the right to privileges, such as family visits or access to the prison library, by conforming to the rules. When prison officials considered a prisoner to have been reformed, he would be transferred to another federal prison to complete the remainder of his sentence. The capacity of the prison was 336, but it never actually contained the full number. At any one time there would have been

something like 260 prisoners held in the cells. Most of these prisoners were not the famous gangsters and racketeers of the day, although Al Capone and George 'Machine Gun' Kelly both spent time there, but were inmates considered to be in need of reform. Probably the best known of the inmates was Robert Stroud, the Birdman of Alcatraz, who, contrary to this name and to the title of the book and film of his life, did not actually keep birds on Alcatraz. Originally convicted of manslaughter in 1909, he was sentenced to death for the murder of a prison guard in Leavenworth Federal Penitentiary in 1920, which was commuted to life imprisonment after his mother petitioned President Wilson. While serving this sentence he began to study canaries, going on to write two books about them, but was transferred to Alcatraz in 1942 where he was not allowed to continue keeping birds. He was transferred to a medical facility in 1959 and died there in 1963 after having served 54 years in prison. The film, starring Burt Lancaster, in a somewhat fictionalised and sanitised version of his life, brought Alcatraz even further into the public's attention than it had been already.

There is no clear evidence of any successful escapes from the prison, although a total of five people are still listed as being 'missing presumed drowned' after attempting to escape. It is not known for certain if any of these five survived, including Frank Morris and John and Clarence Anglin, the subjects of the Clint Eastwood film *Escape from Alcatraz*. The possibility of these escapes having been successful is often put forward as the main reason for the closure of the prison in 1963, but, in fact, it was closed because it was expensive to run and was causing pollution in San Francisco Bay. After the prison was abandoned various uses for the island were proposed, including converting the prison buildings into a hotel, but nothing came of any of the ideas. In 1969 the island was occupied by Native Americans, who described themselves as 'Indians of All Tribes' and were protesting over the treatment of Native Americans and laying claim to

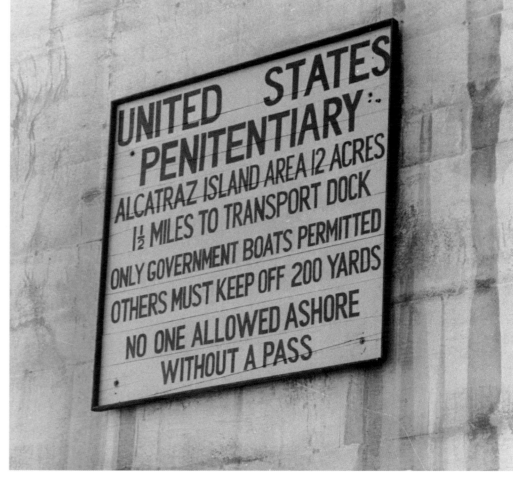

the island. The protest lasted for 18 months and did not succeed in its immediate aims, but it is now thought of as one of the starting points of the Native American push towards self-determination.

After the occupation the island returned to its abandoned state for a number of years until it was taken over by the National Park Service. Today there are no permanent residents, other than the numerous seabirds, but the remaining abandoned buildings are a prominent reminder of its notorious past.

FACT FILE

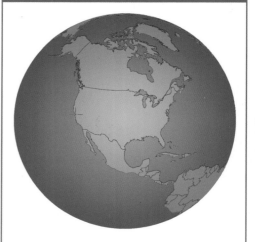

COORDINATES
37°49'35" N, 122°25'22" W

LOCATION
San Francisco Bay Area, California, USA

AREA
18.86 acres (0.0763 km²)

FEDERAL PRISON
1934 –1963

ALHAMBRA PALACE

The Moorish presence on the Iberian Peninsula began in AD 711 and would last for over 700 years. This Muslim caliphate of Al-Andalus in what was otherwise an entirely Christian Europe would become highly sophisticated and cultured and showed tolerance towards the non-Muslim inhabitants of the region. It would, at various different stages, occupy the whole of what is now Spain and Portugal and, at its maximum extent, included parts of the South of France. By the 13th century the Christian reconquista, or reconquest, had taken much of the territory back and, in 1236, Granada, the last remaining part of Moorish Spain under the Nasrid ruler Sultan Muhammed ibn Alhamar, was subjugated by the Christian King of Castile, Ferdinand III. In order to retain Granada, Muhammed had sided with Ferdinand against the Muslim rulers of Seville and, when they had been beaten, Granada had become a vassal state of Castile, paying tribute to Ferdinand in exchange for independence.

The Sultan began work on his palace, the Alhambra, situated on a rocky plateau above Granada, where an older fort, the Alcazaba, already existed, in 1248 and many of the 23 sultans who followed him would extend and alter the palace over the 250-year history of Nasrid rule of the city. Muhammed II, who ruled from 1302 to 1309, built the Generalife, the summer palace of the sultans, lower down on the hill, as a place for relaxation away from the court and where there were two beautifully laid out gardens, called the Court of the Water Channel and the Sultana's Garden. In the second half of the 14th century Muhammed V began a long period of work on the palace, completing many of the buildings that remain today, and this was the last major phase of Nasrid construction. During the late 15th century, King Ferdinand and Queen Isabella of Castile began the Spanish Inquisition, which was aimed initially at converting the Jews and Muslims of Spain to Christianity and would gradually become more intolerant towards all faiths other than their own Roman Catholicism. In 1489 Muhammed XII, who was known as Boabdil in Spain, was summoned to their court and ordered to surrender Granada and, when he refused, they sent a Castilian army to take the city by force. It was under siege for more than two years until, eventually, Boabdil was forced to surrender, putting an end to the last Moorish Sultanate in Spain. As he was leaving Granada, Boabdil is supposed to have stopped for one last look at his beautiful palace and he is said to have shed a few tears. The spot were he stood is still known in Spain as el Utimo Suspiro del Moro, the Moor's Last Sigh.

The name of the Alhambra is said to be a corruption of the Arabic for Red Castle, referring to the colour of the outer brickwork, which appears to glow when the sun catches it. After it was captured by the Castilians, a large palace was built in the middle of the Moorish one, called the Palace of Charles V, and it is completely out of place with the subtle and beautifully designed buildings of the Nasrid period. These are an expression in architecture, the decorative arts and landscape design of an Islamic view of paradise of earth and, as in all palaces in the Islamic world, it is made up of three elements: the royal palace, an area for administration and business, and the harem. During construction, over a period of several hundred years, it became a complex of halls, apartments and open courts, linked by numerous corridors, and many of its rooms are light and airy and decorated with tiling, geometric patterns, Islamic calligraphy and arabesques.

Perhaps the best known feature is the Court of the Lions, an open space with a central fountain, held up on the backs of twelve lions and from which four streams of water emanate, symbolising the four rivers of paradise, and supplying all the water features in the other courts and gardens. The court is surrounded by a wonderful gallery supported by 124 white marble columns, which have arches between them decorated with delicate scrollwork. The Court of the Myrtles has a long pool running along its centre, with goldfish swimming in it and lined by a row of myrtle bushes on either side. The largest and most elaborately decorated room is the Hall of the Ambassadors and this is where the Sultan placed his throne, which was opposite the entrance and had its lighting arranged so that the Sultan could see people coming in to visit him without them being able to see him. The room forms a square and has a dome on top of it, to represent the seven heavens, another common feature of Islamic architecture and another way of representing paradise.

FACT FILE

COORDINATES
37°10'37" N, 3°35'24" W

LOCATION
Spain

CONSTRUCTION
1248 –1354

AREA
35 acres (0.142 km²)

THE AMAZON

The sheer scale of the Amazon, both of the river itself and of its drainage basin, is hard to convey because the numbers involved become so huge it is difficult to appreciate what they mean. It is about 4,000 miles (6,400km) long and, in its lower reaches, can be up to 7 miles (11km) wide during the dry season, expanding to a width of 25 miles (40km) in the rainy season. The mouth of the river is 200 miles (325km) wide and it is responsible for the discharge of a fifth of all the freshwater entering the oceans from all the rivers in the world. The Amazon basin covers about 40% of the entire continental landmass of South America and supports the largest area of rainforest in the world, an important and extraordinary ecosystem which is one of the most species-rich environments on the planet. This huge watershed, which drains water from nine countries, together with the extremely high levels of rainfall throughout this equatorial region, is the main reason for the enormous scale of the Amazon.

It has proved difficult to pinpoint the exact source of the river because of the number of tributaries that flow into it, but, in recent years, the run-off from glaciers in the Peruvian Andes has been identified as the most likely place. It runs westwards and, as it enters Brazil, is known as the Solimões, or the Upper Amazon. From here onwards the river flows through uninterrupted rainforest all the way to the Atlantic Ocean. It is not until it reaches the city of Manaus, the major city and port on the river, that it is actually called the Amazon. From Manaus to the Atlantic, a distance of about 1,000 miles (1,600km), the gradient of the river is extremely shallow, except for a relatively narrow stretch of fast flowing water at the town of Óbidos, where the river is a mile (1.6km) wide and 200ft (60m) deep. As it approaches the ocean, it splits into several channels and, during the rainy season, from November to June, it floods a huge area of land. As the river enters the ocean it is so wide it becomes more like a sea than a river. There are islands the size of small countries in the channels and a huge and fast-flowing tidal bore.

The river, like the rainforests around it, supports a great diversity of life, including the notorious piranha, freshwater dolphins, anacondas and an astonishing variety of fish, including the araipama, the largest freshwater fish in the world. The rainforests are literally teeming with life, an often bizarre range of animals and plants filling a vast array of ecological niches from the forest floor to the canopy high above. An indication of this incredible diversity can be gathered from the fact that there can be more species of trees in a single acre of the Amazon rainforest than there are in the whole of the British Isles. Each rainforest tree supports a community of animals and plants, often ones unique to the area in which they are found.

People have been living in the Amazon basin for many thousands of years. Numerous indigenous tribes have lived by hunting and gathering and have practised shifting cultivation throughout the rainforests and, in areas where they continue to do so, exhibit a remarkable knowledge of their environment and have a minimal impact upon it. More recent settlement has not always been so benign and, while it is hard to criticise landless people for clearing land to grow crops, the profit-motivated destruction of the rainforest, which has destroyed something like 20% of the total area so far, has been and continues to be environmentally disastrous.

Exploitation of the resources of the Amazon began in earnest with the extraction of rubber during and after World War II, which led to the opening up of large areas of the Amazon basin. The building of roads has led to large-scale population movement into the rainforest, causing widespread land clearance for farming and cattle ranching, even though tropical soils are fragile and often highly unsuited to any form of long-term agricultural use. The timber industry, particularly illegal logging activities, also continues to cause extensive damage, although efforts have been made to develop sustainable management practices. The river itself has also suffered from the increasing demands being made on it, through pollution and over-fishing.

It is hard to overemphasise the importance of the Amazon in environmental terms. It is a huge resource of biodiversity, an unparalleled carbon sink and an enormous producer of oxygen. Finding a balance between economic development in the region and the conservation of these precious resources is one of the great environmental challenges of our age.

ANGEL FALLS

South-eastern Venezuela, between the Amazon and Orinoco rivers, is in Bolivar State and remains one of the least explored regions on the planet. In this area, known as the Guayana Shield, there is a unique set of geological features called tepuis, which, in the language of the indigenous Pemón people, means 'Houses of the Gods'. These are table mountains of deeply eroded ancient sandstone, huge rock escarpments that jut out from the rainforests like islands in an ocean of trees. The height and sheer faces of these tepuis, of which there are more than 100 in this region, isolate them from the landscape below, which has resulted in a distinctive array of plants and animals developing on the top of each one of them. Many of these are endemic to their particular location and remain unknown to science. On Auyun Tepui, the Churún river tumbles over the edge of the mountain precipice in a torrent of white water, falling for a total of 3,212 feet (979m), with an uninterrupted drop of 2,648 feet (807m), which makes it the highest waterfall in the world with, also, the highest single drop. Known as Angel Falls, Salto Ángel in Spanish, and as Kerepakupai Merú by the Pemón, meaning 'fall from the deepest place', it is undoubtedly one of the natural wonders of the world.

The story of how the falls came by their English name is a colourful one, although it hardly seems fitting for such a wonderful place to get a name in such a manner. In the 1920s and early 30s an intrepid American pilot named Jimmy Angel made several flights across the region, employed by prospectors to look for places where gold and diamonds may be found. On one of these flights he spotted the falls and, several years later, in 1937, having raised the money for an expedition, set out in a borrowed plane with his wife and a small party of Venezuelans he had talked into going with him. In a manoeuvre best described as being somewhere between a landing and a crash, he set his plane down on the top of Auyun Tepui, right in the middle of a bog. The plane was stuck fast, so the only way they could get out was on foot. Fortunately for all concerned one of the Venezuelans, Gustavo Heny, was an experienced traveller in this difficult environment. They managed to descend the treacherous face of the tepui and walk to safety, but they had seen the falls, which, despite having been described on previous occasions by other people, were named after Angel, who, in subsequent years, became something of a cult hero in Venezuela. Thirty-three years later his plane was airlifted from the site of its crash landing by helicopter and it can now be seen outside the airport in Ciudad Bolívar, the capital city of Bolivar State. Rather bizarrely, a replica of the plane has been placed on the spot of the original landing and can still be seen there today.

Another expedition in 1949, including the photo-journalist Ruth Robertson, who reported on it for *National Geographic*, was somewhat better organised and equipped. This expedition travelled to the base of Auyun Tepui and definitively

established the height of the falls, confirming them as being the world's highest. The resulting article in *National Geographic* brought the falls to the attention of the wider world for the first time.

In 1962 the area became the Canaima National Park and it was designated as a UNESCO World Heritage site in 1994. There are few roads into the Park, transport being mainly by canoe, on foot or by plane. This remoteness has been instrumental in preserving the pristine nature of the area. As one person who made it to the falls felt the need to remark when he got there, there were no souvenir shops or snack bars anywhere in the vicinity. This does not mean that it is completely impossible to go there. Perhaps the best way of seeing the falls, at least for those of us who do not feel adventurous enough to set off on an expedition through the rainforest ourselves, is to join one of the many escorted tours operating out of Ciudad Bolívar. Typically these tours fly into the National Park and transfer people to within walking distance of the falls by canoe. It is also possible to get on a tour in Caracas which includes a fly-past of the falls but, as the tour operators are keen to point out, the falls are often enveloped in cloud, making a good view of them more a matter of luck than judgement. Despite the difficulties and uncertainties involved, people who have seen the Angel Falls rarely come away with any other sense than a feeling of awe.

ANGKOR WAT

Angkor was the capital city of the Khmer Empire, which encompassed modern day Cambodia and, at various different times, parts of Vietnam, Thailand and Laos, between the 9th and 15th centuries ad. As the Empire declined and fell apart, the city was abandoned and gradually reverted to forest or was converted into farmland. The ruins of the city lie on the northern shore of the Tonlé Sap lake and river system near the Cambodian city of Siem Reap and, since 1995, have held the status of a UNESCO World Heritage Site.

Temple building was a feature of the Khmer Empire throughout its history and there are thought to have been somewhere in the region of 1,000 temples in Angkor. Although many of these have been conserved and restored, many more exist now as little more than a few bricks in the grass which mark the spot where a temple once stood. Only one of the temples has been in continuous use since the time it was built, which has meant that it is the best preserved of all the temples in the area. This is Angkor Wat and it is one of the largest and most magnificent religious buildings in the world. Evidence of the regard with which it is held in Cambodia can be seen from the national flag, which has a depiction of the temple at its centre.

Built at the zenith of the Khmer Empire in the early 11th century, during the reign of Suryavaman

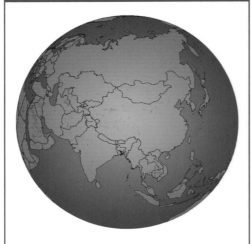

FACT FILE

COORDINATES
13°24'45" N, 103°52'00" E

LOCATION
Angkor, Cambodia

CONSTRUCTION
early 12th century

ARCHITECTURAL STYLE
Khmer

II, it is the epitome of classical Khmer architecture. It was originally built as a Hindu temple, dedicated to the god Vishnu, but was converted to a Buddhist temple at some point in the 15th century and continues to be used as such today.

The temple itself is built of sandstone, unlike many of the earlier temples, which are of brick, and it is surrounded by an outer wall and, beyond that, a moat. A causeway crosses the moat on the western side, which leads to a richly ornate gotura, the entrance building of the temple. The total land area extends to about 200 acres (81ha) and was originally designed, as are many Hindu temples, as a symbolic representation of Mount Meru, the mythological home of the Hindu deities. This is achieved with three layered rectangular galleries, each raised above the next in the manner of a step pyramid. The central, and highest, gallery has five towers, one at each corner of the rectangle with the tallest tower in the middle. This quincunx, as it is known, symbolises the five peaks of the mountain, while the walls and moat represent the surrounding mountain ranges and the ocean. An unusual feature of Angkor Wat is that the temple is oriented to the west, while almost all the other temples in Angkor face to the east. It has not been firmly established why this is so, but it may be because of the temple's dedication to Vishnu or because, when the temple was built, it was intended to be used as the mausoleum of Suryavaman II.

At the time of its building the temple would have been at the centre of Angkor's spiritual community and it provided living quarters for as many as

20,000 people. Ordinary people were allowed to enter the temple but could go no further than the first level, while the second level was reserved for priests who had retired from the outside world to meditate. The third level was accessible only to the king and the high priests.

The walls of the temple are covered in bas-reliefs, flat stones that have been carved in such a way so as to leave a raised picture of the subject on the stone. These bas-reliefs, some of the most extensive anywhere in the world, depict scenes from Hindu mythology, perhaps the best know of which is the Churning of the Sea of Milk, in which Vishnu appears along with his turtle avatar and numerous gods and demons. There are also many devatas, depictions of heavenly nymphs, decorating the walls and, after it was converted to a Buddhist temple, the central shrine, which had previously been open, was walled in and the walls decorated with depictions of the Buddha.

Work on conserving Angkor Wat has been an ongoing project since the end of decades of war and civil strife in Cambodia in the early 1990s. The primary concern of the conservation effort is to stabilise the structure, parts of which have been in danger of collapse, and to prevent any further erosion of the bas-reliefs and devatas. The site is now visited by something like a million people every year, which presents a different conservation challenge, but now that Cambodia appears to be relatively stable, one of the world's greatest examples of religious art and architecture would seem to have a secure future.

THE ARC DE TRIOMPHE

The Arc de Triomphe must be one of the most recognisable examples of monumental architecture in the world today. It is situated at the end of the Champs Elysées, in the centre of the Place Charles de Gaulle, which is still generally known to Parisians by its former name of the Place de l'Etoile, with the Arc de Triomphe usually being called simply l'Etoile. Unfortunately this position also puts it at the centre of an extremely busy and chaotic roundabout, thought to be the largest in Europe, which has 12 streets radiating out from it like the spokes from the hub of a wheel. It is also the centre of L'Axe Historique, a line of wide thoroughfares and monuments beginning at the Louvre and heading westwards out of Paris. There is a museum inside the Arc de Triomphe and steps and a lift up to the top. From here there is an outstanding view of Paris, along the 12 streets radiating out from the Arc de Triomphe and on into the distance.

It was commissioned by Napoleon in 1806 to mark his victory at the Battle of Austerlitz, the decisive battle he fought against a combined Russian and Austrian army which, effectively, put an end to the Third Coalition (a union between Russia and Austria, who were fighting the French Empire on land, and Great Britain, who was fighting the French at sea). The design, by the architect Jean François Chalgrin, was based on the Arch of Titus in Rome and, as such, is often described as being neoclassical. Chalgrin died in 1811 and,

after Napoleon was deposed and exiled to Elba in 1814, work on the monument stopped. It was not finally finished until 1836, during the reign of Louis-Phillippe, the last king to rule France.

It is not easy to get an idea of the size of the Arc de Triomphe from photographs because it is quite a robust, solid-looking structure. It is not until you actually visit it that you realise it is, in fact, impressively large. At 165ft (51m) high and 146 ft (45m) wide it is certainly an imposing building. There are four major statues at the base of each of the masonry blocks that support the arch. Each is by an eminent French sculptor: *The Triumph of 1810* by Jean-Pierre Cortot, *The Resistance of 1814* by Antoine Étex , *Peace* also by Étex, and *La Marseillaise* by François Rude. On the eve of the battle of Verdun, one of the bloodiest and most costly battles of the First World War, the sword in the hand of the female figure symbolising the Republic at the centre of *La Marseillaise*, so the story goes, broke off. The statue was covered over so the French people would not interpret this as a bad omen for the forthcoming battle. Above each of the statues there are friezes and, above them, a long frieze that travels all the way around the building, depicting the symbolic departure and return of the French armies. At the top of the building there are shields inscribed with the names of victorious battles from the Revolutionary and Napoleonic period, and on the inner faces of the arch there are more names of battles and also the

names of French military heroes, with the names of those who died in battle being underlined.

The Tomb of the Unknown Soldier, interred in 1920, lies underneath the arch, along with the Eternal Flame, which is kept burning in memory of all those who died during both World Wars and is rekindled every evening. The simple inscription on the tomb reads 'Ici repose un soldat Francais mort pour la patrie 1914-1918' (Here lies a French soldier who died for his country 1914-1918). Every year on 11 November a ceremony is held here to mark Armistice Day, during which the President lays a wreath on the tomb. It would be fair to say that this brings some balance to the monument, which would otherwise be entirely triumphalist in nature.

Numerous military parades have been held at the Arc de Triomphe, including, infamously, the German army marching through it after the fall of France in 1940, to be followed four years later by the liberating armies of the French and the Allies. The parade to mark French National Day on 14 July starts here and it is also the finishing line of the last stage of the Tour de France. These days it is often seen draped with an enormous French tricolour, which is an obvious sign of a national celebration of one sort or another. Although conceived as a monument to honour victory in war, these days the French themselves view it as more of a symbolic expression and celebration of French national spirit.

FACT FILE

COORDINATES
48°52'25" N, 2°17'42" E

LOCATION
Paris, France

COMMISSIONED
1806

DIMENSIONS
165ft (51m) high – 148ft (45m) wide

ATOMIUM

Belgium, among a number of things it is not particularly famous for, is not overly endowed with internationally well-known landmarks. There are a number of fountains featuring statues of little boys relieving themselves into pools below, there is a beautiful Gothic town hall in Brussels and there is the city of Bruges, known to some as the Venice of the North. It is a country better known for its beer and Tintin than for its buildings, but, perhaps, the exception that proves the rule is the Atomium.

It was originally planned as a centrepiece for Expo 58, the first World's Fair to be held after the Second World War at Heysel Park, on the outskirts of Brussels, and the site of one of the last World's Fairs in Europe, in 1935, before the continent descended into the chaos and destruction of the war. By the mid-1950s, when the Expo was being planned, Belgium was beginning to emerge from the austerity measures and rebuilding period of the immediate postwar years. Sound economic policies, based on the Keynesian model, of a balance between state control and private sector enterprise, combined with aid from the Marshall Plan had seen the country enter a period of recovery and stability. By then it was part of the Benelux Union, a founder member of the European Union and an integral part of NATO, which, as a small country stuck between Germany and France, guaranteed it a much more secure future.

The war had been disastrous for Belgium, with Germany ignoring the country's neutrality, as it had done in the First World War, and unleashing a blitzkrieg in 1940. The Germans occupied Belgium in three weeks, the intention being to use it as a base from which to invade France through the Ardennes, thereby outflanking the French fortifications along the Maginot Line. Belgium endured more than four years of Nazi occupation, until the liberation began by the Allies in late 1944. King Leopold III of Belgium had controversially remained in the country throughout the occupation and had been accused of treason by some Belgian politicians who had left to form a government-in-exile in London. His reputation also suffered by comparison with his father, Albert I, who had become a national hero during the First World War, and by an unpopular second marriage. He went into exile in Switzerland after the war and, although cleared of treason by a tribunal, his return to Belgium in 1951 was met with mass strikes and civil unrest, leading to his abdication in favour of his son, who became King Baudoun I. This constitutional crisis had intensified the already deep divisions within Belgium, with the Flemish-speaking people in the north of the country mostly supporting Leopold and the French-speaking Walloons opposing him.

With a new king and a booming economy, Belgians, in common with much of the rest of the Western world, were becoming more confident and optimistic, and the Atomium, designed by the engineer and metallurgist André Waterkeyn, showed the possibilities of technology and science, which would,

it was thought, lead the way to a brighter future. Its purpose was to represent the arrangement of atoms in the crystal structure of iron, which form what is known as a body-centred cube, but, as it is 335ft (103m) high, magnified, according to Waterkeyn, by a factor of 165 billion. To achieve this, the structure is made up of nine aluminium-clad steel spheres, each 56ft (18m) in diameter and representing an atom of iron, with eight of them positioned at the corner points of the cube and with one in the middle. These are connected with hollow tubes to show the chemical bonds of the lattice structure, which is orientated so the diagonal of the cube is vertical, or, to put it another way, so the whole thing rests on one sphere. A problem came to light immediately with this structure when it was calculated that it would blow over in high winds. Supports were added to the three spheres nearest the ground and these do not represent anything other than structural integrity and safety considerations for the people who go inside it.

There are escalators in the tubes to take visitors to the spheres, where, after a recent renovation, which also replaced the worn aluminium cladding with stainless steel, there are exhibitions and a restaurant. The top sphere has windows in it, allowing for great views of Brussels and the surrounding countryside, proving there is more to Belgium than first meets the eye. There might not be too many famous Belgians, with the exception of the great cyclist Eddie Merckx and the not quite so great actor Jean Claude Van Damme, but there is, at least, one famous building, even if it is not much use for anything.

BIG BEN

The Palace of Westminster, on the north bank of the River Thames and in the heart of London, contains the two houses of the British Parliament, the House of Lords and the House of Commons. The original building, some parts of which dated back to before the Norman Conquest of 1066, was almost entirely destroyed by fire in 1834. The fire is reputed to have started when old tally sticks, an old system of account keeping which involved making notches on a stick, were being burnt in a brazier and the fire got out of control.

The new Palace of Westminster was built on the same spot, taking more than 20 years to complete. The design, by Sir Charles Barry, was in the Gothic Revival style and was selected by a Royal Commission from almost 100 proposals. It included a long river frontage and three towers, the Victoria Tower, St Stephen's Tower and the Clock Tower. The complete building, and particularly the Clock Tower, has become one of the most recognisable buildings in Britain and images of it are now so widespread that it has become a symbol not just of the British Government but of the United Kingdom itself.

The Clock Tower, universally known as Big Ben after the name of the main striking bell, is 316ft (96m) tall in total, made up of the tower itself, which is built of brick with a stone cladding and rests on concrete foundations, and a cast-iron spire. Over the years the stone cladding has been replaced and subsidence, which was causing the tower to tilt,

stabilised, particularly during the construction of the Jubilee Underground line extension, which runs quite close to it. The clock, until quite recently the largest striking turret clock in the world, has four faces, with dials 30ft (9m) across, and strikes on the hour with chimes on the quarter. The mechanism was designed by Edmund Beckett Denison (who later became Lord Grimthorpe) and was built by the clockmaker Edward John Dent and, after his death, by his son Frederick. It was completed some years before the tower was ready, allowing Denison time to experiment with the clock to ensure its reliability. The mechanism he finally settled on is called a gravity escapement, which, because of the separation between the pendulum and the clock mechanism, can be kept very accurate. This is still done now in the same manner as it was when the clock was first installed in 1859 and involves weighting the pendulum with old penny pieces, which went out of circulation in 1971, to adjust its movement. 'To put a penny on it' entered the language as an idiom to suggest some fine tuning was needed, although it is not widely used now.

The original Big Ben was a 14 ton bell cast by John Warner and Sons of Stockton-on-Tees, but it cracked when it was being tested prior to being installed in the tower. An enormous row broke out about whose fault it was and as to whether the bell had been miss-cast or the hammer used to make it sound had been too heavy. The bell was melted down and recast, this time rather lighter in weight, by the Whitechapel Bell Foundry. This bell cracked

shortly after it was installed, initiating another huge row, but, this time, rather than replacing it, the bell was rotated so that the hammer would strike on a different part of it. This is the Big Ben that still sounds in the Clock Tower today.

Various theories have been put forward as to how Big Ben came by its name, such as after Sir Benjamin Hall, the Commissioner for Works for the Clock Tower, or after Benjamin Caunt, a well-known heavyweight boxer of the time, but, wherever the name came from, the sound of Big Ben is now a familiar one throughout Britain. It is broadcast daily on the BBC and has been used for many years during the opening credits of the ITN News as the headlines are being read out. The 'bongs', as they are popularly known, are also extensively used as a countdown to the New Year in London and at parties all over the country.

Big Ben, as a whole, has become associated with reliability and steadfastness, not least because it continued to show the correct time throughout the Second World War, when the Houses of Parliament were extensively damaged in the London Blitz. A few changes have been made over the years, such as replacing the gas illumination of the dial with electric lighting and the winding mechanism with an electric motor. The clock has stopped a few times, and been intentionally stopped occasionally to be repaired, but, in general, it has retained its reputation for being proverbially accurate and reliable.

FACT FILE

COORDINATES
51°30'02" N, 0°07'28" W

LOCATION
Westminster, London, England

CONSTRUCTION
1856

HEIGHT
316ft (96.3m)

BRANDENBURG GATE

Many monuments in the world have either been built with a symbolic purpose in mind or have become a symbol at some point in time, but no other monument can have changed its symbolic meaning as often or in such a contrasting fashion as the Brandenburg Gate (Brandenburger Tor in German). Situated as it is in the middle of Berlin, great historical events have ebbed and flowed through it, particularly during the tumultuous years of the middle and late 20th century, culminating in it now being regarded as was originally intended, as a symbol of unity and peace.

The Brandenburg Gate was built by Carl Gotthard von Langhans between 1789 and 1791 from a commission by Frederick Wilheim II, the King of Prussia from 1786 to 1797. It is located on the Pariser Platz, at the end of the Unter den Linden, and was originally intended as one of a number of gates into Berlin, of which it is the only one still standing. The design, an example of German neoclassicism, is based on the Propylaea, the ceremonial entrance to the Acropolis in Athens, which was built by Pericles in 437 BC. The central part of the gate is made up of 12 Doric columns, 6 on either side, with walls joining the opposing columns through the gate. On each flank are side wings, the guard houses of the gate, which were originally joined on to the city wall, until the wall was demolished in 1868. Above the central columns is the Quadriga, a statue of the winged goddess of peace driving a chariot drawn by four horses, designed by Gottfried von Schadow

and cast in bronze. It was removed after Napoleon captured Berlin in 1806, but returned when he was defeated in 1814, transformed into Victoria, the goddess of victory, with an iron cross held in her hand in place of the original olive branch.

A worse fate was to befall the gate. It was appropriated by the Nazis when they came to power in 1933, marching through it in military parades and using it as a symbol of the Third Reich. The whole area around the gate was destroyed during the Second World War and the gate itself was extensively damaged both by Allied bombing and Russian shelling as they entered the city in 1945. After the war, with Germany divided into East and West, the gate briefly became a sign of unity between the two sides as they cooperated in its renovation. The Cold War intervened and the Berlin Wall left the gate in No Man's Land between the East and the West. Checkpoint Charlie, the iconic crossing point between East and West, was adjacent to the gate, and was, in 1961, the scene of a stand-off between American and Russian tanks, which could have been the spark for a war, but eventually saw the tanks inching away from each other. In the same year John F. Kennedy visited the gate to make his 'Ich bin ein Berliner' speech, which pledged American support for West Germany and, despite numerous reports since, he did not announce to the world in mangled German, 'I am a doughnut'. The Russians, in anticipation of his visit, had draped the Brandenburg Gate with Soviet flags

and banners for the occasion.

So now the gate became a symbol not just of the separation of East and West Germany, but of the Cold War as a whole. In another famous quote the Mayor of Berlin in the early 1980s, Richard von Weizsäcker, said, 'The German question will remain open as long as the Brandenburg Gate is closed'. By 1989 the Cold War had thawed to such an extent that restrictions on travel between East and West Germany were eased. In Berlin this was taken to mean an end to the division of the city and led to a huge party, with people from East and West Germany knocking down large sections of the Berlin Wall with sledgehammers. As ever, the Brandenburg Gate became a symbol for this new freedom, with television pictures of people dancing on it broadcast round the world. In December of that year a crossing point between East and West Berlin was created through the gate and the West German Chancellor, Helmut Kohl, walked through it to be greeted by the East German Prime Minister, Hans Modrow. The following year East and West Germany became formally reunited.

Since reunification the Brandenburg Gate has undergone extensive renovation and large-scale building work has been carried out in the Pariser Platz and the surrounding area. It is to be hope that the Brandenburg Gate's next role will not be one of symbolism for the rampant globalised commercialism that has seen a franchised coffee shop open right next to it.

FACT FILE

COORDINATES
52°30'59" N, 13°22'39" E

LOCATION
Berlin, Germany

CONSTRUCTION
1788–1791

DIMENSIONS
65ft (26m) high, 213ft (65.5m) wide, 36ft (11m) deep.

BURJ AL ARAB

At the Burj Al Arab (the Tower of the Arabs) in Dubai they consider themselves to be the best hotel in the world. While having such an opinion of yourself could be considered to be a little conceited, if luxury and opulence are a measure of such things, then they may have a point. Of course the judgement of the quality of a hotel is an entirely subjective matter, but what cannot be doubted is the extraordinary nature of the building itself.

Dubai is a city state on the Persian Gulf, one of the seven emirates that make up the United Arab Emirates. Its ruler, who is also the Prime Minister and Vice-President of the UAE, is Sheikh Mohammed bin Rashid Al Maktoum and he is one of the richest men in the world, with a fortune estimated as being considerably more than $25 billion (£13 billion). He has been one of the driving forces behind diversifying Dubai's interests away from a dependency on the finite resources of oil, which has included making Dubai a tourist destination. Sheikh Mohammed has been described as the overseer of the project to build the Burj Al Arab. The architect was Tom Wright of the British consultancy Atkins and he has said that his brief was to design a building that would become an iconic or symbolic statement for Dubai, as the Opera House has for Sydney or the Eiffel Tower for Paris.

The design of the building was influenced by the shape of the lanten sail of a dhow, an Arabian sailing ship, billowing in the wind. Building work, carried out by the South African building contractor Murray & Roberts, began in 1994 and the first part of the construction involved establishing an artificial island 919ft (280m) out from the shore. This was achieved by driving concrete piles into the sand on the seabed, which are held in place by friction rather than being driven into rock. Large rocks were then used to create the island itself and the whole lot was then surrounded with more concrete, laid down in a honeycomb pattern in order to protect the foundations from erosion. This work took three years to complete, more time than it took to build the actual hotel.

The hotel itself is built inside a steel exoskeleton held up by a reinforced concrete 'mast'. This consists of a 1,053ft (321m) tower with two wings coming out from it near the top, which form an inverted V going down to the ground. The 'sail' is a huge expanse of a specially produced fibreglass that has been coated with Teflon to protect it from the weather. It faces towards the shore and creates, between it and the wings of the mast, a huge atrium which is 582ft (182m) high and takes up almost a third of the interior space of the building. A helicopter landing pad has also been suspended out over the top of the sail, which has been used for a number of high profile publicity stunts. Tiger Woods has hit golf balls off it into the Persian Gulf and it has been converted into a grass tennis court so Roger Federer and André Agassi could play a game of tennis on it. On occasion it has also been used to land helicopters on.

The sail allows a soft light through into the interior and in the evening it is lit by slowly changing coloured lights. There are 202 suites, all of which are spread over two floors and range from the smallest, with a floor area of 1,800sq ft (169sq m) and costing in the region of $900 (£475) a night, to the Royal Suite, which is the size of a large house, with a floor area of 8,400sq ft (780sq m). Anyone who could actually afford it would probably not bother to ask the price, which is reputed to be in the region of $28,000 (£15,000) a night. For this you get a master bedroom with a rotating four poster bed in it and a second bedroom, each with adjoining marble bathrooms, a private lift, a dining area, a lounge and a library. Furnishings include marble flooring, mahogany furniture, a marble and gold staircase and, apparently, leopard print tufted carpets. All suites come with butler service and a pillow menu, allowing you to choose between 13 different sets of pillows and duvets, and there are chauffeur-driven white Rolls-Royces to take you shopping, although this comes at an extra charge.

There is a choice of eight different eating options, from the Al Muntaha restaurant, situated on the 27th floor on a cantilever overhanging the sea, to a snack in the foyer. Should this all be rather beyond your wallet, but you would still like to look around, the only way of doing so is to pay $50 (£28) to get into the building.

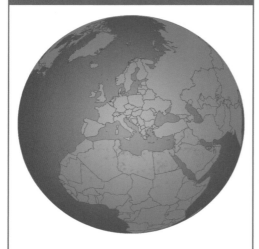

FACT FILE

COORDINATES
25°08'28" N, 55°11'08" E

LOCATION
Dubai City, United Arab Emirates

TOTAL HEIGHT
1,053ft (321m)

ARCHITECT
Tom Wright

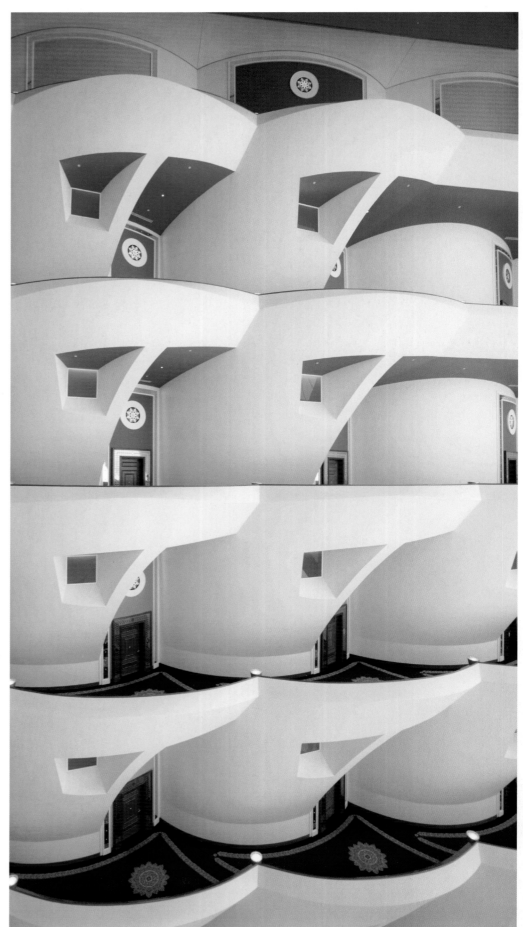

CHARTRES CATHEDRAL

The city of Chartres has a population of 42,000 and is about 50 miles (80km) south-west of Paris. It is in the Beauce, a flat agricultural region between the rivers Loire and Seine, often referred to as the granary of France, and it is the main market town in the region and a centre for the perfume-making industry. But it is famous on account of its cathedral, the Cathedral of Our Lady of Chartres, which is the largest in France and one of the finest Gothic cathedrals in Europe.

The reason why a modest town in rural France should have such a magnificent cathedral relates to its association with the Virgin Mary, which has made it a centre for Marian pilgrimage from at least the 9th century, and possibly from considerably earlier. Archaeological evidence suggests a Gallo-Roman church on the site by the 4th century, but there are stories suggesting it had been a centre for pagan worship in the pre-Christian period. Although there is no evidence for this, it would not have been unusual for the Early Church to position a place of worship of their own on such a site. Further stories relate to the presence of a sacred well where the birth, possibly even the virgin birth, of a divinity was celebrated. Joseph of Arimathea, who, according to the Gospels, was the man who begged Pontius Pilate for the body of Jesus after the Crucifixion and gave up his own tomb for

the burial, is said to have visited Chartres and, on hearing of these associations, to have dedicated the church there to the Virgin Mary. In yet another story, Charles II of France, who was also the Holy Roman Emperor, but was rather unkindly known as Charles the Bald, gave an important relic, a tunic said to have belonged to the Virgin, to the cathedral in 876. There is no way of knowing the truth or otherwise of any of these stories now, but they do give an idea of how deep rooted this association with the Virgin Mary goes. The relic, the Sancta Camisia, remains in the Cathedral Treasury today and continues to attract pilgrims from all over the world.

After a succession of fires destroyed previous cathedrals, culminating in a fire that destroyed almost the entire building and a large portion of the town as well, the bulk of the existing one was built between 1194 and 1220. The design was based on the plans of the earlier cathedral and incorporated those parts that had not been destroyed in the fire, such as the west frontage and the crypts. What makes this particular cathedral so extraordinary is

that it has hardly been touched since, except for a few minor alterations and the rebuilding of one of the spires after it was hit by lightning in the 16th century. The cathedral that stands there today is much the same as it was at the beginning of the 13th century.

Chartres Cathedral is essentially cruciform in plan with a 427ft (128m) nave running east to west and two short transepts to the south and north. More than 2,000 sculpted figures decorate the exterior, with particularly fine examples around the porches, including some dating back to 1140. The large number of flying buttresses around the exterior walls, the first use of this feature in Gothic architecture, spreads the weight of the ceiling away from the walls. This allows for a much higher ceiling, which is 121ft (36m) in the nave, and for narrower columns to support it from the inside, than had previously been possible. The flying buttresses, together with an innovative design for the vaulting in the ceiling, which spreads the load even further, also allow for the inclusion of many more stained-glass windows than in older buildings,

a feature for which the cathedral is justly famous. There are more than 150 altogether, the largest number to have survived together from the 13th century, and they depict narrative scenes from the life of Christ and the Apostles and, of course, the Virgin Mary. The east end of the cathedral is unusually rounded and has an ambulatory with five semicircular chapels radiating out from it, and in the nave there is an extensive labyrinth inlaid in the floor, built in about 1200 and one of the very few still in existence.

Chartres Cathedral has survived the religious wars of the 16th century, the French Revolution and the Nazi occupation. It is now a UNESCO World Heritage Site and, when standing in the nave looking towards the domed apse, with coloured light shining through the high columns, which has the effect of lifting the observer's eyes upwards towards the glory of God, it is possible to appreciate why this cathedral is considered to be one of the finest examples of medieval religious art and architecture.

FACT FILE

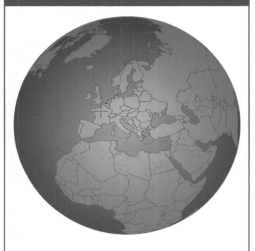

COORDINATES
48°26'50" N, 1°29'16" E

LOCATION
Chartres, France

CONSTRUCTION
begun: 1145
destroyed by fire: 1194
completed: 1220

FLOOR-PLAN
117,058sq ft (10,875sq m)

NUMBER OF STAINED-GLASS WINDOWS
176

CHICHEN ITZA

FACT FILE

COORDINATES
20°40'58" N, 88°34'9" W

LOCATION
Chichen Itza, Vallodolid, Yucatán, Mexico

TOTAL HEIGHT
98ft (30m)

NUMBER OF STEPS
365

CONSTRUCTION
Between 11th and 13th century

The Yucatan Peninsula in southern Mexico is a huge limestone shelf stretching out into the sea, separating the Caribbean from the Gulf of Mexico. These days it is probably best known for two things: the popular tourist destination of Cancun, which lies on its tip, and the extensive ruins left by the Mayan civilisation, which rose and fell in what is called the pre-Columbian period, the time before Europeans arrived in the Americas.

The unusual geology of the Yucatan has dictated where settlements have been established. Water runs through limestone rather than on its surface and, in the Yucatan, in places where the water is quite close to the surface and the limestone above it has collapsed, sink-holes, known as cenotes, have formed. As these are the only sources of a regular water supply, settlements have grown up around them. The extensive ruins of the Mayan city of Chichen Itza is situated in central Yucatan, close to three of these cenotes.

The Mayan civilisation arose in central Guatemala something like 3,500 years ago and gradually spread out, covering what is now southern Mexico, Guatemala, northern Belize and western Honduras by AD 200. It is thought that the Maya never actually formed into a cohesive empire, but existed as numerous city states which often fought wars with each other. By the Classic era, between AD 250 and AD 900, they had developed writing, mathematics, a calendar, astronomy, and a complex system of agriculture. They lived in a highly stratified society dominated by a nobility made up of the religious, military and political elites. Their architecture and their craftsmanship with stone, without the use of metal tools, are remarkable and can be seen all over the region in the ruins of vast cities, many of which include temple pyramids and royal palaces, which were highly decorated with carved stone and painted murals.

The first building phase in Chichen Itza belongs to this Classic era, between the 6th and 9th centuries. These buildings are to the south of the site and include those known as the Nunnery, the Temple of Phalli and the Red House. The architecture is described as being in the Puuc style and is characterised by many representations of the Mayan rain god Chaac. The Nunnery, the largest of this group at 54ft (17m), is so called because its numerous chambers reminded early Spanish visitors of nuns' cells, although it is now thought to have been either a ceremonial building or a palace of the governing elite.

During the 9th century Chichen Itza declined, along with the Mayan civilisation in general. Various theories for this decline, including war, civil strife, famine, disease or some form of ecological catastrophe, have been put forward to explain the decline, but whatever the actual cause, Chichen Itza was only visited sporadically until it was reoccupied after AD 1000 by a Yucatan Mayan group called the Itza. It is during this period, called the Post-Classic era, that the second building phase at Chichen Itza occured. The buildings are decorated with images of the god Kukulcán, the plumed serpent, which is seen as a Toltec influence, although how far this influence went is not known. It is during this period that the monumental buildings that characterise the site today were constructed. The largest is the Temple of Kukulcán, also known as El Castillo, which is a 77ft (26m)-high step pyramid with staircases of 91 steps on each of its four sides, which lead to the temple on the top. At sunrise and sunset on the spring and autumn equinoxes, the sun casts a shadow onto the north staircase, which takes the form of a plumed serpent and appears to slither down the steps as the sun moves, towards a huge stone serpent's head at the bottom.

The Ballcourt, which is 545ft (166m) long, features stone carvings down the side showing teams of ball players, including one where the captain of the losing team has had his head cut off. Some of the other buildings include the Temple of Warriors, the Plaza of a Thousand Columns and the Observatory.

Chichen Itza became all but abandoned again at some point in the 13th century. Again, the reason for this decline is not known, although a power struggle with another group of Maya which resulted in the defeat of the Itza is one possible explanation. Today there remains a large Mayan population in the Yucatan region, who still speak the Mayan language and certainly don't consider themselves to be the remains of a fallen civilisation. As Rigoberta Menchu, the human rights campaigner and recipient of the 1992 Nobel Prize for Peace, who is a Maya, has put it, 'We are not myths of the past, ruins in the jungle or zoos. We are people and we want to be respected, not to be victims of intolerance and racism.'

STATUE OF CHRIST THE REDEEMER

FACT FILE

COORDINATES
22°57'05" S, 43°12'39" W

LOCATION
Tijuca Forest National Park, Corcovado Mountain, Brazil

CONSTRUCTION
1931

HEIGHT
125ft (38m)

The great statue of Christ the Redeemer overlooks Rio de Janeiro, arms outstretched to form the shape of a cross, ready to embrace all people and offering them a deliverance from sin. Some see this open-armed stance as being a sign of the friendly and welcoming nature of the people of Brazil and others, perhaps because the statue's head bends forward slightly, think of it as the shepherd watching over his flock.

The statue stands on the top of Corcovado, which is Portuguese for hunchback, a 2,330ft (710m) granite mountain in the Tijunca National Park. It is 125ft (38m) tall in total, including the 28ft (8m) base, has an arm span of 91ft (28m) and it weighs 1,145 tons. The statue has a steel framework which supports an inner core of concrete. The outer layer is a mosaic of pale cream soapstone, laid over the concrete. Soapstone is a popular material with sculptors because it is easy to carve, does not crack readily and is weather resistant, but it is quite soft and can be damaged easily. It is the largest statue built in the art deco style and one of the most famous examples of this design movement in the world.

The idea of erecting a statue of Christ was first put forward in 1921, as a means of marking the centenary of Brazilian Independence from Portugal in the following year. As well as Corcovado, the Sugarloaf and St Anthony's Hill were also considered for the location, Corcovado being chosen because it is the tallest of the three. A petition for permission to erect the statue was started, collecting more than 20,000 names. The Brazilian President at the time, Epitácio Pessoa, assented to the request, and a foundation stone was laid on 4 April 1922. A competition was then held to find the best project to actually build the statue, which was won by the engineer Heitor da Silva Costa, and fund-raising began to pay for the work. The design was drawn by the Brazilian artist Carlos Oswald, whose initial image showed Christ carrying a cross and holding a globe in his hands, but this proved unpopular with the Brazilian public and it was changed to the present one. It was built in sections by the French sculptor Paul Landowski and transported by train up the mountain to be assembled on the spot.

The statue was finished in 1931 and inaugurated on 12 October in front of the head of the provisional government, Getúlio Vargas, who had led the 1930 revolution and would remain in power in Brazil until 1945. An ambitious plan to have Guglielmo Marconi, the Italian physicist best known for his work on radio communications, to switch on the lights by radio link from his yacht in the Bay of Naples, came to nothing when bad weather interfered with the signal and the lights had to be turned on at the site. Since then the statue has been renovated a number of times, notably on the occasion of Pope John Paul II's visit to Brazil in 1980, and in 2000 when the lighting system was replaced and protected from salt corrosion, which has been the main problem with the statue. The original mortar used in the construction of the statue had salt in it and, over the years, this has corroded the underlying metal frame. The solution to this problem came from a technique used in the shipbuilding industry and involved the installation of an electrified titanium mesh under the outer soapstone mosaic. The system, known as cathode protection, works because the mesh has a positive electric charge, which attracts the negatively charged salt particles, drawing them away from the metal.

In 2003 a system of elevators and escalators was installed from the station on Corcovado up to the statue itself, access to which had previously entailed visitors walking up a stairway of 222 steps, and in 2006 the Archbishop of Rio de Janeiro, Cardinal Eusébio Oscar Scheid, consecrated a chapel under the statue, which can be used for baptisms and marriages. The trip up to the statue from Rio on the Corcovado Rack Railway has become almost as well known as the statue itself. It starts from the station in Cosmo Velho and travels up through the Tijunca Forest, the largest expanse of urban forest in the world, and then out onto the mountain. The panoramic views of Guanabara Bay, Rio's natural harbour, the Sugarloaf and the mountains beyond are spectacular to say the least. The city sprawls out around the bay and it is possible to pick out such well-known landmarks as the beaches of Copacabana and Ipanema and the Maracanã Stadium, where passions of a different order to those inspired by the Statue of Christ the Redeemer are played out.

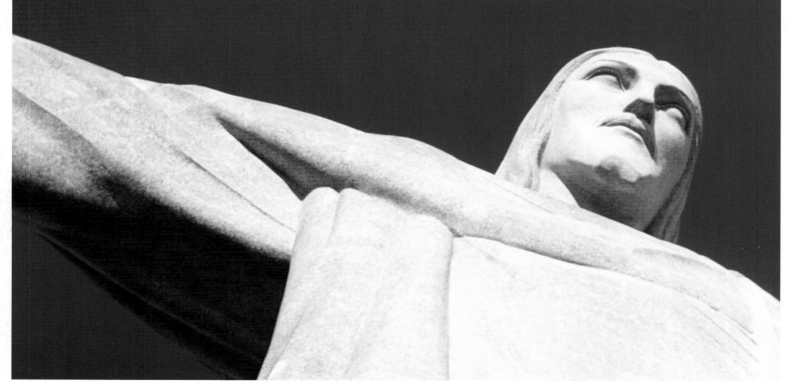

THE CN TOWER

The Council for Tall Buildings and Urban Habitat was founded at Lehigh University in Bethlehem, Pennsylvania, in 1969 and moved to the Illinois Institute of Technology in 2003. It is the compiler of a list of the world's 100 tallest buildings and, to achieve this aim, has developed a set of criteria establishing the terms of reference it uses, making itself the authority on such matters. Currently, the tallest structure in the world is the KVL9-TV mast near Fargo in North Dakota which is 2,063ft (629m) high and is supported by guy-wires. The Warsaw Radio Mast in Poland was 2,115ft (645m), making it the tallest structure ever built, but it collapsed in 1991. Fortunately, no one was hurt. The Petronius Platform, an oil rig in the Gulf of Mexico, has been advanced as the tallest free-standing structure (as opposed to the tallest building) at 2,001ft (610m), but 240ft (75m) of it are underwater and it is partially supported by buoyancy, which rules it out of the running. Due for completion in 2008, the Burj Dubai has been specifically designed to break the record for all the categories of tallest building and tallest structure.

The exact height it will rise to when it is finished is not being divulged, but, if some reports are to be believed, it will be over 3,000ft (935m) tall.

Meanwhile, as of 2007, the CN Tower in Toronto, at 1,815ft (553.33m), holds the title of the tallest free-standing structure on land, a position it has held for more than 30 years, taking over from the Ostankino Tower in Moscow in 1976. It was conceived by CN, who were originally known as the Canadian National Railway but had diversified their business interests by the 1970s, as a large TV and radio platform to overcome broadcasting problems created by Toronto's rising skyline in the 1960s and early 70s. As the plans were developed, the proposed tower gradually got taller and taller, until it was realised that, the way things were going, it could become the world's tallest structure. From then on the plans were changed to make this possible and, although access to the public had always been part of the plans, the design was also modified to include a higher viewing deck in anticipation of the publicity it would attract by breaking the record.

Two firms of architects were involved, John Andrews International and WZMH Architects, and the structural engineers were NCK Engineering. Building work started on 3 February 1973, with the digging of the foundations, which, amazingly for such a tall building, are only 48ft (15m) deep with the main shaft of the tower penetrating into them to a depth of 19ft (6m). The tower is made of reinforced concrete and was built by what is known as the slipform method. Essentially, this involved building a metal platform around the base of the tower into which concrete was poured and, as this concrete became sufficiently hard, moving the platform upwards on huge hydraulic jacks and pouring more concrete in. Using this method allowed the concrete pouring to continue almost continuously and the building rose by about 20ft (6m) a day. Needless to say, an enormous amount of concrete was used altogether. It has been estimated that the combined weight of the concrete and the reinforcing steel is about 132,000 tons.

The finished building was officially opened to the public on 1 October 1976, although it had been in use for several months before that. While the tower had been in construction, plans to develop the land around it had fallen through, leaving the tower rather isolated in a mostly disused industrial area. Since then extensive development has taken place, known as CityPlace. The tower itself now belongs to the Canada Lands Company, a government-owned company to which it was transferred prior to the privatisation of CN in 1995. There are two main visitor areas, the SkyPod at 1,150ft (351m) and comprising of seven floors, which include an outdoor observation deck and a revolving restaurant called 360, and the Space Deck, the world's highest observation deck, at 1,465ft (447m). It takes the elevator about one minute to get from the ground to the SkyPod and there is also a staircase, with 2,579 steps, up to the same spot. The staircase is not open to the public, except in the case of an emergency, although it is used occasionally for charity events. The record for the fastest climb up to the SkyPod was set in 1989 by Brendan Keenoy, an Ontario Police Officer, and it is 7 minutes and 52 seconds. No doubt he trained for the attempt by chasing the local criminals.

FACT FILE

COORDINATES
43°38'33" N, 79°23'13" W

LOCATION
Toronto, Ontario, Canada

CONSTRUCTION
1973–1976

HEIGHT
1,815ft (553m)

ARCHICTECT
WZMH Architects and John Adrews International

NUMBER OF FLOORS
181

COLOSSEUM

For one building to become particularly identified with Rome, a city with an unparalleled historical and architectural heritage stretching back more than 2,500 years, gives some measure of the extraordinary nature of the Colosseum. It is also emblematic of the Roman Empire, being a building of great architectural beauty and technical achievement, the largest amphitheatre in the Roman world, built for the purpose of staging gladiatorial combat, often to the death, and other blood-thirsty spectacles involving executions and the mass slaughter of huge numbers of wild animals. There is no definite proof of Christians actually being fed to lions there, but it is not beyond the realms of possibility.

The period in Roman history immediately prior to the construction of the Colosseum, which began around AD 70, had been a disastrous one for the Roman Empire. The rule of Nero, who famously 'fiddled while Rome burned' and was the last in the line of emperors descended from Julius Caesar, had seen the Empire descend into chaos, riven with internal revolts and threatened on all sides, in the west by what the Romans called 'the barbarians' and in the east by the Persians. Nero committed suicide in AD 68 and civil war broke out between factions within the government and the army who were supporting rival claims for the imperial throne. By the end of AD 69, a year in which there had been four different emperors, Titus Flavius Vespasianus, an experienced and successful military leader, had assumed power, becoming known as

the Emperor Vespasian, the first in the line of the Flavian dynasty. He brought firm rule and stability back to the Empire, restoring discipline to the army and reforming the government. An inscription found in the Colosseum credits him with building it and says that he paid for it out of the spoils of war, building it as a monument to the recent victory in the east, known as the Revolt of the Jews. It was built on land that had been appropriated by Nero for his palace, so it can also be seen as Vespasian drawing a line under the recent past while, at the same time, enhancing his popularity with the Roman public. The Colosseum, or the Flavian Amphitheatre as it is also known (although the Romans themselves called it the Amphitheatrum Caesareum, the hunting theatre), opened in AD 80, by which time Vespasian had died and been succeeded by his son Titus.

The Colosseum was built mainly of travatine stone, held together with iron clamps, but concrete and brick were also used extensively. It is 157ft (48m) high and has three tiers of arcades and an attic above, which has windows in it. A movable canvas awning, called the velarium, hung from the top of the attic and was used to shade the crowd from the sun or when it was raining. It is estimated that it could hold 50,000 people and there are 80 entrances on each level, know as vomitoria (derived from the same root as the word vomit), which allowed people to leave quickly after a show. As with theatres today, the cheaper seats were at the top and the best ones were reserved for the Emperor and his circle. The arena itself was 272ft

(83m) long and 157ft (48m) wide. It had a wooden floor, which was covered in sand and, below it, their was a warren of tunnels and cages where gladiators and wild animals were held prior to their appearance in the arena.

The Roman ruling classes were obliged by law to organise and pay for games in the arena. As well as the gladiatorial bouts and the wholesale slaughter of people and animals, including lions, elephants and crocodiles, it was also used to put on a variety of spectacles, often using elaborate sets to re-enact famous battles or to recreate natural scenes, complete with wild animals. There are accounts of the arena being flooded to stage a naval battle, but it is not known how this was done.

It continued to be used into the 6th century, long after 476, the date usually given for the fall of the Roman Empire. Since then extensive damage has occurred to it through a series of earthquakes, particularly a large one in 1349 which caused a major collapse of one side of the building, and it has been stripped of large amounts of stone, often used to construct other buildings in Rome. The interior marble façade has entirely gone, having been burnt to make quicklime, and there are numerous holes all over the remains of the building where the clamps used to hold the stones together have been dug out of the walls. More recently, extensive restorations have been carried out, particularly between 1992 and 2000, but despite, or perhaps even because, of the ravages of time, the Colosseum remains one of the greatest buildings in the world.

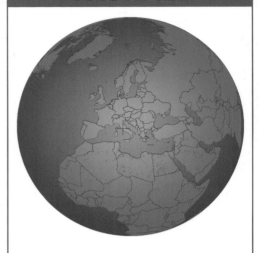

DEAD SEA

There is a very good reason why the Dead Sea is named as it is. There are no fish in it, or any other marine life for that matter, except for a few micro-organisms. This is because it is too salty to support anything apart from the very few who can tolerate such saline conditions. It is more than eight times saltier than sea water, with a salinity level of about 30%, such high levels having come about because the River Jordan, the main river running into it, contains some salts, which, since there are no rivers running out of the Dead Sea, become concentrated through evaporation. This high level of salt increases the relative density of the water, which increases its buoyancy, allowing people who have come to stay in one of the health resorts along its shores to float in the water, lying back unaided reading the newspaper. At least, that is what they are always doing when they have their photographs taken.

The Dead Sea is 1,371ft (418m) below sea level, the lowest point on the Earth on land, with the exception of some depressions in the Antarctic, which are, of course, permanently covered in ice (the Bentley Subglacial Trench is the lowest of these at 8,383ft (2,555m) below sea level) and would be below water if the ice melted. It is in the Jordan Rift Valley, part of the Great Rift Valley that runs from southern Africa to Turkey, and is on the border between Israel's West Bank and Jordan. The rift valley is the reason why the Dead Sea is so far below sea level. It lies on the boundary of two

of the Earth's plates, which are gradually moving apart, stretching the Earth's crust and causing the ground to sink. This process is ongoing and the Dead Sea continues to get lower every year. The weather in the area could best be described as being as near to permanently sunny as makes no difference.

Human occupation of the area goes way back into prehistory. Jericho, near the River Jordan and just north of the Dead Sea, is thought to be the oldest continuously inhabited town in the world, with people living there for the previous 11,000 years. There are a large number of other archaeological sites and many places with biblical associations around the shores. The Dead Sea Scrolls were found in caves near Qumran by a Bedouin shepherd in 1947. These texts, some of which date back to before the birth of Christ and include parts of the Hebrew Bible, are considered to be of great historical and religious significance because there are virtually no other surviving Biblical documents of a comparable age. The rock plateau of Masada overlooks the Dead Sea and is best known as the place where a group of Jewish Zealots held out against besieging Romans in AD 74, until their position became hopeless and they committed mass suicide rather than surrender. To the south-west of the Dead Sea is Mount Sedom, a 700ft (210m) hill entirely composed of rock salt, which some think is the site of the biblical cities of Sodom and Gomorrah.

Today the Dead Sea is perhaps best known as a health resort and spa. Herod the Great is thought to have come to the Dead Sea for the waters, although you would have thought he would have had more need of a salve for his conscience than for his body. People come to the area because of the very low levels of allergens, such as pollen, in the air and to take mud baths, as well as for the waters. The health resorts also say that it is safer to sunbathe at the Dead Sea because of a reduced level of ultraviolet rays. There are also hot springs associated with specific ailments and treatments based on the high atmospheric pressure, it being so far below sea level, which seems to benefit people with respiratory problems and cystic fibrosis.

There is a specific environmental problem occurring in the Dead Sea at the moment, caused by the water of the River Jordan being used for irrigation and drinking water. With very little running into the Dead Sea, the water level has been dropping for a number of years, by as much as 3ft (1m) a year, so that, in the last 20 years, its surface area has shrunk by 20%. The proposed solution to this problem is to build a canal through the Sinai Desert to link the Dead Sea to the Red Sea. Opponents of the scheme think it will create more environmental problems than it will solve, although, so far, it has shown that it is possible for the Israeli Government, the Palestinian Authority and the Jordanians to co-operate, on this one issue at least.

FACT FILE

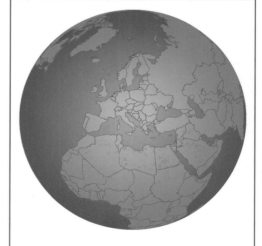

COORDINATES
31°20' N, 35°30' E

LOCATION
South-West Asia, bordered by Israel, the West Bank and Jordan

DEPTH
1,082ft (330m)

SALINITY
30% (8x that of normal sea water)

DEATH VALLEY

Badwater in Death Valley doesn't sound like a good place to be. The name pretty much tells you all you need to know about it. There is a spring-fed pool there, but the water is too salty to drink. And it is hot there. Very hot. It is not a place to get stranded in for long, that's for sure.

Death Valley is in the Mojave Desert, about 80 miles (145km) east of Las Vegas, and it is orientated in a north to south direction. It is about 130 miles (210km) long and 12 miles (19km) wide, with a relatively flat valley floor and steep mountains rising abruptly around it. It is the lowest point on the continent of North America, and the lowest point in Death Valley is, you've guessed it, Badwater, which is 282ft (82m) below sea level. The temperature, which would be hot anyway, is further increased by the radiating effect of the surrounding mountains. In the summer months it can become one of the hottest places anywhere on the surface of the Earth, with temperatures of 120°F (50°C) being common. The hottest temperature ever recorded was at the, again, appropriately named Furnace Creek in 1913 when it reached 134°F (56.7°C). As if that is not enough, it is also one of the driest places on the continent, receiving less than 2in (5cm) of rain a year, a result of the valley being in the rain shadow of the Sierra Nevada mountains. Of course the same facts that make it such a harsh environment are the ones that make it so extraordinary. This has been recognised in the designation of the whole area as the Death Valley National Park, which covers over 5,000 square miles (13,500sq km) and includes extensive areas of the mountains surrounding the valley as well as the valley itself, the largest protected area in the United States of America not including the parks in Alaska.

The geology of Death Valley is extremely complex. Seismic activity has been occurring here for hundreds of millions of years and has resulted in many unusual rock formations, such as the polished marble walls of Mosaic Canyon or the faults and folds of the Amargos Chaos, as it is known, where it has taken geologists many years to untangle the sequence of geological events. As well as the arid valley floor itself, there are also rugged canyons, salt pans and extensive areas of sand dunes, such as the huge wind-sculpted dunes around Stovepipe Wells. At first sight it may seem as if the area is devoid of all life, but, away from the salt pans and the sparse vegetation of the valley floor, it is home to a wide range of plants and animals which have adapted to the extremes of the environment. The creosote bush has small waxy leaves to minimise water loss and can survive long periods of drought, mesquite has long tap roots to draw up water from deep down and, higher up, there are Joshua trees, which are very slow growing and can live for thousands of years. There are bighorn sheep, coyotes and cougars and something like 50 species of desert-adapted small mammals. The Death Valley pupfish is the last known survivor of an ancient lake that dried out thousands of years ago. It is adapted to the hot salty water of a particular section of Salt Creek, which flows all year round, and is not found anywhere else in the world.

People have lived in the area for more than 10,000 years and the Timbisha, who are Shoshone, still do. About 50 of the 300 Timbisha people live near Furnace Creek and, in 2000, 7,500 acres of land were given back to them in the Timbisha Shoshone Homeland Act, together with the right to carry on with their traditional lifestyle in much of the rest of the National Park. In 1849 the California gold rush saw wagons entering the valley for the first time, the prospective 49ers having lost the trail taking them to California. It took these unfortunate people weeks to get out and, when they finally did, a woman is supposed to have looked back and said 'Goodbye Death Valley', giving it a name. Borax, used to make soap and detergents and for various industrial purposes, was found in the valley and extraction begun and, a few years later, gold was also found. Short-lived boom towns sprang up, such as Rhyolite, in the early years of the 20th century. At its height more than 5,000 people lived there, but it had been abandoned by 1916, a ghost town gradually disappearing into the desert.

Death Valley is a place of extremes. It is arid and desolate and, at the same time, beautiful and full of life.

FACT FILE

COORDINATES
36°14' N, 116°46' W

LOCATION
Death Valley National Park, California, United States of America

LENGTH
140 miles (225 km)

WIDTH
5–15 miles (8–24km)

HIGHEST RECORDED TEMPERATURE
134°F (56.7°C)

DELPHI

The town of Delphi is on the lower southern slopes of Mount Parnassus in central Greece, facing the Gulf of Corinth, which separates mainland Greece from the Peloponnese. It is a small town, with narrow winding streets, set between two huge limestone cliff faces, known to the Ancient Greeks as the Phaediades, the shining ones, because they reflect the glare of the sun. There are many hotels, bars and tavernas in the town, catering for the huge number of visitors who come to look around the ruins of the Temple of Apollo and the many other buildings of the archaeological site adjacent to it. People were visiting this site in large numbers in ancient times too, although the purpose of their visit was rather different. At that time Delphi was the most important religious centre in Ancient Greece and people came from all over Europe to consult its oracle, to ask it questions about the future and to determine their actions by the answers it gave.

The spring at Delphi had been a sacred site long before the temple was built, perhaps associated with Gaia, the Earth Goddess, but, by the 8th century BC, it had become dedicated to Apollo, the god of the sun, who is also associated with healing and archery. One of many legends says that Apollo came to Delphi in the form of a dolphin, the Greek word for which gives Delphi its name, and killed Python, the serpent who guarded the sacred spring, and took it over as his own. From then on, the cult of Apollo developed at Delphi and a shrine was built on the spot. It was revered as the centre of the world and the site of the omphalos stone, literally the navel of the world, from which the prophecies arose.

Many of the classical writers, such as Herodotus and Plato, mention the oracle and from their writings it is possible to gather what happened there. Pythia, the high priestess of the oracle, would, after a ritual of purification, enter the adyton, the inner sanctum, of the temple, where the omphalos stone was. She sat on a tripod over the spring, holding laurel leaves in her hand and staring into a cauldron of the spring water. A pneuma, a gas or vapour, arose from the cleft in the rock from which the spring poured, enveloping her and she would enter into a trance, becoming possessed by Apollo, who would communicate the prophecy to her. People who came to consult the oracle, having first washed their hair in the sacred spring, would give a gift of money and sacrifice a goat at the temple and, if the signs were right, would be given a prophecy in response to their question. Some of these prophecies survive, having been written down by the recipients. On being consulted when Athens was under threat of invasion by the Persians in 480 BC, the oracle told the Athenians to put they trust in 'wooden walls' and said 'Pray to the Winds and they will prove to be the mighty allies of Greece'. This was taken to mean that the Greeks would defeat the Persians at sea, which was what happened at the naval battle of Salamis.

As well as the oracle, people came to Delphi for the Pythian games, which were on a par with those held at Olympia, and included poetry and plays as well as athletic events. The remains of the theatre and stadium can be seen at the site today. Various Greek states built their treasuries along the Sacred Way to the temple, to give thanks to the oracle and to commemorate victories, and there were also numerous votive statues. Of the other buildings, the circular Tholos at the Temple of Athena is probably the best known and some of its Doric columns have been re-erected on the site.

The oracle continued to be consulted through into the Roman period, but, in the 4th century AD the Roman Emperor Theodosius I, who had made Christianity the official religion of the empire, decreed that pagan temples should no longer be used and Delphi fell into decay. It was excavated in the late 19th century by French archaeologists, who, finding no trace of a cleft or the presence of gas under the temple, declared the stories about the oracle to be false. More recently, scientists have found that there is an intersection of two geological fault lines directly under the temple site. They speculate that it could have been the source of the gas, which they think was ethylene, a gas that, in the correct quantities, can induce trances and hallucinations, although it is dangerous in high doses. They don't have much to say about the prophecies, but they don't dismiss them out of hand either.

FACT FILE

COORDINATES
38°29' N, 22°30' E

LOCATION
Mount Parnassus, Greece

TIME PERIOD
6th century BC (main activity)

DATE DESTROYED
373 BC (earthquake)

DOME OF THE ROCK

The history of Jerusalem is one of conflicts and conquests stretching back to before the time of King David (*circa* 1000 BC). It has come under the control of the Persians, the Greeks and the Romans. In the medieval period it was the object of the Crusades, having become an Arab caliphate in AD 638, and it changed hands between Christians and Muslims a number of times, before it ended up as part of the Ottoman Empire. With the collapse of the Ottoman Empire at the end of the First World War, it became a British Mandate. It was partitioned between Israel and Jordan after the Arab–Israeli war of 1948 and captured in its entirety by the Israelis in 1967 during the Six Day War, which is pretty much how things stand today.

Within the sprawling modern city of Jerusalem, enclosed by walls built by the Ottomans in the 16th century on much older foundations, is the Old City, a warren of narrow streets and the site of many of the holiest places of three of the world's major religions: Judaism, Islam and Christianity. It is divided into four quarters based on these religions, with the fourth quarter being Armenian, who are mostly Christian, but form their own distinct community.

The Temple Mount, as it is known to Jews and Christians, rises above the streets of the Old City. It is the most holy place in Judaism and is the site of the Temple of Jerusalem. The first temple, built by King Solomon in the 10th century BC, was destroyed by the Babylonians and rebuilt in 515 BC, only to be destroyed again, this time by the Romans, in AD 70, who then exiled the Jews from Jerusalem, beginning the Jewish diaspora. The Ark of the Covenant, containing the stone tablets on which the Ten Commandments were written, was placed in this temple by Solomon. The Western Wall, sometimes known as the Wailing Wall, was a retaining wall of the second temple and faces the Jewish quarter of the Old City. It is the holiest site accessible to Jewish people, who pray in front of it and deposit slips of paper with prayers and wishes written on them into cracks in it.

The same area is known to Muslims as Al Haram es-Sharif (the Noble Sanctuary) and is the third holiest site in Islam, after Mecca and Medina. The Dome of the Rock stands in the middle of Al Haram, within the walls of the El-Aksa Mosque, which encircle almost all of the area, and it is one of the oldest Islamic buildings in the world, dating from AD 691. It is octagonal and has a gilded dome, which is visible for miles around. It was built by the Caliph Abd al-Malik over the rock on which Abraham planned to sacrifice his son Isaac, which is also thought of as the spot from which the Prophet Muhammad ascended into Heaven.

The Church of the Holy Sepulchre stands in the Christian quarter of the Old City and is thought by Christians to be the site of Golgotha, the Hill of Calvary, where Christ was crucified and, also, where he was buried, the tomb now being under the dome of the Resurrection rotunda. It was

originally built in AD 325 by the Roman Emperor Constantine the Great and has been destroyed and rebuilt several times since. On one of these occasions, in 1009, when it was razed to the ground and the foundations dug out, its destruction became the catalyst for the Crusades. The church is used by the Greek Orthodox, Armenian Apostolic and Roman Catholic Churches, who all hold daily services there under an agreement to share the church called the Status Quo, and the Coptic, Ethiopian and Syriac Orthodox Churches also have shrines within it. The Via Dolorosa, the way of sorrows, traces the last steps of Jesus and comes to an end in front of it.

The winding cobblestone streets of the Old City are too narrow for cars and have remained virtually unchanged for centuries. Houses, many with interior courtyards, are closely crowded together. The streets throng with people, and the markets and stalls, known as souks, are busy and noisy. There are supposed to be 226 monuments from all the three religions packed into what is an area of only a third of a square mile (1sq km). It has been fought over for more than 3,000 years and the differences between the communities who jostle together here seem to be as intractable now as they ever were. Jerusalem's turbulent history is what has led to its great diversity, both of people and heritage, but it is hard to foresee a time when this diversity will be a strength, rather than a source of distrust and animosity, as it is now.

DUOMO

The city of Florence, the capital of Tuscany in the north–west of Italy, has often been described as the birthplace of the Renaissance. Beginning in the 14th century, it was, as the name implies, literally a rebirth, the beginnings of a rediscovery of the arts and sciences of the classical Greeks and Romans that had been lost in the upheavals of the medieval period. By the 14th century Florence had become a very wealthy city, primarily through the wool trade, and it was dominated by several rival families who had become extremely rich through trade and commerce, including the Albizzi and Alberti and, most particularly, the Medici, who had made their money in banking. As happened in a number of other Italian city states, rivalry between each other and with other cities was partly expressed through the sponsorship of the arts and sciences and some of the great names of the Renaissance, and the world in general, were associated with Florence at this time: Leonardo da Vinci, Michelangelo, Botticelli, Galileo, and the political philosopher Machiavelli, whose writings on the attainment of power and political pragmatism are, unfortunately, as relevent now as they were to the Medici family then.

In the field of Italian Renaissance architecture, one name in particular stands out, Filippo Brunelleschi, and, although he was responsible for many buildings in Florence and building work on the Duomo had begun almost 100 years before he was born, it is for this, the Basilica di Santa Maria de Fiore, to give it its full name, that he is mostly remembered. Work began on the Duomo in 1296, to a design attributed to Arnolfo di Cambio, to replace the previous cathedral, the Santa Reparta, with a much larger building, in response to the magnificent cathedrals of Siena and Pisa then being built. Construction work continued for many years, interrupted on various occasions, including on the death of di Cambio and during a major outbreak of the Black Death in 1348, which decimated the population of Florence, as it would in many parts of Europe. Giotto, another highly influential figure in the Renaissance, was one of the many architects who worked on it during this period, being credited with the campanile. He continued the use of coloured marble, in geometrically vertical and horizontal designs, for the exterior, following the pattern set by di Cambio's redecoration of the nearby 11th-century octagonal baptistery, which

is, perhaps, best known for its bronze doors, designed by Lorenzo Ghiberti and called the Gates of Paradise by Michelangelo.

By 1419 most of the structural work had been finished, with the exception of the dome, which, at that time, existed as a temporary wooden structure. A competition was held to find a design for a permanent replacement and it was won by Brunelleschi, who beat Ghiberti, whom he had previously worked for and who had beaten him in the competition to design the doors of the baptistery. Several years before, Brunelleschi had made extensive studies of the Pantheon in Rome, along with Donatello, the Florentine sculptor, and he used the knowledge he had gained to develop his own solutions to the complex problems posed by the dome of the Duomo. The octagonal drum below the dome could not have any supporting buttresses, meaning it would have to be built without it exerting any significant lateral thrust. The structural integrity of the concrete the Romans had used for the Pantheon's dome solved this problem for them, but Brunelleschi was building his dome in brick. He solved it by having the dome rest directly on the drum, independently of the roof,

and then strengthening the base of the dome with iron to contain the lateral thrust. He then went on to develop ingenious methods to build the dome without the need for a wooden supporting structure, a revolutionary change in architectural practice.

The dome was finished in 1436 and Brunelleschi went on to design a lantern for it, but he died before it had been built. It would be almost 30 years before his friend Michelozzo completed it, in 1469, and a gilt ball and cross were then placed on top of that by the artist Andrea de Verrochio, who raised it into position using an apparatus said to have been designed by one of his apprentices, Leonardo da Vinci.

The other well known feature of the Duomo is the façade of coloured marble, which was actually put up in the late 19th century and designed to fit in with di Cambio's and Giotto's work on the baptistery and campanile. It has been criticised as being overly decorative and elaborate, but, whether this is true or not, the Duomo remains one of the crowning achievements of the Renaissance, because of its wonderful dome and its architect, Filippo Brunelleschi.

EASTER ISLAND

The Polynesians were, by any standards, master mariners. They covered vast distances in their outrigger canoes and colonised hundreds of islands in the central and south Pacific. By about AD 900 they had arrived on Easter Island, known in the indigenous language as Rapa Nui, and it is about as isolated as it can get. It is 2,237 miles (3,540km) from South America and more than 1,000 miles (1,600km) from the next nearest inhabited island. What happened on the island between the Polynesian colonisation and the coming of the first Europeans, a Dutch ship, which arrived on Easter Day 1722, leading to the European name for the island, has been the subject of intense debate and speculation ever since.

These days there are about 3,700 people on the island, which is about 14 miles (23km) long and 7 miles (11km) wide. Most of them live in the only town, Hanga Roa, and about 60% are of Polynesian descent, with most of the rest being Chilean. At its height there are thought to have been between 10,000 and 15,000 people on the island, but, by the time the Dutch arrived, the population had dropped to about 3,000. By that time most of the huge statues, the Moai, for which the island is famous, had been knocked over and abandoned.

Something like 890 Moai have been found so far around the coastline of the island. The largest one to have been erected was 33ft (10m) tall and weighed 75 tons, but there is a much larger one in the only quarry on the island, which had not been finished when work on the Moai stopped. They stand on a platform, called an Ahu, each one of which belonged to a particular village or clan, and they face inland. The heads, which are massive compared to the truncated bodies, are highly stylised, being elongated with a stern, some say mournful, expression. Each one originally had a Pukaos on its head, which could either have been a hat or stylised hair, and eyes made from coral. The body of the statues is made from a brown stone, a tuff of compressed volcanic ash that is quite easy to carve, while the Pukaos were made from a reddish-coloured tuff. They are thought to have represented ancestors or, perhaps, protective spirits of some sort, which would look after the village or clan that had erected them. But they were all abandoned suddenly, with unfinished statues in the quarry and some that appear to have been abandoned while being transported to the site they would have been erected on.

One explanation for what happened suggests that, after arriving on the island, the people gradually cut down all the trees, which had originally covered much of it. This meant they could no longer build canoes, isolating them on the island and limiting the amount of fishing they could do. With no trees, the wind eroded the soils, making farming progressively harder and harder. As resources on the island became ever more scarce, they began to fight among themselves for possession of those resources and, at some stage, turned against their ancestor gods, who had failed to protect them, intentionally toppling the statues and gouging the eyes out.

Sometime in the 17th century, the remaining people, having turned against their ancestor gods, or, perhaps having been forced to do so as a result of civil war, began to worship a previously minor god and this developed into what is known as the Birdman Cult. A competition was held every year between clans in which a representative from each clan would swim out to a small island to collect a sooty tern egg and bring it back to the main island. The winner would be appointed 'Birdman of the Year' and may have had a role in deciding how resources were allocated in the following year. This continued to go on until the 19th century, when it was stopped by missionaries. At about the same time many islanders were seized by American and Peruvian slave traders, to work in the guano mines in Peru, and many more died of disease. By the time Chile annexed the island in 1888 there were only a few hundred people left.

There is a further mystery on Easter Island, which, if it is ever solved, has the potential to explain what happened there. The islanders used shark's teeth, or possibly obsidian flakes, to inscribe wooden tablets with what looks like hieroglyphics. Known as rongo-rongo, it has, so far, resisted all attempts to decipher it, but, if it turns out to have been a written language, and if someone does actually manage to decipher it, then it is possible that the people themselves will tell us the real story.

FACT FILE

COORDINATES
27°7'14" S, 109°21'5" W

NATIVE LANGUAGE
Rapa Nui

AREA
63sq miles (163.6sq km)

VOLCANOES
Poike, Rano Kau and Terevaka

POPULATION
3,791 (2002 census)

EDINBURGH CASTLE

Castle Rock is the remnants of the basalt plug of a long extinct volcano, eroded down by Ice Age glaciers, which have also left a long tail of moraine on its eastern side, and weathered further by the wind and rain into rocky crags and cliffs. It is one of a chain of similar geological features over which Edinburgh spreads, including Arthur's Seat to the east, and the castle itself stands on the edge of the precipice of the rock, which protects it on three sides with sheer rock faces. It has a commanding view across the city towards the Firth of Forth and the surrounding countryside and this view is one of the reasons why there has been a fortification here since at least the 1st century AD, when the Romans, on a brief visit to the area north of Hadrian's Wall, reported on a hill fort of the Votadini, the Iron Age occupiers of the region. The other reason for a castle in such a position is, of course, for the occupiers of the castle to be visible themselves, to show everybody where the power lies and who is in charge. Its position has meant that, over its history, it has been all but impregnable to direct assault, but it also has an Achilles' heel. There is no water supply on the top of the hill, making the castle vulnerable if any of its attackers were to put it under a prolonged siege.

The castle has not actually been attacked in anger since 1745, during the Jacobite uprising led by Bonnie Prince Charlie aimed at restoring the Catholic House of Stuart to the thrones of England and Scotland. The uprising captured the city of Edinburgh, but failed to take the castle and ended with the decisive victory of the Hanoverian army under the command of the Duke of Cumberland, the younger son of King George II, at the Battle of Culloden in the following year. In the aftermath of the battle the Duke ordered the execution of all the Jacobite prisoners and wounded, who were mostly Scottish clansmen, earning himself the name of 'the Butcher' in the process, and he went on to ruthlessly suppress Jacobite sympathisers throughout Scotland. Bonnie Prince Charlie escaped the battlefield and evaded capture for the next five months before fleeing Scotland into exile, with the help of the Jacobite heroine Flora MacDonald, from which he would not return.

Although the castle has not been needed as a fortress since, and despite it becoming the foremost tourist attraction in Scotland in terms of the number of visitors, it retains its military associations. It is currently the headquarters of the 52nd Infantry Brigade, which includes the Royal Gurkha Rifles, although they are actually based in Kent, the Royal Regiment of Scotland, several regimental museums and the Army School of Piping. The army continues the tradition of the One O'Clock Gun, the firing of an artillery piece from one of the castle's batteries, originally done to provide an accurate time signal for ships in the Firth of Forth and Leith Harbour in the days when clocks were not very accurate, although the purpose now appears to be to surprise unaware tourists and to signal that it is lunchtime to the people of Edinburgh. The gun is also fired at midnight on New Year's Eve as part of the city's Hogmanay celebrations, the official events of which often get cancelled these days because of bad weather, although this does not appear to stop most people from having a huge party anyway.

The Esplanade in front of the castle is the site of the annual Military Tattoo, held in August and forming one part of the Edinburgh Festival, an informal name for what are, in fact, a number of entirely separate festivals occurring at the same time. These days one of the best known is the Edinburgh Fringe, which encompasses a huge range of the performing arts, from prestigious stagings of Shakespeare's plays to bunches of students with nothing better to do than mess about. The tattoo itself involves performances by military bands and display teams, mainly from the Scottish regiments of the British Army, but including all sorts of other guests from all over the world. The highlight is the finale of the evening, the massed pipes and drums, when all the bands join together for spectacular and incredibly noisy renditions of Scottish favourites like the *Skye Boat Song* and *Flower of Scotland*. The flag is then lowered to the sound of the Last Post and this is followed by a lone piper on the castle ramparts, piping a lament for fallen comrades. As the final note fades, an enormous firework display erupts, all those present, performers and public alike, sing *Auld Lang Syne* and, with handshakes all round, everyone goes home happy.

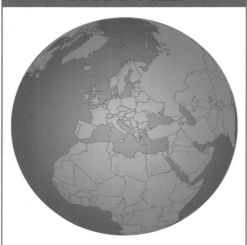

FACT FILE

COORDINATES
55°56'55" N, 3°12'03" W

LOCATION
Edinburgh, Scotland

HEIGHT
400ft (121.92m) above sea level

HUMAN HABITATION
Dates back to early 9th century

FOUNDATION
Basalt plug of an extinct volcano, which rose 340 million years ago

EIFFEL TOWER

During the planning stages for the 1889 Exposition Universelle, a French version of a Great Exhibition or World's Fair, a design competition was held to find a structure that would form the entrance to the exhibition and demonstrate to the rest of the world French prowess in science and technology. Gustave Eiffel won with what he called La Tour de 300 Metres (the 300 Metre Tower). Before it was even built for the exhibition, critics were calling it a tragic street lamp and had contemptuously dubbed it Le Tour de Monsieur Eiffel (Mr Eiffel's Tower), intending to suggest something along the lines of Eiffel's Folly, but the name came into popular usage, as the Eiffel Tower, and it has stuck ever since. Originally intended to stand for 20 years and designed to be easily dismantled, it is still going strong and is more popular than ever. It is the most visited monument in the world, with more than 6.5 million people going up it every year, and it is also one of the most recognisable buildings, second only, perhaps, to the pyramids.

Although Eiffel is the principal name associated with the tower, a number of other people were also involved. Maurice Koechlin and Emile Nouguier, who both worked for Eiffel, were the structural engineers who brought the project to fruition, and the architect Stephen Sauvestre was appointed to make it more aesthetically pleasing. It was built using wooden scaffolding with small steam cranes attached to the tower itself, which moved building materials up the tower in stages. The design is, essentially, of a large pylon, built of four columns of latticed iron girders, separated at the base and coming together at the top. More than 7,000 tons of iron were used, held together with something like 2.5 million rivets. The uprights were engineered to offer the least possible wind resistance and the whole structure was painted to prevent the iron rusting. It is entirely repainted every ten years, requiring 60 tons of paint, and has changed colour a number of times, starting out as a red-brown colour and, since the last time it was painted, it is now bronze. It is slightly higher now than when it was first built, because of the addition of a larger radio antenna in 1959, and it now stands at 1,063ft (324m).

The elevators were an original feature of the building and have been updated a number of times since, although some of the winding machinery has not been changed. There are stairs all the way to the second level, a total of 719 steps, and almost half the visitors to the tower choose to climb them, although not all of them make it all the way, deciding to stop at the first level or take the lift on to the second. There are stairs going right to the top, but these are no longer open to the public.

The tower has had a long history of use as a radio transmitter, which is one of the main reasons it was not demolished in 1909. During the First World War it was used to dispatch military signals, including during the Battle of the Marne, when it was used to coordinate a fleet of 600 Paris taxis, used to transfer reinforcements to the front, then only 30 miles from Paris. It was also the place where the German signals that led to the exposure of notorious spy Mata Hari were intercepted, although there is also some suggestion that she was, in fact, a double-agent working for the French.

In 1940, just before the Germans entered Paris, the lift cables were cut. No spare parts could be found after the occupation and German soldiers were forced to climb to the top to fly a swastika. Within hours of the liberation in 1944 the lift was working again.

Since then the tower has had a somewhat less eventful history. It has been used in major national celebrations, including during the Millennium, when a spectacular fireworks display, with fireworks shooting off the top of the tower and going off down its entire length, was one of the highlights of the celebrations from around the world. In 2003 a new lighting system was installed, which has proved controversial. The lighting design is effectively under copyright, so anyone taking photographs of the tower at night, including individuals, should seek permission before doing so. Outbreaks of petty-mindedness have, however, failed to dent the tower's popularity and, to ensure this continues, the attractions are constantly being updated. One of its two restaurants holds a Michelin star and, during the winter, an icerink is laid down on the first level, but, for fans of the kitsch, a souvenir scale model of the tower can still be bought in the gift shop.

FACT FILE

COORDINATES
48°51'30" N, 2°17'40" E

LOCATION
Paris, France

CONSTRUCTED
1889

HEIGHT
1,063ft (324m)

EMPIRE STATE BUILDING

The 1920s, or the Roaring Twenties as they are often known, were a time of great optimism in America, fuelled by a financial boom and a cultural blossoming. Towards the end of the decade a competition had developed in New York to construct the tallest building in the world. On 23 October 1929, Walter Chrysler, the founder of the eponymous car manufacturing company, thought he had won the race when, at the last minute, a spire was added to the Chrysler Building, making it 119ft (36m) tall, beating its rival, the Manhattan Company Building. In the following week the Wall Street Crash occurred, sending shock waves throughout the financial markets of the world and precipitating the Great Depression of the 1930s. This did not stop the competition, however, as, unknown to Chrysler, John Raskob, who had long been associated with General Motors, was planning the Empire State Building, along with the financier Pierre DuPont and Alfred Smith, a former Governor of New York.

Raskob was a man in a hurry. The architect, Walter Lamb of Shreve, Lamb and Harmon, drew up the plans in two weeks and the builders, Sharrett Brothers and Eken, no doubt helped by Smith's political experience, began work almost straight away. In keeping with the project, building work progressed incredibly quickly. From the starting point in January 1930 to its opening in May 1931, construction took 410 days and continued at a rate of four floors a day. There were 3,400 workers on the project, many of whom were European immigrants and people from the Mohawk Nation, particularly from the community in Grand Rapids, Illinois. There are many great photographs, taken by Lewis Hines while suspended off the side of the building in a basket, of these skywalkers, as they were known, up in the high steel, casually walking along the steelwork or sitting on one of the girders hundreds of feet above the ground having their lunch with their feet dangling into the emptiness below.

By the time the building opened the Great Depression was in full swing and many of the offices remained empty, but it had achieved Raskob's ambition, as it was the tallest building in the world by a considerable distance. It stands at 1,464ft (443m), including its antenna, and was not beaten until 1973, by the Sears Tower in Chicago. The spire at the top had been intended as a mooring point for airships, but was never used as such because high winds experienced at the altitude would have made it too dangerous. It is built in the Art Deco style, with a classic façade of limestone and granite, and its characteristic setbacks, giving it the appearance of a very elongated step pyramid, are a result of planning legislation requiring tall buildings to reduce the shadow they would otherwise cast. It has 6,500 windows and there are 73 elevators. The lobby is a classic of Art Deco design. It is three storeys high, with a marble, granite and brushed stainless steel interior and features an aluminium relief of the building behind the main desk. There are 2.2 million sq ft (220,000sq m) of office space in the building

and it is home to more than 1,000 businesses. It has two observation decks, one on the 86th floor, which is open and relatively large, and a smaller enclosed space on the 102nd floor. From here, as well as panoramic views of Manhattan and the rest of New York, on clear days it is possible to see for 80 miles (130km) into New Jersey, Pennsylvania, Connecticut and Massachusetts. Not surprisingly, and despite the queues at the ticket office, it is one of the most popular tourist attractions in New York.

One Saturday morning in July 1945 a US Air Force B-25, which was flying over New York in heavy fog, hit the building, crashing into the 79th floor where the offices of the National Catholic Welfare Council were situated. Fourteen people were killed and one of the elevator operators survived a fall of 75 floors. Despite all this, the building was open again on Monday morning.

Over the years it has featured in about 100 films, including *Sleepless in Seattle* and *An Affair to Remember*, but, most famously, in the 1933 film *King Kong*, where, in the final scenes of the film, Kong escapes his captors, finds Fay Wray and climbs the building. He puts her down at the top and is attacked by aeroplanes, which buzz around him like flies, and, having been shot many times, falls to his death. In some ways the film can be compared to *Romeo and Juliet*, in that it is a story of forbidden love which has tragic consequences, except, of course, in *King Kong*, one of the lovers is a great big monkey.

FACT FILE

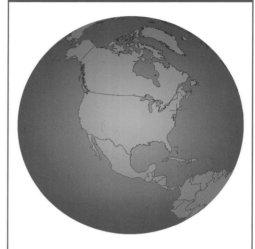

COORDINATES
40°44'54" N, 73°59'09" W

LOCATION
350 Fifth Avenue, New York, USA

CONSTRUCTION
1929–1931

HEIGHT
1,472ft (449m) antenna/spire

WORLD'S TALLEST BUILDING
1931–1972

FORBIDDEN CITY

The Yuan Dynasty, who were ethnically Mongol and were, in effect, the heirs of Genghis Khan's Mongol Empire, ruled China until 1368, when the future Hongwu Emperor, who was Chinese, led a revolt against them and established the Ming Dynasty. Initially the capital of the Ming Dynasty was Nanjing, but the third emperor, known as the Yongol Emperor, who had usurped the throne from his nephew, the Jianwen Emperor, in 1402, had been advised that the palace in Nanjing was vulnerable to attack and he decided to move the capital back to Beijing, where it had been under the Yuans. Work on a palace in Beijing began in 1406 and was on an epic scale, with, it is thought, 200,000 people working on the buildings. It was finished in 1420 and, although extensively rebuilt after fires and wars over the centuries, the resulting palace is what we know today as the Forbidden City, known as such because no one could enter it unless they had the permission of the emperor.

There are something like 800 wooden buildings, which have characteristic yellow tiled roofs, yellow being the sign of the emperor, in the Forbidden City and it is enclosed by high walls and a moat. It covers an area of 124 acres (72ha), making it the largest palace complex in the world. It is rectangular and arranged along a north to south axis, which connects the two gates on either side of the buildings. The south gate, the Meridian Gate, leads into the palace grounds and then through another gate onto Tiananman Square, where the public access into the palace is situated. The palace is divided into two areas, an Outer Court and an Inner Court. The Gate of Supreme Harmony is reached through the Meridian Gate and this opens onto the Outer Court, where there are three main buildings on the central axis. The Hall of Supreme Harmony is the largest of these, and also the largest wooden building in China. It was used for public ceremonies, such as weddings and coronations, and stands on a three-tiered marble base. Behind this hall, again on the central axis, are two more smaller halls, The Hall of Medium Harmony and The Hall of Protective Harmony, and then the gate into the Inner Court, which is where the emperor lived. The main building in the Inner Court is called The Palace of Heavenly Purity and it is here that the day-to-day affairs of state were dealt with. On either side of the central axis there are numerous buildings, which decline in importance the further they are away from the axis.

The layout of the palace has been seen as symbolic of the divine nature of the emperor and as an attempt to create an image of Heaven on Earth. It has also been seen as an expression of the human body, with the halls of the Inner Court as the brain, where all the important decisions are made, the central axis as the spinal column leading out from the brain to the rest of the buildings, lesser parts of the body which are, nevertheless, important to keep the whole body functioning properly. In a further interpretation, the central axis, which passes through a total of seven halls and courts, is thought

FACT FILE

COORDINATES
39°54'56" N, 116°23'27" E

LOCATION
Beijing, China

AREA
2,362,205sq ft (720,000sq m)

BUILDINGS
800 (8,886 rooms)

CONSTRUCTION
1406–1420

to represent the body's journey from this world to the next as it passes through the seven heavens.

The Ming Dynasty oversaw huge advances in China, with agriculture, trade and the arts all flourishing. The exceptionally fine porcelain of the period is an example of how culturally advanced China had become, but, by the 17th century, stagnation had set in. The Manchu Qing Dynasty toppled the Mings during that century and continued to use the Forbidden City as their palace until 1912, when China became a republic, ending 2,000 years of imperial rule. The last emperor, Puyi, was required to stay within the Forbidden City, until finally being expelled in 1924, when the Palace Museum was established. By this time, the Forbidden City had been an imperial palace for five centuries and had accumulated an enormous wealth of treasures going back to the early Ming Dynasty. These treasures were removed before the Japanese invaded China in 1937 and many of the artefacts ended up in Taiwan, where they remain today in the National Palace Museum in Taipei.

During the Cultural Revolution of the late 1960s, when the Red Guard destroyed many historical monuments, the Forbidden City was guarded by soldiers on the orders of the Premier of the People's Republic of China, Zhou Enlai, possibly the only person in China at the time with the authority to prevent the destruction that would have ensued had the Red Guard been allowed in and, thereby, saving one of the greatest of all imperial palaces.

GALAPAGOS

The Spanish word galapogo means tortoise and, in 1535, when Spanish ships first arrived in the archipelago of islands they had found on the equator, some 600 miles (965km) off the coast of South America, they named them after the giant ones they found there. By the time the HMS Beagle arrived, 300 years later on 15 September 1835, a few of the islands had become inhabited, but, other than that, they were much as the Spanish had found them. The ship spent a total of 36 days in the Galapagos and Charles Darwin, who had joined the ship four years previously as a companion for the captain, Robert Fitzroy, and as a naturalist, spent his time there exploring the geology of the four islands he visited and making collections of the plants and animals he found there, many of which were new to science.

There are 13 main islands in the archipelago, including Isabella, Fernadina, Santa Cruz and San Christobel, and many smaller islands and islets. They were formed from volcanic activity under the ocean, the result, it is thought, of a magma plume rising from within the Earth, pushing the Earth's crust upwards. Some of the magma has broken through the crust, forming volcanoes, which have formed the islands. The tectonic plate on which the Galapagos lie, called the Nazca Plate, is moving very slowly towards South America and, as it does so, the islands move away from the magma source that formed them. As the magma continues to rise to the surface, another island is formed. This means that the oldest islands in the archipelago, which, being about 10 million years old, are still very young in geological terms, are in the east, while, in the west, the islands are still being formed. This can be seen on Isabella, the largest island and one of the most westerly, where there are a number of active volcanoes.

The climate, as Darwin remarked, is surprisingly temperate and dry considering the islands lie on the equator. This is a result of the Humboldt Current, which brings cold water up from the Antarctic, and a phenomenon known as upwelling, where cold water rises from the deep ocean. The water around the islands is often too cold to swim in, but it is full of fish and other marine life. The direction of the Humboldt Current is reversed during El Niño years, roughly one in seven, bringing warm water and heavy rains.

The combination of remoteness from the mainland, the relative youth of the islands and of the changeable climate, is what has led to the remarkable array of plants and animals, the giant tortoises and iguanas, the finches and mocking birds. Many of them are endemic to the archipelago and, often, to a particular island, and it is this that makes them so special. Although there are not as many different species on the Galapagos as are found on the mainland, they have, after finding their way to the islands, gone through a process called speciation, in which isolated populations of a species of animal or plant evolve away from the original species, leading to the formation of a new species. The differences between species of the same family on the different islands is what interested Darwin. The formation of the Theory of Evolution is often portrayed as if Darwin had a eureka moment on the Galapagos, but it was not like that at all. In some cases he did not even realise that there were different species on different islands until he was back in London, where his collection, and those of Captain Fitzroy and other members of the Beagle's crew, was classified and the results pointed out to him. His notebooks show that he began to formulate his theory after this, but it was not until 24 years later, with the prompting of Alfred Russell Wallace, who had independently come up with a similar theory, that he published The Origin of Species, starting the controversy that continues today.

The special and unique nature of the Galapagos has been recognised for many years. They have been protected by legislation since 1934 and these days 97.5% of the total area is a National Park. They are now a UNESCO World Heritage Site and Biosphere Reserve and the seas around them are a Marine Protected Area. The main threat comes from introduced animals, particularly goats and cats, but there are also problems associated with the increasing human population of the islands and with an ever larger number of tourists visiting them. It is a place of outlandish volcanic terrain and of plants and animals found nowhere else on Earth. To damage such a place would be an incomparable crime and, surely, it cannot be allowed to happen.

FACT FILE

COORDINATES
0° N, 91° W

NUMBER OF ISLANDS
13 main volcanic islands, 6 smaller islands, 107 rocks and islets

OLDEST ISLAND
5–10 million years old

VOLCANOES
2,648ft (807m)

GIANT'S CAUSEWAY

The northern coast of County Antrim, in Northern Ireland, can be a wild place. When storms roll in off the Atlantic, as they often do, waves can crash over the tops of the sea walls protecting the fronts of the small holiday towns of Portstewart and Portrush and batter into the houses on the other side of the promenades. The landscape here is one of green rolling hills and small farms and, on the coast, where the hills meet the sea, there are high cliffs and headlands and narrow rocky bays cutting into the land. It is a treacherous coast and there have been many ships wrecked along it. In 1588 the *Girona*, a ship of the Spanish Armada, returning to Spain after being defeated by the English Navy, was blown ashore at Lacada Point. More than 1,000 people were aboard and only a handful survived. Bodies were washed up in the nearby bay, Port na Spaniagh, where, contemporary reports say, there was a pile of white bones just above the shoreline for many years afterwards, known locally as the Spanish Bones.

A stone's throw from where the *Gironda* floundered, Giant's Causeway juts out into the sea, separating Port Ganny from Port Noffer. On seeing the causeway, it is immediately obvious how it got its name. It looks like a rough pathway made of hexagonal flagstones, laid flush against each other, heading out to sea in the direction of Scotland, and worn smooth and rounded at the edges, as if by the passing of feet, rather than by the abrasion of the wind and waves over millions of years. When the Bishop of Derry visited the causeway in 1692, claiming to have discovered it, which is rather like saying you have found something that has not been lost, he came up with three possible explanations for how the causeway had been formed: by men with hammers and chisels, by natural forces, or, as the locals had probably told him, by giants.

The rock making up Giant's Causeway is basalt, an igneous rock formed when lava from volcanoes cools and solidifies. During the Tertiary Period, about 65 million years ago, there were at least three lava flows in this area, including one that formed Giant's Causeway. The hexagonal columns were formed as a result of the lava cooling quickly, which can happen, for example, when lava flows into the sea, causing the rock to crack. Under the particular conditions of cooling that occurred during the formation of the causeway, the rock cracked to form a geometrical pattern, in a similar way to how crystals are formed. Although not particularly common, there are a number of other examples of this process, including at Fingal's Cave on the Scottish island of Staffa. Here the rock columns are set into a cliff face above the sea and form the entrance to the cave.

There are many different legends about the causeway, although none of them come from the actual canon of Irish mythology as it has been written down. They are popular stories, which take characters from mythology and adapt them for the purposes of the story, as storytellers have always done everywhere, and are no less valid for doing so. Perhaps the best of the stories comes from *The Legend of Knockmany* written in 1845 by William Charleton. It doesn't really have much to say about the causeway, but does feature the giant Finn MacCool, the Anglicised version of the Irish warrior-hero Fionn mac Cumhail, who is supposed to have built it. Finn is working on his causeway when he hears that Culcullin, the Scottish giant, is looking for him to find out who is the strongest. Finn goes home to his wife Oonagh, trembling in fear, saying he will be 'skivered like a rabbit'. Oonagh, knowing that Culcullin's strength comes from the power in his middle finger, hatches a plan to outwit him. Finn dresses as his baby son and hides in the cradle, while she bakes two loaves of bread, putting stones into one of them. When Culcullin arrives, spoiling for a fight, she tells him that Finn is not there and offers him the bread with the stones in it. He tries to eat it, but breaks his teeth on the stones and has to stop. Oonagh now gives bread from the other loaf to the baby, or so Culcullin thinks, who eats it all. Culcullin thinks he had better leave before the father of such a baby gets back, but asks if he can feel the baby's teeth before he goes. He puts his finger into the baby's mouth and Finn bites it off. Culcullin has now lost all his strength and Finn jumps out of the cradle and beats him easily in the ensuing fight.

FACT FILE

COORDINATES
55°15'00" N, 6°29'07" W

LOCATION
County Antrim, Northern Ireland

NUMBER OF BASALT COLUMNS
40,000

TALLEST BASALT COLUMN
36ft (12m)

FORMATION
Palaeogene period

GOLDEN GATE BRIDGE

The Golden Gate is the mile-wide strait of water that separates San Francisco from Marin County at the mouth of the San Francisco Bay. There are ten rivers running into the bay and out into the Pacific Ocean through this narrow channel, which becomes a swirling mass of currents as the ocean tides force water back through it. The English name was already in use before the 1848 gold rush in San Francisco had begun and, it has been suggested, the name actually refers to the Golden Horn in Istanbul, the harbour at the mouth of the Bosporus, which separates the Black Sea from the Sea of Mamara and is also known for its treacherous currents. A ferry ran from San Francisco to Sausalito in Marin County up until 1937, when the Golden Gate Bridge was opened. Since then, its sleek design and distinctive colour, known as international orange and originally used to make the bridge more visible in the fog, together with its appearance in numerous films, have made it the most recognisable bridge in the world, with the possible exception of Tower Bridge in London.

The idea of building a bridge across the Golden Gate had been around since at least 1917, but was given great impetus by the structural engineer Joseph Strauss, who became involved in 1921. He had designed many bridges before, but nothing on anywhere near the scale of the Golden Gate Bridge. Initially his designs were rejected, mostly on aesthetic grounds, but, after ten years of redesigning and campaigning, and with the help of the engineer Charles Ellis, the bridge designer Leon Moisseif and the architect Irving Morrow, who was responsible for the Art Deco look of the bridge and chose the colour, building work began.

The design of the bridge required the main towers to be sited in the strait, which caused a number of delays and led to the project going considerably over budget. This first attempt involved using divers, but this proved too dangerous in the current. A jetty was built out to the site of the foundations from the shore, but a freighter ran into it in the fog and then it was blown down in a storm. Once the foundations were finally finished, the two suspension towers were built on them. Joseph Strauss was much more safety conscious than was usual at the time and insisted on measures such as harnesses and hard hats for the workers. A huge net was also slung under the bridge to catch anyone who fell off and it is credited with saving 19 lives. Despite this, 16 people were killed when part of one of the towers collapsed. The main suspension cables, each comprising 27,000 galvanised wires spun together into cables, were strung between the towers and were sealed and clad in steel to prevent them rusting. The suspension cables were then installed, going down from the main cables to the suspended deck, on which the roadway was laid. When it was opened in 1937 it was the longest suspension bridge in the world, a title it held until the Verrazano-Narrows Bridge in New York was built in 1964.

In 1989 the Loma Prieta earthquake, which measured 6.9 and killed 62 people in the San Francisco area, struck. The Golden Gate Bridge survived relatively intact but part of the Bay Bridge collapsed and led to what has been called seismic retrofitting at the Golden Gate, which became particularly pertinent when it was calculated that an earthquake of the magnitude of the 1906 quake, which was 7.9 and killed 3,000 people, would have destroyed the bridge. It is now being equipped to survive an 8.3 earthquake and, as the engineer in charge of the project has explained, anything higher than that and there will be no need to worry about the bridge because San Francisco will have been flattened anyway. The retrofitting involves, in effect, completely rebuilding the bridge piece by piece while, at the same time, increasing its ability to dissipate seismic forces and separating each section of the bridge with isolation bearings. As long as the next earthquake doesn't hit before the project is finished, the bridge should be standing for many years to come.

A further problem has been to try to reduce the number of people committing suicide by jumping off the bridge, which now runs at around one suicide every two weeks. There have been proposals to fit suicide barriers, which have come to nothing so far, and pedestrians are no longer allowed onto the bridge at night, but, unfortunately, people still choose this beautiful bridge, 220ft (67m) above the currents of the Golden Gate, as the place to end it all when they can go on no further.

FACT FILE

COORDINATES
37°49'3" N, 122°28'42" W

LOCATION
San Francisco, California and Marin County, USA

TOTAL LENGTH
8,991ft (2,740m)

DESIGN
Suspension, truss arch & truss causeways

GRACELAND

These days Memphis is probably best known for two things: as the place where Martin Luther King was assassinated, at the Lorraine Motel on 4 April 1968; and as the place where Elvis Presley lived, from when he moved to Memphis with his mother, from Tupelo Mississippi, in 1948, when he was 11, to when he died, in the bathroom of Graceland, the house he had lived in for 20 years, on 16 August 1977, at the age of 42.

Memphis already had a long association with music by the time Elvis paid $3.25 to record an acetate at Sun Records as a birthday present for his mother in 1953. Jug bands and blues bands had been playing in the bars on Beale Street since the 1860s and blues musicians had been coming up to Memphis from northern Mississippi and the Delta for many years. In the early 1950s, Muddy Waters, Howling Wolf and B.B. King, to name a few, could be heard playing on Beale Street, while the country and rockabilly scenes were also taking off, with

Johnny Cash, Jerry Lee Lewis and Carl Perkins. Sam Philips at Sun Records was recording many of them and, in July 1954, after an assistant had heard one of the acetates Elvis had recorded, Philips got him into the studio to sing *That's All Right* by the delta blues singer Arthur 'Big Boy' Crudup. It was an immediate hit and more recording followed, together with touring and appearances on television. By the end of 1955, Elvis was managed by Colonel Tom Parker and had released *Heartbreak Hotel* for RCA Records, going on to become a huge worldwide star in 1956. The house where he had been living in Memphis, at 1034 Audubon Drive, was not private enough for someone as famous as he had become and, in early 1957, he bought Graceland, which is set back from the road in its own grounds. He moved in with his mother and father and, on his discharge from the army in March 1960, brought his future wife Priscilla back from Germany to live with him there.

The house sits on the top of a hill in the suburb of Whitehaven, about 8 miles (13km) from downtown Memphis. The property was originally established as a farm in the 1860s, with the present house being built in 1939. It is built of limestone in the Southern Colonial style and has Corinthian columns forming the entrance portico. Many people who visit it comment on how much smaller it is than they had expected, being a large two-storey house with about 20 rooms rather than the enormous mansions owned by many rock musicians and film stars.

It was opened to the public in 1982, by Priscilla and their daughter Lisa Marie, and, since then, it has become the second most visited house in America, after the White House. Visitors can take a tour of the parts of the house Elvis would have shown to them. These include the music room, the dining room, the TV room and the trophy room, where Elvis kept all his awards and his gold and platinum

records. Perhaps the most famous room is the jungle room, where he relaxed with his friends, the Memphis Mafia. Elvis had this room decorated and furnished to remind him of Hawaii and it has lush green carpets, wood-panelled walls and exotic furniture, which probably didn't look as garish then as they appear now. The upstairs parts of the house, which Elvis thought of as his own private space, including his bedroom and bathroom, have not been touched since he died and remain closed to the public. The tour finishes with an opportunity for visitors to pay their respects to Elvis at his grave in the garden. Also buried here are his mother, father and grandmother and there is a memorial to his twin brother, Jesse Garon, who was stillborn.

Over the road, the Elvis Presley Boulevard, there is a complex of buildings containing a museum of memorabilia, his collection of cars and his two aeroplanes, the *Lisa Marie* and *Hound Dog II*. The house and museums continue to draw visitors from all over the world, some of whom regard their visit more as a pilgrimage than a trip to a tourist attraction. The Japanese Prime Minister, Junichiro Koizumi, a lifelong fan, when taken to Graceland by President Bush during an official visit, needed little persuasion to demonstrate his Elvis impersonation. What Priscilla and Lisa Marie, who were showing the party around the house, thought about this impression has not been recorded, but at least it does give an indication of how enduring and widespread Elvis's reputation remains and how, for many people around the world, Elvis is still the King.

FACT FILE

COORDINATES
35°2'46" N, 90°1'23" W

LOCATION
Memphis, Tennessee, USA

PUBLIC MUSEUM
1982

NATIONAL HISTORIC LANDMARK
27 March, 2006

GRAND CANYON

The pathway from the car park to one of the National Park's viewing points on the South Rim of the Grand Canyon winds through a stand of trees which blocks the view until, suddenly, there it is, one of the most spectacular sights in the natural world. People who have not been to this spot before stand there open-mouthed, overwhelmed by what is before them, before walking on to the ledge of the viewing area. From there, looking down at the ribbon of water at the bottom that is the Colorado River, more than a mile below, and across the gorge itself at the layer upon layer of differently coloured rock strata, the variegated vista, on the far side, it is difficult to credit that geologists consider this enormous canyon to be quite a young feature. It is thought to be no more than 6 million years old, with the majority of the erosion having taken place over the past 2 million years. This may sound like a long period of time, but when you compare it to the age of the rocks at the bottom of the canyon, which are something like 2 billion years old, it is, in geological terms, the blink of an eye.

The canyon is in the semi-arid region of northern Arizona and cuts through 277 miles (446km) of the Colorado Plateau, an area of geological uplifting caused by pressure from within the Earth and the movement of continental plates. The Colorado River began to flow on something like its present course about 6 million years ago, beginning the processes of erosion that have formed the canyon. One of these processes is called downcutting,

where the fast-flowing waters of the Colorado cut into the bedrock of the channel, and the other is lateral erosion. The sides of the canyon are subjected to the abrasive action of wind and rain, are undermined by the river and by flash floods, and where ice forms in the winter months, which can cause rocks to crack and break up. The rock strata exposed, beginning at the top with the youngest rock, includes Kaibab limestone, which is about 230 million years old, and is followed by successive layers of sedimentary rock, mostly more limestone, sandstone and shale, continuing down to what is known as the great unconformity. Here there should be more layers of sedimentary rock, according to the dating of the rocks above and below, but these layers are missing, an absence that has not been fully explained as yet. The rocks below the unconformity are metamorphic, pre-existing rocks which have been changed under huge pressure and temperature, and are made up of granite and, right at the bottom, the Vishnu schist. Altogether this represents one of the most complete pictures of geological time that exists anywhere in the world.

Human presence in the canyon stretches back 10,000 years, including the Anasazi, who are sometimes known as the Basketmakers and, in a later period, the Pueblo people. The canyon was abandoned some time in the 13th century, during a long period of severe drought, and remained unoccupied until, at various times, the Paintes, Cerbat and Navajo arrived. The US Army moved

the majority of these people to reservations in 1882, as part of a plan to end the Indian Wars, but some ancestors of the Cerbat, the Hualapai and Havasupai, still live in the immediate area.

The first Europeans to see the canyon were a party of Spanish soldiers in 1540. More than 300 years later, in 1869, an expedition led by John Wesley Powell, a Civil War veteran who had lost part of an arm at the Battle of Shiloh, began a full survey of the canyon. As it became more widely known, it was protected under law, becoming a National Park in 1919, including a large area of the Colorado Plateau surrounding the canyon. In recent years the park has been involved in a number of high profile conservation efforts, including the reintroduction of the Californian condor, one of the rarest birds in the world. This huge bird, which can have a 9ft (2.8m) wingspan and, while beautiful when seen at a distance soaring on thermal air currents, is quite stunningly ugly when seen up close, had dwindled to a population of nine birds in the wild. A captive breeding programme over many years saw numbers increase until it was possible to release some back into the wild, including into the park. There are now 60 birds in the area of the canyon and, while they remain a critically endangered species, there is hope for their continued survival.

The Grand Canyon may not be the largest or deepest canyon in the world, but it remains one of the most beautiful and spectacular places on the planet.

GRAND PALACE BANGKOK

The current King of Thailand, Bhumibol Adulyadej, who is also known as Rama IX, is the ninth monarch of the Chakri Dynasty, established by Buddha Yodfa Chlaloke, or Rama I, in 1782, after he came to power following a *coup d'état* against the previous monarch. Rama I moved the capital of Thailand from Thonburi to Bangkok shortly after he became king and began building the Grand Palace and the Wat Phra Kaew, the Temple of the Emerald Buddha, the most important and sacred Buddhist temple in Thailand, which stands within the palace grounds. Building work continued on the palace for many years and there are now around 100 buildings within its walls, which enclose about 60 acres (27ha). It continued to be the official royal residence for many years, the additions becoming increasingly opulent with each successive monarch, until King Bhumibol ascended to the throne in 1946. He moved the residence to the Chitralada Palace after the mysterious death of his older brother, King Rama VIII, who was found shot dead in his bedroom. The exact circumstances of his death have never been firmly established and, because of the reverence and respect with which the king is held in Thailand, it is never discussed there. The grounds of the palace, the museum and some of the buildings are now open to the public, but the buildings that continue to be used for state and ceremonial occasions are generally not, except on special occasions.

When Rama I decided to move his capital to Bangkok it was little more than a fishing village on the east bank of the Chao Phraya River. It is now a sprawling modern metropolitan city with one of the fastest growing economies in the whole of South-East Asia. The palace is on the west bank of the river, which forms one of the borders of its grounds. The buildings within the royal compound are a mix of traditional Thai-style architecture and those which show some degree of influence from Western architecture. The largest building is the Chakri Maha Prasat Hall, which was built by Rama V in 1882 using British architects and Thai workers. It has three wings in the Italian Renaissance style with traditional Thai stucco roofs, which are topped by layered and heavily ornamented spires, known as mondrops. The central mondrop contains the ashes of each Chakri king, while the flanking ones contain the ashes of royal princes. The middle wing is still used for official receptions, such as to receive foreign dignitaries.

Of the many other buildings, a few are particularly notable. The Dusit Maha Prasat is a traditional Thai-style pavilion, again with a highly ornate roof, built by Rama I to be used after his death for the lying in state of his body, a function the building retains today for the King and members of the royal family. The coronation of monarchs takes place in the Paisal Taksin Hall, which houses the coronation throne and the octagonal seat where the monarch receives the people's invitation to rule. Between these two seats is an altar containing a symbolised figure of Thailand called Phra Syam, which is traditionally invoked for the good of the state. The most Western-style building is the Borom Phiman, which dates from 1903 and was built by the then king, Rama V, as a residence for the heir apparent and is now used to house visiting heads of state.

The Wat Phra Kaew is built in the style of a Thai monastery, except it does not include any living quarters for monks. The interior is highly decorated, with many statues and mural paintings depicting the life of the Buddha, and its Assembly Hall, which is divided down the middle for the purpose, is also the private chapel of the King. Within this chapel is the Emerald Buddha itself, an 18in (45cm) high jade figurine of the sitting Buddha, which rests on a high golden altar. Legend says that it was made in India in 43 BC by Nagasena, who was a Buddhist sage, of comparable standing to one of the Apostles in the Christian Church, and it is considered to be the first representation of the Buddha to be brought to Thailand. After many years in different hands, it returned to Thailand after it was captured by Rama I, before he ascended to the throne, during a military campaign in Laos. Three times a year, in a ceremony of the changing seasons conducted by the King, the gold clothing of the Buddha is changed. It is an object of national veneration, which is considered to bring good fortune to Thailand, and crowds come to pay respect to the memory of the Buddha in front of it on days when the temple is open to the public.

FACT FILE

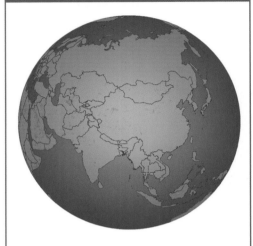

COORDINATES
13°44'57"N, 100°29'30" E

LOCATION
Bangkok, Thailand

ROYAL RESIDENCE
18th century to the mid-20th century

AREA
716,535sq ft (218,400sq m)

GREAT BARRIER REEF

A barrier reef can develop where the shallow water of a continental shelf extends out for a distance from the coast and then drops off quite suddenly into deeper water. Reefs develop where there is both a suitable climate and waves of a sufficient size to keep the water oxygenated and to bring in nutrients, but not so big as to break up the reef. As it develops the reef has the effect of a harbour wall, protecting the shore from the action of waves and creating a lagoon inside it. This is what has happened over the course of 20,000 years in the Coral Sea off the coast of Queensland, although here it has occurred on a truly epic scale, resulting in the Great Barrier Reef, which stretches from just north of Brisbane for the entire length of the Queensland coast and on up to the Torres Strait Islands, between Australia and Papua New Guinea, a distance of around 1,600 miles (2,600km).

The reef is made up of coral, a tiny marine organism that forms into colonies. It grows as polyps, each generation on top of the previous one and, as the polyps grow, they produce a hard exoskeleton of argonite, a type of calcium carbonate, which remains after the polyps have died. Over many thousands of generations, and where the colonies grow close together, the argonite becomes the rocky base of the reef, while the polyps continue to grow, gradually enlarging it. The Great Barrier Reef is an accumulation of reefs built up in this manner, something like 3,400 altogether, and it also includes around 300 coral islands, known as cays. There are around 400 species of coral in the reef, making it the most diverse area of coral in the world as well as the largest, and they are of numerous different shapes and sizes, including fan, antler and brain coral. They are also of a variety of colours, which is the result of a symbiotic relationship with algae, so each reef is a myriad of greens, yellows, reds and blues. In late spring, in the few nights following on from a full moon, the coral spawns, filling the water with eggs and sperm, a spectacle that has been likened to a gigantic underwater snowstorm.

As well as a large number of coral varieties, there is a quite incredible diversity of marine life associated with the reefs. There are 30 species of whales and dolphins, including both the humpback and killer whales and the bottle-nosed dolphin, living around the reef, as well as tiger sharks, dugong, both green and loggerhead turtles, and something like 1,500 species of fish, with more being discovered every year. The giant clam, which can be up to 5ft (1.5m) wide and weigh 400lb (180kg), is the largest of an incredible 4,000 species of mollusc and there are also more than 200 birds, many of which nest on the cays, including the white-bellied sea eagle and the roseate tern.

Corals are, in general, quite delicate and will die off quickly if subjected to changes in water quality, as can happen when sediment from agriculture runs into the ocean. Pollution from towns and cities along the Queensland coast, such as Cairns and Townsville, and from fertilisers and pesticides used in, for example, sugar cane farming, which is common in Queensland, also has the potential to be very damaging. As well as these general problems, there are a number of specific threats, such as that posed by the booming population of Crown of Thorns starfish, which eat the coral polyps in great numbers and can kill extensive areas in short periods of time. Bleaching has also killed large areas, where the polyps die off, leaving the exposed reef devoid of life. It has not been established exactly what causes this, but it is thought to result from a rise in sea temperature, which affects particular species of coral, as a result of global warming. As with many marine ecosystems around the world, there have been problems associated with over-fishing, the increasing number of ships in the area and the increasing number of tourists.

Almost the entire area covered by the barrier reef is now within the Great Barrier Reef Marine Park, one of the largest protected areas of marine environment in the world. The park oversees all commercial activities that make use of the reef, including fishing and tourism, and has developed long-term management plans for protecting the reef for many years to come. Some areas of the park are now managed jointly with the Aboriginal peoples who have lived on the islands for many generations. Their knowledge of the area and non-destructive use of resources provide a model of environmental management for us all.

FACT FILE

COORDINATES
18°17'10" S, 147°42'00" E

LOCATION
Coral Sea, off the coast of Queensland in north-east Australia

AREA
136sq miles (344,400sq km)

NUMBER OF REEFS
3,000 individual reefs and 900 islands

GREAT WALL OF CHINA

The building of defensive great walls was an old idea by the time the present Great Wall of China was built, beginning in the 14th century, during the Ming Dynasty, but the purpose was the same. The nomadic tribes of Mongolia and Manchuria had been harassing the northern borders of China for more than 2,000 years and a wall to keep them out had first been built in the 8th century BC, during what is known as the Spring and Summer Period of Chinese history. The first emperor of a unified China, Qin Shi Huang, had also built a wall, beginning in 221 BC. It was much further north than the Ming wall and was made of stones and pressed earth and it has almost entirely eroded away now. In 1368, when the Ming Dynasty came to power, after almost 100 years of Mongol rule in China during the Yuan Dynasty, ending with their expulsion by the Mings, the wall as we think of it today was begun. Impetus to continue the building work was no doubt renewed after the defeat in the Battle of Tumu Fortress in 1449, when, to the north of the wall, as it existed then, a large Chinese army was beaten by a much smaller force of Mongol cavalry and the emperor, who, against all advice, had been leading his army, was taken prisoner. Building continued into the 17th century and it was used as a defence against the Manchus. Unfortunately for the Mings, in 1644 a rebel general opened one of the gates in the wall to let the Manchu army through, an event generally considered to be the beginning of the end of the Ming Dynasty. The ensuing Manchu Qing Dynasty,

being the people whom the wall was built to keep out, did not need it and it fell into disuse.

At its pinnacle the wall began on the Pacific coast at what was known as the Old Dragon's Den, which is now in the city of Qinhuangdoao in Hebei Province, and ran roughly along the border of Inner Mongolia for almost 4,000 miles (6,400km) to Lop Nor in the arid north-west of China. Large parts of the wall are in a state of disrepair today, but some parts have been preserved and, in some cases, renovated and it is these that are accessible to tourists today. One of the sections relatively accessible from Beijing is known as the North Pass at Juyongguan, originally built to protect Beijing itself. Here the wall has been restored to look much as it would have done in its original state. It is 25ft (7.8m) high, an imposing barrier to anyone trying to cross it, and is mostly built of brick, with stone used for the foundations, the fortifications along the wall and in the gateways. The walkway along the

top is wide, something like 16ft (5m), giving an idea of the quantity of brick needed to build the wall, which tapers out towards the bottom, and there are ramparts along the sides. At regular intervals along the wall there are solid-looking watchtowers, more like small castles than towers, built into it, which would have held the garrisons responsible for particular sections of wall. It runs for as far as the eye can see in either direction, up and down hills and valleys and, wherever possible, following ridges, making best use of the local topography for defensive purposes and to command the terrain in front of it. The watchtowers are often situated on hills, to give a clear view of the wall and so that signals could be sent back to the barracks behind it if reinforcements were needed.

Standing on the wall, it is easy to see the idea behind it. The nomadic tribes of the north characteristically fought on horseback, employing lightning raids and hit and run tactics and, when

they did fight battles, doing so on open ground, where they could outmanoeuvre their opponents, tactics at which they were, according to military historians, unequalled. This sort of warfare, however, could make no headway against a highly fortified and defended wall, where their prowess on horseback was nullified. To invade China, the nomadic tribes would have had to assault the wall directly first, engaging in a static siege battle against the superior numbers of the Chinese within the fortifications of the wall.

The wall proved to be highly effective at protecting China's northern borders, until the Ming Dynasty was betrayed from within, and stands today as testimony to their immense power and their ability to mobilise an enormous number of people for huge building projects. It remains to this day as the longest man-made structure in the world, although the number of people who died during its construction was not recorded.

FACT FILE

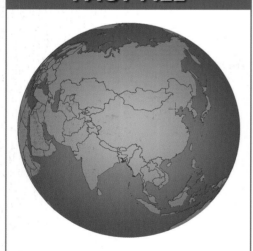

COORDINATES
40°19'58" N, 116°28'39" E

LENGTH
Over 3,948 miles (6,352km)

RECORDS
World's longest man-made structure

CONSTRUCTION
Took place between 5th century BC and the 16th century AD

GUGGENHEIM MUSEUM BILBAO

Bilbao, the largest city in the Basque region of northern Spain, is going through a major phase of urban renewal, prompted by the decline of its traditional industrial base situated around the port, which included shipbuilding and steel manufacturing. The city has also seen a reduction in its population in the metropolitan areas and the Basque Government, in an effort to halt this decline, has attempted to transform its economy, from one dependent on heavy industry to a mixed economy that includes services, culture and the information industry. As part of this process, in the early 1990s, the construction of a landmark building that would give the city international recognition was proposed. The Basque Government, in collaboration with the Guggenheim Foundation, commissioned the architect Frank Gehry to design such a building, the Guggenheim Museum Bilbao.

Frank Gehry, who is originally from Toronto but now lives and works in California, worked for architectural firms for many years designing what could be described as traditional buildings. In 1967 he started his own business and, at some point, radically changed his approach to the discipline. This new style has been described as being of the deconstructivist school of postmodern architecture, a description Gehry himself rejects. As with most postmodern thought, it is almost impossible to say what deconstructivism actually entails, but essentially it involves the subversion of preconceived ideas of what the structure of a building implies to the observer. This is achieved by designing buildings that do not conform to the geometric shapes of more traditional architecture

and by using building techniques and materials it has previously not been possible to use. The presence of the building within the space it occupies becomes its central theme and the spaces themselves, the parts of the building that are not built, become as important as the actual building. This forces the observer to look at the building without reference to previous buildings, which have no relevance to its design.

The Guggenheim Museum stands on the waterfront in central Bilbao. At first sight it appears to be an abstract sculpture, whose curving geometrical shapes clash with each other, creating odd angles and elevations. Looked at from the other side of the river, the shape of a ship, with buildings or, possibly, mountains rising above it, begins to emerge from this chaos of shapes. As well as symbolising the cultural heritage of Bilbao, the curving lines of the building evoke the spiral structure of Frank Lloyd Wright's design for the Guggenheim in New York. These extraordinary shapes were achieved using computer-aided design and visualisation, fixing the building specifically within the time period of the available technology. It is built from three main materials, limestone, titanium cladding and glass. The titanium, which is used in very thin sheets, gives the outside shell a highly distinctive look, reflecting sunlight and taking on the appearance of fish scales.

The entrance to the museum from the city centre is reached by descending a long flight of stairs, bridging the different levels between the city and the river and ensuring that such a large building does not dominate the landscape. The interior revolves around a central atrium, a huge

empty space with glass walls, which, together with skylights in the high sculpted ceiling, lets in shafts of daylight, illuminating the interior in the manner of a Gothic cathedral. Curved walkways, lifts and stairways lead to the galleries, which take different forms to comply with the original specification of having three exhibitions: a permanent collection, a temporary collection, and a collection of living artists. The space created for the temporary collection is particularly notable, being an elongated rectangular gallery that extends underneath the La Salve Bridge, culminating in a tower on the far side, which integrates the bridge into the building.

The permanent collections include a number of site-specific installations, including works by Richard Serra. These huge steel sculptures include *Snake*, three parallel sheets of steel curving through one of the galleries, which was created for the opening of the museum in 1997, and a series of seven sculptures called *A Matter of Time*. On the outside of the building is *Puppy* by Jeff Koons, a 12ft (3.5m)-high sculpture of a puppy covered in flowers, which has been described as a monument to the sentimental and shows that museum curators can have a sense of humour too.

Since its opening the museum has attracted a great deal of comment, most of which has been favourable. Some critics find the building too impersonal, as if it were designed with postmodern architecture in mind rather than people, and others think the building overshadows the works of art on display inside, but, if its original purpose was to put Bilbao on the international stage, then it has succeeded in a spectacular way.

FACT FILE

COORDINATES
43°16'07" N, 2°56'03" W

LOCATION
Bilbao, Basque Country, Spain

ARCHITECT
Frank Gehry

STYLE
Deconstructivism

PUBLIC OPENING
1997

HADRIAN'S WALL

The Roman Emperor Hadrian succeeded Trajan in AD 117 and immediately set about consolidating the expansions to the empire that had occurred under the previous emperor, when it had reached its greatest territorial extent. He began a series of prolonged tours, taking him to the extremities of the empire, both to see for himself what the situation was in those areas and to show himself to his legions. In AD 122 he arrived in Britannia, as the Romans called it, which had recently been through a period of rebellion, and he ordered the building of the wall that bears his name. Having determined that invading Caledonia, now Scotland, would have been difficult and expensive, he decided on the wall to protect the northern fringe of the empire and as a demonstration of Roman power to the Britons. There may well also have been a number of other reasons for the wall: it would allow the Roman army to control movement on both sides of it; the soldiers could collect taxes from people entering or leaving the Roman Empire, in the manner of a customs post; the work would keep the soldiers busy in an otherwise relatively quiet period; and it would act as a clear indication of the borders of the empire.

The Roman legions took highly skilled stonemasons with them wherever they went, who would have shaped the stones, which were quarried in the immediate vicinity of the wall, and supervised the building work of the soldiers. According to inscriptions found on the wall, it was built by the 2nd, 6th and 20th Legions over a period of ten years and, at its height, the work involved more than 10,000 people. There was a total of 17 forts along the wall, some of which had existed before it was built and each with a garrison of several hundred men, and there were gates at regular intervals. These intervals were so regular that, on occasion, the gates would open straight onto the sheer face of a cliff. Building began in the east, at what is now Wallsend in Newcastle, on the River Tyne, and continued for 73 miles (117km) across country to the Solway Firth near Carlisle. The first sections to be built were something like 15ft (4.5m) high and 10ft (3.5m) wide, but by the time the wall got to Branton Fort, plans were changed and the wall became lower and narrower. The final sections of the wall, which may have consisted of lengths of earth bank as well as stone wall, have all but disappeared now, the stone having been carted off to be used in other buildings.

The wall remained in use for 300 years, until the Roman withdrawal from Britain in AD 410. By this time the soldiers of the wall are thought to have integrated into the local population and they continued to man the wall for some period after the Romans had left, but it gradually fell into disuse. Large sections of the wall remain today, particularly the middle parts, and the route it follows now forms a long-distance walking path. Extensive archaeological digs have been carried out in some areas, particularly in the remains of the forts, and some amazing artefacts have turned up.

At Vindolanda, an auxiliary fort just south of the wall, built some years before it and used during the construction as a base for the people actually doing the building, digging has been carried out for many years. The soils in this area, being anaerobic, have preserved many wooden and leather objects that do not usually survive extended periods buried underground, including bowls, leather shoes and boxwood combs. The most incredible find, however, has been the Vindolanda tablets, of which 900 have been unearthed so far. These are Roman letters and they give a more personal insight into life at the fort than can usually be gathered from archaeology alone. The tablets are made up of two thin pieces of wood, about postcard size, and held together with leather strips so they fold over. On the inner sides messages have been written, using the Roman cursive script, which is very difficult to read, with the addresses written on the outer sides. In one famous example, Sulpicia Lepidina, the wife of the commander of a nearby fort, writes to Claudia Severa, the wife of the commander of Vindolanda, inviting her to a birthday party and saying she hopes Claudia can come because she is finding life in the fort very boring and would appreciate the company. In another tablet, the writer uses the word 'Brittuculi' to refer to the local people, the first known example of a Roman nickname for the British and, it is now known, not a very polite one at that.

FACT FILE

COORDINATES
54°59'33" N, 2°36'05" W

LOCATION
Northern England, UK

LENGTH
200 Roman miles (183.8 modern miles, 300 kilometres)

CONSTRUCTION
Started around AD 122, complete within ten years

HAGAR QIM

The archaeological record shows that Malta was inhabited from at least 5000 BC and by about 3500 BC, during the Chalcolithic, or Copper Age, a culture of temple building had developed on the islands. More than 30 of these temples remain throughout the Maltese Islands, including those known as Tarxien, Ggantija, the Hypogeum and Hagar Qim. They are considered to be the oldest free-standing stone structures in the world, 1,000 years older than the pyramids, and show that the people who built them, sometimes called the Temple Builders, were very highly skilled at working with stone. Then, at around 2500 BC, temple building appears to have stopped abruptly and there is no further archaeological evidence of people living in Malta until the Phoenicians arrived in about 1000 BC. Archaeologists have been investigating the temples since the 19th century and, as well as uncovering the temples themselves, they have found some extraordinary artefacts, most famously the so-called 'fat lady' figurines, but major questions remain concerning what the temples were used for and why these people expended so much effort to build such elaborate structures.

Hagar Qim, which is pronounced along the lines of 'Hajar Eem', is one of the most impressive of the temples and also, in fact, one of the most impressive stone buildings remaining from prehistory. It stands on top of a hill on the south coast of Malta, overlooking the sea, and it is roughly rectangular in shape. The outer walls are built from huge horizontally laid stones, dressed to fit together perfectly, with huge standing stones, known as orthostats, at the four corners, the largest of which is about 22ft (7m) high and weighs 20 tons. Small stone models of temples found at other sites all have roofs on them, so it is reasonable to assume that Hagar Qim would also have had a roof when it was originally built. A terraced forecourt extends out from the main doorway, which leads into a central court with four or five, it's not entirely clear, small rounded rooms, known as apses, radiating off from it. The doors into several of these apses have been carved through the middle of a single stone slab, which has the effect of isolating anybody inside them from the central court. There are what look like stone tables, often described as altars, in several of the apses and there was a larger and more elaborately carved alter in the central court, which is now in the National Museum of Archaeology in Valletta. The seven fat lady figurines found in the temple are also now in the museum, including the Venus of Malta, a 5in (13cm)-high female figure, which is missing its head and feet. It was modelled in clay and was then baked until it was hard and, unlike all the other figurines found so far, it is of a standing figure and is quite naturalistic in its design.

An attempt to answer the thorny question of what the people who built Hagar Qim actually used it for can only be one of speculation based on what is there now, as the people who built it disappeared without trace 4,500 years ago. One interpretation is that, as the temple shows no sign of having been lived in and would have taken an enormous communal effort to build, it would most likely have been used for spiritual and ritual purposes. The ability to organise a communal effort would suggest that the society was structured, perhaps including a 'priest' class, who would have conducted the rituals in the temple, which, like ritualistic behaviour all over the world, would have involved some form of interaction with the spiritual realm. The layout of the temple, with an open public forecourt, a more exclusive enclosed central court and secluded apses, is further evidence of a structured society, with people of higher rank having access to the temple, but only the priests themselves being allowed into the apses, where they would commune with their deities. Finds of animal bones from other temples suggest that the altars were used for animal sacrifice and this, together with the fat lady figurines, may have played a role in fertility rituals, a common occurrence in early agricultural societies. The remains of a huge sculpture of a woman found in the temple at Tarxien would suggest the worship, at least in part, of female gods, possibly a Mother Earth figure, although this inference is, perhaps, pushing the speculation further than the available evidence really allows. What does become apparent, however, is the complex and involved nature of the spiritual lives of these people. Hopefully, at some stage, new archaeological finds will shed more light on what they were doing at Hagar Qim, why they stopped using it and what became of them after it was abandoned.

FACT FILE

COORDINATES
35°49'40" N, 14°26'32" E

LOCATION
Southern edge of Malta

EXCAVATED
1839

LARGEST TEMPLE
6.4m long, 5.2m high, estimated weight 20 tons

HAGIA SOPHIA

The Hagia Sophia, known as the Ayasofya in Turkey, stands on a hill in Istanbul, looking out over the Bosporus and the Sea of Mamara. It was commissioned by the Emperor Justinian, of the Eastern Roman Empire, now known as the Byzantine Empire, in AD 532 and by the time it had been completed, six years later, it was regarded as the greatest church in the world. Although it has not been a church for more than 500 years, and, in its history, has suffered at the hands of man and nature, it remains one of the world's great buildings.

The original architects, Anthemius of Thralles and Isidorus of Miletus, designed a rectangular building which supported one of the largest domes in the world at that time and achieved this remarkable feat in such an elegant manner that the dome almost appears to float over the basilica below rather than be supported by it. To do this they employed a number of innovative methods to rest the circular base of the dome on the columns, or piers, at each of the fours corners of the basilica, allowing the weight of the dome to spread downwards while restraining its lateral force, which is, in effect, its tendency to flatten itself out. Each side of the basilica is supported by semi-domes, which are themselves supported by further semi-domes known as exedras, and the piers rise up into the arches of these semi-domes forming an architectural feature called a pendentive, which looks like a triangular segment of a sphere. These pendentives meet over the arches of the semi-domes to form the circle on which the dome rests, so the weight flows through the piers and semi-domes to the ground. The floating impression is enhanced by a row of windows just above the rim of the dome, allowing light to flood in, and this has been achieved by using ribs as an internal support for the dome, which flow down from the top to meet the rim on either side of each window.

On seeing the completed interior Justinian is supposed to have said, 'Solomon I have surpassed you', referring to the Temple of Jerusalem which had been destroyed 1,000 years earlier. Twenty years later the dome was destroyed in an earthquake and its replacement fell again in 563. This time it was rebuilt by Isidorus the Younger, the nephew of one of the original architects, who raised the dome and strengthened the external buttresses. These modifications held it up until 989, when a third, and much larger, earthquake caused part of it to cave in and it was restored yet again. The interior was ransacked in 1204, when crusaders sacked Constantinople and converted it into a Roman Catholic cathedral, during the short-lived Latin Empire. The Byzantines retook the city in 1261 and it reverted to its original Eastern Orthodox roots, but, almost 200 years later, Constantinople was conquered again, this time by the Ottoman Turks under Mehmet the Great, who converted it into a mosque. The Ottomans were tolerant of other religions and did not destroy the Christian iconography decorating the interior of

FACT FILE

COORDINATES
41°00'30" N, 28°58'48" E

LOCATION
Istanbul, Turkey

CONSTRUCTION
532–537

CENTRAL DOME
102ft (31m) wide and 184ft (56m) high

their mosque, although they did plaster over much of it. During the reign of Sulieman the Magnificent, the four minarets, which give it such a distinctive silhouette today, were built. They were designed by the greatest of all Ottoman architects, Mimar Sinan, who is said to have become obsessed with the building and tried to emulate it again and again in the mosques he built.

The Ottoman Empire lasted until after the end of the First World War, long enough for the British and French to partition it along the lines of a secret accord signed by the two countries, known as the Sykes-Picot Agreement. The Turkish War of Independence saw the emergence of the Republic of Turkey in 1922 and its first president, Kemel Ataturk, turned the Hagia Sophia into the Ayasofya Museum. Restoration work has continued since then and has often proved controversial because the original Christian art has often been covered over with fine examples of Islamic art. In the museum today there are many early Christian mosaics, including depictions of Christ, the Virgin Mary and John the Baptist. In one example, the Virgin is seen with Justinian on one side and Constantine, the founder of Constantinople, on the other. Among the marble columns there are some of purple porphyry and one of the stone columns, known as the weeping column, is clad in brass and the moisture seeping from it is thought to cure a wide range of ailments. Perhaps the properties of its damp should come as no surprise in a building that has survived such vicissitudes in its history.

HERMITAGE MUSEUM

The State Hermitage Museum is one of the foremost museums and art galleries in the world. It stands on the banks of the River Neva, which runs through St Petersburg and out into the Gulf of Finland. Five of the Hermitage's seven buildings make up a hugely impressive river frontage: the Winter Palace, the Hermitage Theatre and buildings known as the Great, New and Small Hermitages. The other two buildings are the General Staff Building and the Menshikov Palace and, all together, they display a vast range of art works and antiquities from the museum's collection of almost 3 million items.

The museum is particularly strong in Italian Renaissance and French Impressionist paintings, including the *Benois Madonna* and the *Madonna Litta* by Leonardo de Vinci, two of a handful of original paintings by Leonardo that still exist, and there are significant works by Raphael, Titian and Caravaggio. All the Impressionists are represented, including Renoir, notably the *Portrait of the Actress Jeanne Samary*, Monet, Cezanne and Gauguin, with several of his Tahiti paintings. There is a room devoted to Rembrandt, with a number of the self-portraits, *The Descent from the Cross* and the recently restored *Danae*. The museum holds 37 paintings by Matisse, including the two panels *Music* and *Dance*, and 31 by Picasso, from the early blue period, through cubism and into the later works. A few of the other painters whose work is in the collection include Rubens, van Gogh, El Greco and Velazquez. There are sculptures by Michelangelo and Rodin, jewellery by Fabergé and the finest collection of

ancient artefacts from central Asia to be found anywhere in the world, including some magnificent pieces of Scythian gold. These few highlights hardly scratch the surface of the collections, some parts of which can now be seen in galleries in London, Amsterdam and, slightly more surprisingly, in the Venetian Hotel and Casino in Las Vegas.

The buildings of the Hermitage are often said to be works of art themselves, particularly the largest and most opulent of them, the Winter Palace, which was the winter residence of the tsars and has fine interior decoration and architectural detail. It was commissioned in 1754 by the Empress Elizabeth, who was Peter the Great's youngest daughter and had come to power following a *coup d'état* in 1740, and it was designed by Bartolomeo Rastrelli. It is in the rococo style, which it typifies by the lightness of its design and in its colours, which are light green and white. It was finished in early 1762, but it came too late for Elizabeth, who had died at the beginning of the year. She was succeed by Peter III, who was, by reputation, an immature and feckless man, and he moved into the newly completed palace with his wife Catherine. The marriage had been arranged by the Empress Elizabeth and was not a happy one, the two of them having taken many lovers in the 16 years of their marriage. Peter proved an unpopular and capricious emperor and, while he was away from the palace, the Leib Guard, his personal bodyguard, revolted against him and installed Catherine as empress. It has been assumed that Catherine initiated this coup and also that she was involved when Peter died three days later, in what

was described as a shooting accident. Catherine was a much more popular ruler, becoming known as Catherine the Great, and she was a great patron of the arts. She began the collection that would later form the nucleus of the Hermitage Museum in 1764, buying up collections from around Europe as they came onto the market, including that of Robert Walpole, the first Prime Minister of Great Britain, who was said to have had one of the finest collections in Europe.

The Winter Palace continued to be the residence of the tsars until the October Revolution of 1917, led by Vladimir Lenin and the Bolsheviks, which began with a siege of the palace. On gaining power the Soviets established the State Hermitage Museum, but Stalin, who considered art to be bourgeois and decadent, allowed the sale of a number of masterpieces from the collection, including Raphael's *Alba Madonna*, which was sold to an American banker and is now in the National Gallery of Art in Washington.

During the Second World War much of the collection was taken to the Urals for safe keeping and, during the Siege of Leningrad, the Hermitage became accommodation for thousands of people and was bombed on numerous occasions. With the Soviet victory in 1945, a large number of works of art were removed from Germany to Russia, where they remain. The restitution of the works is a contentious issue for many Russians, who consider them to be legitimate reparations for the suffering inflicted on the Russian people during the war.

FACT FILE

COORDINATES
59°56'26" N, 30°18'49" E

LOCATION
St Petersburg, Russia

CONSTRUCTION
1754–1762

ARCHITECT
Francesco Bartolomeo Rastrelli

CURRENT ITEMS OF ART
over 3,000,000

HOLLYWOOD HILLS

For a glorified advertising hoarding to have become an instantly recognisable landmark, you would have thought it would have to be selling something pretty amazing. Certainly not real estate, but that is what the Hollywood sign was originally about. The 50ft (15m)-high white letters rising out of the scrub on the side of Mount Lee in Griffin Park, which had originally spelled out HOLLYWOODLAND, was just a big publicity stunt to try and shift some property in an area of Los Angeles just below it. In 1923 Harry Chandler, the owner of the *Los Angeles Times*, was involved with the syndicate, the Hollywoodland Real Estate Group, who owned the land and, after a friend of his had pulled a similar stunt a few months earlier, he thought he might as well give it a try. The syndicate paid $21,000 to have the sign erected and, no doubt, after it was up they must have waited for the money to come rolling in. The land they were selling was going to be a gated community in Beachwood Canyon, upmarket properties aimed at the wealthy and, to be fair to them, they did sell some. The houses are there, and are sought-after now, but it wasn't long before the Wall Street Crash, followed by the Great Depression and then the Second World War. The gates of the community are still there on Beachwood Drive and their old offices are occupied now by a different real estate business, but they only sold 50 acres of the 500 on offer.

That is the story of how the sign got to be there, but we all know this is not why it is still there now, more than 80 years later. It is still there because of the movies, not because of the real estate, and it is all to do with glamour and money, with film stars and the dreams of ordinary people, because, in America, anyone can become rich and famous, anyone can be in the movies. This may not be true in America any more than it is anywhere else in the world, but that doesn't stop people believing it and, if you go to Los Angeles, you cannot miss the sign to Hollywood. It is right there in front of you, spelled out in great big white letters.

The film industry had become firmly established in Hollywood by 1923. Film-makers had moved out to California to avoid the stranglehold Thomas Edison, who owned the patents to almost all of the film-making processes, held over the industry, and they found the California weather to be much more conducive to filming than it had been on the east coast. In 1915 the Supreme Court cancelled Edison's patents and the industry took off, with the likes of Cecil B. De Mille and D.W. Griffith, who had started out making films in barns, establishing the studio system that would dominate Hollywood for the next 40 years. By the early 1920s, movie-making was big business and real estate was booming along with it. In 1927 Warner Brothers released *The Jazz Singer*, the first picture with synchronised sound, and the boom got even bigger. The Depression did not hit it as hard as most other businesses. Going to the movies was cheap and a distraction from the grim realities of recession, and Hollywood entered its golden years with classic films like *Casablanca*, *Gone with the Wind*, *It's a Wonderful Life* and *The Wizard of Oz*.

By 1944 the Hollywoodland Real Estate Group had gone bust and the sign had become the property of the Los Angeles City Council. It was falling down and all its light bulbs, which had blinked throughout the night when it had first been put up, had been stolen. In the postwar years television began to threaten the film industry and the Hollywood Chamber of Commerce were looking for ideas to promote it. They took over the sign, removed the last four letters, repaired the rest of it and gave it a new coat of paint, but replacing the bulbs would have cost a fortune so they decided against it.

It was looking the worse for wear and tear again by 1978 and an auction was held to raise funds to replace it. Alice Cooper bought the 'O' and the singing cowboy Gene Autry came up with the required $28,000 for one of the 'L's. A shiny new sign was put up, the one that stands there today. It is regularly maintained now and, in the billion dollar movie industry of today, it is a reminder of where it all came from and, in the story of Peg Entwistle, one of those who didn't make it and, in 1932, threw herself to her death from the top of the sign, of the human side of the business as well as the glamour.

FACT FILE

COORDINATES
34°08'02" N, 118°19'18" W

LOCATION
Los Angeles, California, USA

HEIGHT OF LETTERS
45ft (13.7m)

ORIGINAL SIGN
Real estate advertisement, *Hollywoodland*, 1923

CURRENT SIGN
Unveiled on Hollywood's 75th anniversary

HOOVER DAM

On 30 September 1935, in the middle of the Great Depression and only a few months after the worst wind storms of the Dust Bowl, President Franklin D. Roosevelt made a determinedly upbeat speech at the dedication of the Hoover Dam. He pointed to it as a symbol of recovery and progress and said 'This is an engineering victory of the first order, another great achievement of American resourcefulness, American skill and determination', and there can be no doubt he was right in this assessment. Throughout the speech he referred to it as the Boulder Dam, its original name before it was changed in 1930 and, while he thanked many of the people who had been involved in its construction, he did not mention Herbert Hoover, under whose presidency the building work had started and who had been involved in getting the project off the ground in the first place. The dam reverted to being called the Hoover Dam in 1947, but the personal animosity between FDR and the man he had beaten in the 1932 presidential election was not going to be given a day off, not even

to celebrate the completion of such a notable project.

There were many practical reasons for building a dam on the Colorado River and these had been recognised for years. The river was prone to flash flooding, particularly in the spring when melt water flowed into it from the Rocky Mountains. A dam could be used to control the river, while, at the same time, the lake created behind it would hold a reliable supply of water for agricultural irrigation and for the rapidly increasing population of Southern California and, as the water was released, it could be used to generate hydroelectric power. Herbert Hoover, a mining engineer before turning to politics, was the Federal Government's representative on a committee set up in 1922 to work out a scheme for equitable use of the river's waters between the Basin states (Arizona, Nevada, Colorado, California, New Mexico, Utah and Wyoming) and the resulting agreement laid the groundwork for the construction of the dam. Hoover was president himself by the time the required legislation had been passed in 1930, and,

by then, embarking on such large public projects had become politically expedient too, with the Government being seen to be getting the country back to work during the Depression.

The site of the dam had originally been in Boulder Canyon, but, early on, was changed to Black Canyon for sound engineering reasons. The consortium that won the contract to build it, the Six Companies, whose Chief Executive, Frank Crowe, was also its Chief Engineer, was keen to get the project under way immediately and did not wait until the town to house the workers, Boulder City, was finished before beginning preparatory work. Unemployed men flooded into the area, often bringing their families with them, and Ragtown, a ramshackle tented city, grew up.

The first job was to divert the river away from the site of the dam and this was achieved by driving two tunnels through the bedrock of the canyon on either side of the river and diverting the water into them using a cofferdam. Once this was done the dangerous jobs of blasting down to the bedrock on the site itself and preparing the walls of the canyon

were started. Concrete pouring began in June 1933 and, for this to be done quickly, techniques had to be developed to get the concrete to set. The dam was built of a series of interlocking blocks, the concrete for each of which being poured on site and then cooled to set it quickly using cold water from an on-site refrigeration plant. While this was being done the hydroelectric power station was being built and the architect George Kaufmann had been employed to give the dam an Art Deco look after the original plans had been criticised for their bland concrete exteriors.

The availability of cheap labour and the rush to build the dam led to what can only be described, even by the standards of the day, as terrible disregard for the workers. Officially there were 96 deaths in industrial accidents, from rock slides, blasting accidents and falls, but this does not include people who died as a result of carbon monoxide poisoning, brought on by working in the tunnels and listed by the Six Companies as being pneumonia, or from diseases contracted in the unsanitary conditions of Ragtown. As much as it is a great engineering achievement, the largest dam of its day and still one of the largest gravity-arch dams in the world, it is also a monument to the desperate times of the Great Depression and to the ordinary people who lived through those times and, on occasion, died because of them.

FACT FILE

COORDINATES
36°00'56" N, 114°44'16" W

LOCATION
Borders of Arizona and Nevada
– Colorado River

CONSTRUCTION
1931–1936

MATERIAL REMOVED DURING EXCAVATION
1,500,000yd³ (1,150,000m³)

MAXIMUM HYDROELECTRIC POWER
2,074 megawatts

KNOSSOS

The Bronze Age civilisation that developed on Crete, known as the Minoan civilisation after the mythical King Minos, existed between about 2600 and 1400 BC. Of the extensive archaeological remains from the Bronze Age, Knossos, which stands on Kephala, a hill 3 miles (5km) inland from the modern Cretan capital of Heraklion, is the largest and most extensively excavated site.

Knossos was known before Sir Arthur Evans began his excavations there in 1900, but it is his name that has become inseparable from it. As well as uncovering the Great Palace, as he called it, he was also responsible for the restoration of sections of it. Some people consider this restoration was necessary for the preservation of the site and now makes it more accessible to visitors, while others would argue it was an exercise of the imagination rather than anything to do with archaeology. Evans was looking for the site of King Minos' labyrinth, as described in the Greek myth of Theseus and the Minotaur, and in the palace he uncovered, which has more than 1,000 rooms and can easily be described as labyrinthine, he considered he had found it.

The site of Knossos had been occupied since the Neolithic, going back at least to 6000 BC, while the earliest Bronze Age remains date to about 2000 BC. The original building, the Old Palace as Evans called it, appears to have been destroyed by earthquakes on a number of occasions, each time being rebuilt on more elaborate lines, resulting in the Great, or New, Palace, built by 1700 BC. This was also modified and extended many times over the next 300 years until being destroyed and abandoned, along with the surrounding buildings and town, by about 1380 BC.

The palace covered about 6 acres (2.5ha) and the buildings, which were several storeys high, were arranged around the four sides of a central court. On the west side of this court were the buildings containing what is thought to have been the sacred areas of the palace, including the Throne Room, another one of Evans' names. This is a surprisingly small room with a low ceiling, considered to be the central room of any ritual activity. It contains a large alabaster seat, the throne, which rests against one of the walls, opposite what looks like quite a large bathing area. The walls have stone benches around them and are decorated with frescos of griffins, which have large cat-like bodies and bird's heads. In one of the rooms leading off from the Throne Room the figurines known as the Snake Goddesses were found. These are small glazed earthenware statues of bare-breasted women who are holding snakes in each hand. At least one of them had been intentionally broken before being buried in a stone-lined pit, suggesting their use in some form of ritual.

Many of the rooms in the palace were used for storage and contained large clay vases, known as pithoi, which contained produce such as grain, olive oil, beans, and dried fish. Evidence of olive presses and wine making has been found on the site and, from the number of storerooms, it would appear to have had a highly productive agricultural society. A feature of these buildings are the many frescos decorating the rooms and halls. The ones that can be seen today have been reconstructed from the fragments remaining of the originals and, while they cannot be assumed to be exactly correct representations, are still wonderful images. Famous ones show people leaping over bulls, men boxing and dolphins. Men and women are represented differently, the men being darker coloured than the women, and the fact that there are many more images of women than men and no images of any form of warfare at all has led to intense speculation concerning the nature of Minoan society. It has been suggested that it was a peaceful society dominated by women, perhaps ruled by a high priestess. While there may be a certain amount of wish fulfilment in this interpretation, the evidence does point to an equality between the sexes absent from the later male dominance of Ancient Greece.

Many theories have been put forward to explain the apparent rapid decline and disappearance of the Minoan civilisation. A huge volcanic eruption on the island of Thera, now Santorini, causing a tsunami and changing the climate of Crete, could have been devastating for the Minoans, although the date of the eruption is a hotly debated problem with this theory. Other ideas, of invasion by the Mycenaeans from mainland Greece or a decline in maritime trade, at which the Minoans are thought to have been at the forefront, are equally contested, but, for whatever reason, this highly developed society collapsed and the palace of Knossos was abandoned.

FACT FILE

COORDINATES
35°17'52" N, 25°09'49" E

LOCATION
Near Heraklion, Crete

DISCOVERED
1878 by Minos Kalokairinos

PREHISTORIC CLASSIFICATION
Bronze Age

KREMLIN AND RED SQUARE

In the immediate aftermath of the October Revolution in 1917, civil war broke out in Russia between the communist Red Army and the White Guard, a loose association of forces who had opposed the Bolsheviks after they had overthrown the Tsar in St Petersburg. Vladimir Lenin transferred the new government to Moscow, where the Russian capital had been until 1712, to distance it from the heartland of support for the Whites and where it has stayed since, with Moscow becoming the capital of the Soviet Union on its formation in 1922. Several assassination attempts had been made on Lenin's life before his arrival in Moscow and this, no doubt, must have influenced his decision to take up residence in the highly fortified compound of the Kremlin. With the dissolution of the Soviet Union in 1991, it became the official residence of the President of the Russian Federation, with, in 1992, Mikhail Gorbachev moving out and Boris Yeltsin, its first president, moving in.

The Kremlin is a triangular complex of buildings surrounded by high walls and it stands on the River Moskva in the heart of Moscow. On its west side there is a public park called the Alexander Garden, containing the Tomb of the Unknown Soldier and the Eternal Flame, which are dedicated to the soldiers of the Red Army who were killed in the Great Patriotic War, as the Second World War is known in Russia. On the east side is Red Square, the name it has been known by in Moscow for several hundred years and not, as is commonly thought, a name given to it by the communists, although Lenin, on moving into the Kremlin, must have enjoyed the coincidence. Lenin's Mausoleum stands on the square, a step pyramid-like building where his embalmed body continues to be on public display more than 80 years after his death in 1924, and, during its opening hours, there is a permanently long queue of people outside waiting to get in.

One of the most distinctive buildings in Russia, St Basil's Cathedral, occupies one end of the square and, if the stories are to be believed, was saved from demolition by over-zealous Soviet administrators, who were planning to increase the area of the square to allow for even larger military parades than were already occurring, by Josef Stalin himself, not a man generally associated with an appreciation for symbols of bourgeois decadence. The cathedral was commissioned in 1555 by Ivan the Terrible to commemorate his victory in the siege of Kazan and, although Islamic architecture is often cited as an influence, its onion-shaped domes and tented roofs follow a tradition of Russian Orthodox church building, if with considerably more decoration than was usual. The other two sides of the square are occupied by the beginnings of the Kitay-Gorod commercial district, with the huge State Universal Store, known as the GUM, facing the Kremlin, and, at the opposite end of the square from St Basil's, by the State Historic Museum. This is a large brick building bearing some resemblance to St Pancras Station in London and described as being built in the Russian Revival style, a catch-all phrase applied to 19th-century Russian buildings which, if this case is a typical example, look as if the architects, if there were any, have thrown the kitchen sink at them.

Borovitsky Hill, which is often simply called the Kremlin Hill, has, according to archaeological evidence, been occupied for more than 2,000 years and been the site of a fort since the 12th century. It developed as a walled town, with the current walls being built towards the end of the 15th century, during the reign of Ivan the Great, when the Kremlin became the centre of a unified Russia and the city began to develop around it. A number of the buildings also go back to this period, including three of the four cathedrals within the complex, which stand around Soboyana Square and share a single campanile, known as the Ivan the Terrible Bell Tower. There are also a number of palaces, all built after the capital had moved to St Petersburg. The tsar's residence in Moscow was the huge Great Kremlin Palace, which overlooks the river and, after the revolution, was used for meetings of the Supreme Soviet. In the 1990s it was restored at enormous expense and is now a museum of Tsarist Russia. The Senate Building faces Red Square and is the president's official residence. Next to it is the Arsenal, where the Kremlin Regiment is based, who have responsibility for the security of the Kremlin and form the guard of honour at the Tomb of the Unknown Soldier. Of the other buildings in the complex, one stands out for all the wrong reasons. It was built in the early 1960s and it is, not to put too finer point on it, a concrete monstrosity.

FACT FILE

COORDINATES
55°45'05" N, 37°37'04" E

LOCATION
Moscow, Russian Federation

AREA WITHIN THE KREMLIN WALL
2,960,075sq ft (275,000sq m)

TALLEST BUILDING WITHIN KREMLIN
266ft (81m). Buildings taller than this at the time were forbidden.

LAKE BAIKAL

COORDINATES
52°47'17" N, 107°25'03" E

LOCATION
Russia

WATER VOLUME
5,521mi³ (23,600km³)

MAXIMUM SIZE
395 miles (636km) length
50 miles (80km) width
5,369ft (1,637m)

To the Buryat people of southern Siberia Lake Baikal is known as Dalai Nor, the Sacred Sea, and when they are fishing on this vast expanse of crystal clear water they think it is unlucky to refer to it as a lake, considering the word demeans it and its use causes the violent storms that sweep across the lake from time to time. Little was known about it outside of this remote part of central Asia until the early years of the 20th century, when the Trans-Siberian Railway arrived in Irkutsk, the main city in the region, and skirted Baikal's eastern edge as it continued on to Vladivostok. It is the largest and deepest freshwater lake in the world, containing as much water as all five of the Great Lakes of America put together, and it forms a great crescent, 395 miles (696km) long, in the deepest rift valley on the Earth. The water is more than a mile (1.6km) deep and there are 4 miles (7km) of sediment below that, which has accumulated over more than 20 million years, making Baikal the oldest lake in the world as well. The rift continues to grow, as separating tectonic plates move away from each other, leading to frequent earthquakes in the area, and also to hydrothermal vents in the floor of the lake and hot springs around its shores. There are more than 300 rivers flowing into it, but only one running out, the Angara River, which is more than a mile wide at the point of its formation on the shore of the lake and has a current like a tidal race.

Many large enclosed bodies of water, such as the Black Sea, form into layers, with the top few hundred feet supporting life but, below that, they are virtually lifeless. The water in Baikal is constantly circulating, thought to be due to the gravitational pull of the sun and the moon and the warming effect of the vents, and this keeps all of its water sufficiently oxygenated to maintain life right to the bottom. The lake is enclosed on all sides by high mountains, isolating it from the world beyond, and this, together with its great age and its unusual physical properties, has led to the enormous diversity of plants and animals living in it and an incredibly high incidence of endemism. The nerpa, or Baikal seal, is the only truly freshwater seal in the world and the only mammal living in the lake. It only occurs in Baikal and how it got there remains, like so much else about the lake, something of a mystery. Of the lake's 52 species of fish, the omul, which is also not found anywhere else, is the main

catch of the commercial fishermen of the lake. It is a large white fish and, when it has been smoked, is considered a delicacy of the region.

The great abundance and diversity of life can conceal the fact that this is a fragile environment, life in the lake having evolved in such conditions of purity as to make them highly sensitive to disturbance and pollution. The opening up of the region by the railway has led to the commercial exploitation of its natural resources and, in 1966, to the construction of the Baikalsk Pulp and Paper Mill on the shore of the lake. In the industrial process of making paper, the mill uses chlorine as a bleaching agent and the effluent it emits from this process forms a plume of pollution that spreads out into the lake. Large areas of forest have been cleared to provide the pulp for the mill and this has resulted in increased levels of sediment running into the lake as well as damage to the taiga, the Siberian forest, itself. In recent years plans to build

an oil pipeline within half a mile (0.8km) of the lake were being proposed, but were stopped when the Russian president, Vladimir Putin, personally intervened, instructing the company involved to find an alternative route for the pipeline to avoid any threat of pollution to the lake. This is a sign of the changing attitudes of the Russian Government since the end of the Soviet era, when huge damage was done to the Russian environment through unchecked industrial development.

The Pearl of Siberia, as the lake is sometimes known, remains for the most part in a pristine condition, despite the pollution released into some areas of it. Some people have expressed the opinion that, as it is so large, it is capable of absorbing the impact of this pollution, but the environmental disaster of the Aral Sea is a stark reminder, if one is needed, of the consequences of such a short-sighted attitude.

LEANING TOWER OF PISA

The Campo dei Miracoli (the Field of Miracles) is a walled area in the centre of the Italian city of Pisa. Within the walls there are four buildings which all date back to the medieval period, including a beautiful cathedral, the Duomo, a separate building containing the font, the Baptistery, and a walled cemetery, the Camposanto Monumentale. The fourth building is a free-standing bell tower, or campanile, and, due to its having been built with inadequate foundations which stand in a loosely compacted subsoil, it has become one of the most recognisable buildings in the world. It is, of course, the Leaning Tower of Pisa, which, assuming it was intended to stand up straight when it was originally built, would, had it been built properly in the first place, now only be known as the bell tower of the cathedral.

In the 12th century Pisa was a powerful city state and had become wealthy through maritime trade and the exploits of its navy. In 1113 the city,

along with a number of its allies, captured the Balearic Islands from the Moors and the riches it gained from this, together with other such spoils of war, were used to build the Campo dei Miracoli as a statement of its wealth and power. The tower was the last of the buildings to be commissioned and, according to an inscription on the inside, work began on 9 August 1173. There is some doubt as to the identity of the architect, who is traditionally said to have been Bonanno Pisano, but several other names have also been put forward. It was almost 200 years before the tower was fully finished, with the work initially stopping when the tower was only three storeys high because the lean had already begun. Work did not begin again for about 100 years because the Pisans were almost continually engaged in war with one or other of the different Italian city states and, it is thought, this long delay allowed the subsoil on which the tower stands to stabilise. Had it been completed

in its entirety at the first attempt, it would almost certainly have fallen over. The second phase was carried out by Giovanni of Simone, who attempted to compensate for the lean by continuing the building with a slight curve away from it, but he also had to stop, this time at the seventh storey. Finally, the building was completed in 1372 by Tommaso di Andrea Pisano, who added a Gothic belfry to the tower, which had been built in the Romanesque style with its characteristically rounded arches.

It is built of marble blocks, constructed to form two concentric walls around a hollow centre. A spiral staircase runs up the building within the cylindrical body, giving access to the arcaded storeys and to the belfry at the top. Although it is hard to know from what point to measure it to give its height, it is something like 185ft (55m) tall.

In one famous incident, the veracity of which is by no means certain, Galileo, who was born in Pisa in 1564, is supposed to have dropped two different

sized cannon balls from the top of the tower to demonstrate that two bodies of different mass would descend at the same speed, independent of their masses. This had already been proved some years previously, but Galileo was the first person to have used experimentation to show it was definitely the case.

Attempts over the years to correct its lean have almost always been unsuccessful, and have sometimes made it worse. By 1990 the lean was 5.5 degrees from perpendicular and an engineer who examined it was surprised that it had not already fallen over. It was closed to the public and secured with steel cables while a plan was worked out to stabilise it. The problem was solved by placing lead weights on the north side of the building, the opposite side to the lean, and then digging out tons of soil from under that side. The north side of the tower slowly sank into the cavity being created under it, pulling the tower back towards the perpendicular by 17in (45cm), and correcting the lean to within acceptable levels. The intention was not to correct the lean completely, which would have done the fame of the building and the tourist trade in Pisa no good at all, but to make it safe enough for people to climb to the top of it again without thinking it might fall over while they were inside. It was reopened to the public in 2001 and should now be safe from collapse for the next 200 years, at which point another ingenious scheme for its preservation will be required.

FACT FILE

COORDINATES
43°43'23" N, 10°23'47" E

LOCATION
Pisa, Italy

CONSTRUCTION
Started 9 August, 1173. Continued in three stages for 199 years

HEIGHT ON HIGHEST SIDE
183.27ft (55.86m)

LOCH NESS

The waters of Loch Ness are deep and murky and the reports of a monster in them have a long history. Rarely seen, and the sightings even more rarely believed, the Loch Ness Monster, or Nessie, may be a figment of the imagination, but people, some of them reasonably sensible, have been seeing something in the loch going back for 1,500 years. At some point in the 6th century St Columba, the monk who reintroduced Christianity into Scotland during the Dark Ages, is reputed to have saved someone who had been swimming in the loch and had been attacked by an unidentified creature. Sightings, although not unknown, were a bit thin on the ground after that, until a road was built along the shores of the loch in 1933. Suddenly reports started to come in, thick and fast, of an enormous animal with a long neck and humps on its back, and these sightings made the front pages of the newspapers. Photographs and film followed, often of a rather dubious nature, but the story had been reborn and reports of sightings continue to this day, fuelled, some cynics say, by the burgeoning tourist industry in this beautiful part of Scotland.

Loch Ness is the largest of an interconnected series of freshwater lakes in the Great Glen, a geological fault that runs right the way through the Scottish Highlands, from Inverness on the Moray Firth to Fort William at the head of Loch Linnhe. These lochs, together with the Caledonian Canal, link the North Sea to the Atlantic Ocean and, although this route was never particularly well used by commercial vessels, it is now popular with people in pleasure crafts. The loch is 23 miles (37km) long and is particularly notable for its great depth, reaching down to about 800ft (245m). The water draining into it comes through the surrounding peat bogs and has been stained to a deep brown colour by the peat. This is why the water is so dark, with visibility often down to less than 15ft (5m), which leads to a relative paucity of life in the loch, as sunlight cannot penetrate very far into it. The only island in the loch, called Cherry Island, is an example of a crannog, an artificially enlarged island, which was probably created in the Iron Age, when it would have been fortified and have had a causeway running out to it.

Over the years there have been a number of expeditions to the loch which have set out to establish once and for all whether there is a monster in it or not. Using a range of increasingly sophisticated equipment, including submersible vehicles, sonar and underwater cameras, they have met with what could be, at best, described as mixed levels of success. In one of these expeditions in the 1970s, led by Robert Rines, an American lawyer, photographs were taken which, it was claimed, showed the fins of a plesiosaurus, an aquatic dinosaur that became extinct during the Cretaceous–Tertiary extinction event some 65 million years ago. Explanations of how this cold-blooded dinosaur could have survived in the cold water of a land-locked Scottish loch and through the Ice Ages, when the loch could well have frozen solid, have not been very convincing. Some of the other explanations, of it being a primitive whale or a species of long-necked seal, have not solved the mystery either and the suggestion that Nessie is actually an extremely large eel is, frankly, just plain crazy. In a rare outbreak of rationality in the debate, a Swedish naturalist, Bengt Sjorgen, has linked the sightings of Nessie to the ancient Celtic mythologies surrounding kelpies. These, according to the myths, were supernatural shape-shifting water horses who would lure people into riding on their backs and then dive into lochs which were deep enough for them to vanish into completely and for their unwary riders never to be seen again. According to Sjorgen, these myths have been adapted over the centuries to fit with a modern audience, so what people see now is an image they can relate to, one they may have seen on television, such as a dinosaur or a particular type of animal.

Modern folk tale the monster may well be, but anyone visiting the loch who fails to catch a glimpse of it will not be disappointed by the natural beauty of the loch itself and the Scottish Highlands around it. Those who don't have the time, or just can't be bothered, to come and have a look for themselves, can check out nessie.co.uk, which is Nessie's official website, where she (apparently Nessie is a lady monster) keeps her fans up to date on what she's been doing by writing a regular blog.

FACT FILE

COORDINATES
57°18' N, 4°27' W

LOCATION
Inverness, Scotland

HEIGHT ABOVE SEA LEVEL
52ft (15.8m)

SURFACE AREA
21.8sq miles (56.4sq km)

MAX DEPTH
754ft (230m)

LOUVRE

The Louvre first opened its doors to the public as a museum on 10 August 1793, during the period of the French Revolution known as the Reign of Terror. Louis XVI, the former King of France, had been executed in January of that year and the Government, the Committee of Public Safety, had come under the control of Maximilian Robespierre. Thousands of people were being accused of counter-revolutionary activities and then tried and executed with the guillotine. The Louvre had been a royal palace since a castle had been built on the site in 1190 and opening it as a museum, where the public could see the art collections of the royal family and of aristocrats who had been executed or had fled abroad, can be seen as a revolutionary act.

The buildings of the Louvre and its collections were enlarged during the turbulent years of French history in the 19th century. Towards the end of the Paris Commune, established in 1871 as a socialist government of Paris and only lasting for a few months, the Tuilleries Palace, the west wing of the Louvre, was burnt down shortly before the French army retook the city. The gutted building stood for a number of years before it was demolished, opening the Tuilleries gardens and the central courtyard of the Louvre, as they are today. For the bicentennial celebrations of the French Revolution in 1989, President François Mitterrand commissioned the Chinese–American architect Leoh Ming Pei to build the glass pyramid that now stands in the courtyard. Although highly controversial when it was first put up, it has solved the problem of access to the Louvre, providing an entrance to the reception hall below it. Shortly afterwards the Ministry of Finance, which had occupied the Richelieu wing of the building since the late 19th century was, much to the annoyance of the civil servants, moved out and the entire building was given over to the museum.

The museum holds one of the finest collections of art and antiquities in the world, including some of the most famous. The *Venus de Milo*, possibly the most widely recognised statue in the world, was found in pieces on the Aegean island of Milos in 1820 and has been attributed to the relatively unknown Alexandros of Antioch. On arrival at the Louvre it was reassembled, but the left arm, which was of a lower quality than the rest of the statue, was left off, the right arm having not been found with the statue in Milos. The plinth, bearing the name of the sculptor, was lost, possibly after the experts who had initially attributed the sculpture to Praxiteles, one of the greatest of all the classical Greek sculptors, had become embarrassed by their mistake. The wonderful *Winged Victory of Samothrace* stands on the sweeping Daru staircase and is one of the greatest surviving masterpieces of the Hellenistic period of Greek history, dating back to around 200 BC. It was also reassembled from fragments, which did not include the head or the arms, although one of the hands was subsequently found at the site of its discovery on Samothrace. It depicts the open-winged goddess Nike in a naturalistic pose, leaning forward slightly with her clothes flowing back from her body, as if she is leaning into the wind.

The Department of Paintings includes a wide range of European art from the 13th century to 1848, the year of the abdication of King Louis-Philippe and the establishment of the Second Republic, whose president, Napoleon III, would seize dictatorial power in the *coup d'état* of 1851. Without doubt the best known painting of the extensive collection and, arguably, the most famous work of art in the world today, is the *Mona Lisa*, or *La Gioconda* as it is sometimes known, painted by Leonardo da Vinci in the early years of the 16th century. The painting is famed for the proverbially enigmatic smile of the female subject, the identity of whom has been the subject of endless scholarly debate, although the original identification, of it being Lisa Gherardini, the wife of the Florentine cloth merchant Francesco del Giocondo, is as convincing as any of the later proposals. The painting leapt to the attention of the world in 1911 when it was stolen from the Louvre. Guillaume Apollinaire, the French poet who had called for the Louvre to be burnt down, was arrested and Pablo Picasso, known to detest the painting, was questioned, but, as there was no evidence against either, they were both released without charge. Several years later it was found in the flat of an employee of the Louvre, who had stolen it as part of a confidence trick to sell forgeries by claiming they were the original missing painting, and it was returned to the museum, where it remains to this day.

FACT FILE

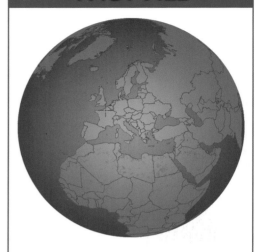

COORDINATES
48°51'41" N, 2°20'06" E

LOCATION
Paris, France

ESTABLISHED
1793

CONSTRUCTION OF PYRAMID
1989

VISITOR FIGURES
8,300,000 (2006)

MACHU PICCHU

In his best-selling book *The Lost City of the Incas* Hiram Bingham, who was more of the Indiana Jones school of archaeology than the academic disciple, related the story of how, in 1911, he discovered Machu Picchu, an Inca city standing on the top of the mountain of the same name, which overlooks the Urumbamba Valley in the Peruvian Andes. He had been looking for Vilcabamba, the last stronghold of the Incas after the destruction of their empire by Spanish Conquistadors, and, having been told of some ruins in the area, made an arduous ascent of the mountain with a local guide to make the discovery. In another interpretation of events, Bingham was led to the ruins, which were well known to the locals and were, in fact, inhabited at the time of the 'discovery', then, when he had returned to America, made extravagant claims of feats of exploration in an unknown region of the world, which cast him in the role of hero. The truth of the matter probably lies, as it so often does, somewhere in between the two extremes, but what can be said for certain is that Bingham brought Machu Picchu to the attention of the world and that, now, his name is inextricably linked with it.

Machu Picchu is thought to have been built in around 1440 by Inca Pachacuti (the word Inca is used for the ruler of the empire as well as for the empire itself) and it was inhabited for about 100 years, until the Spanish conquest of 1532. There are something like 170 buildings spread out across the top of the mountain, room enough for perhaps 1,000 inhabitants altogether, and they are constructed of the white granite so characteristic of Inca buildings throughout the empire. The level of craftsmanship of the Inca stonemasons is astonishing. Even today, more than 500 years later, the dry-stone walls fit together perfectly and there are numerous stone staircases cut directly into the rock of the mountain, making use of its natural aspect to best advantage. The water system is a sophisticated one, bringing water to the city from the adjoining higher ground and using it to feed fountains and stone troughs and then to flush the drainage system and to irrigate crops growing on the mountainside below.

The view across to the towering peak of Huayna Picchu and the mountains beyond is breathtaking and it can be no coincidence that Machu Picchu is positioned to take best advantage of this view. Looking down from the city, towards the River Urumbamba thousands of feet below, terraces cut into the sides of the mountain and have been shorn up with stone retaining walls. These were used to grow a range of agricultural produce, but particularly maize. There are buildings within the city itself that were clearly storehouses for this produce and there is evidence of the brewing of chica, corn beer, which is still made in the Andes today. Other parts of the city were divided into sectors where craftsmen, such as weavers, potters and gold - and silversmiths, lived and there is also a separate area for the nobility. In one area, described as the sacred district, there are temples standing around a large central courtyard. These stand out for the superior finish of their stonework, comparable to the best work in the Inca Empire, so, it has been assumed, these must have been the most important buildings in the city. They include the Temple of the Sun and the Temple of Three Windows, and there is also a stone, the Intihuatans, which has been sculpted for the purpose of making astronomical observations.

Over the years there have been many theories as to why the Inca built Machu Picchu, some of which make more sense than others. One recent idea, by archaeologists who have spent many years studying the site and have also found references to it in Spanish colonial documents from the period of the conquest, is that it was a country retreat for the Inca nobility, a place for contemplation and recreation, and the site may have been chosen for its outstanding natural beauty rather than for any sacred or religious reasons. Other ideas suggest the city was a sanctuary for the Inca equivalent of nuns, or, perhaps, a specific place of worship of the sun or other Inca deities.

Whatever the actual reason, there can be no doubting the aesthetic values of the Inca or their architectural skills. It attracts people from all over the world, so much so that UNESCO think it is being damaged by the level of tourism it experiences. It would be a shame indeed if the desire to visit this wonderful place felt by so many people would be the cause of its gradual destruction.

FACT FILE

COORDINATES
13°09'47" S, 72°32'44" W

LOCATION
Urumbamba Valley, Peru

FIRST NON-INDIGENOUS SITING
1911, by archaeologist Hiram Bingham

HEIGHT ABOVE SEA LEVEL
7,972ft (2,430m)

MONT-SAINT-MICHEL

The small rocky island of Mont-Saint-Michel rises out of the bay where the Couesnon River runs out into the English Channel, and the Benedictine abbey on the top of the island appears to be continuous with the natural shape of the island, bringing it to a point with the spire of its church. In 1879 the natural land bridge that connected the tidal island to the mainland was converted into a permanent causeway so the island would no longer be cut off every time the tide came in.

The Couesnon used to form the border between Normandy and Brittany and its constantly changing course, as it flowed out through the huge expanse of sandbanks in the bay, led to disputes between the two regions. The border has been firmly established for many years now and the course of the river fixed by turning it into a canal to prevent the erosion of its banks, but this has also stopped the river from carrying its sediment out to sea and the bay has silted up, leading to the formation of extensive mudflats. This, together with the causeway, which prevents the incoming tide from sweeping sediment from around Mont-Saint-Michel, is gradually causing the island to become integrated with the mainland. A huge engineering project, begun in 2006, aims to reverse this and involves the construction of a dam on the river and the replacement of the causeway with a footbridge. The aim is to allow the tides, which Victor Hugo described as coming in with the speed of a galloping horse, to clear the sediment that has built up in the bay. It is due for completion in 2012 and, when it is finished, Mont-Saint-Michel should begin to return to its natural state, that of a tidal island surrounded by the sea for part of the day, while remaining accessible to the millions of people who visit it each year.

In the early 8th century St Michael the Archangel is said to have appeared to the Bishop of Avranches in a series of visions and instructed him to build an Oratory on the island, perhaps in place of a pre-Christian shrine. The island became a place of pilgrimage, the Miquelots coming from all over Europe to pay homage to St Michael and, under the patronage of the Duke of Normandy, the Benedictine Order began building an abbey in the 10th century. Over the centuries work continued, with successive stages being built on top of the previous buildings. The Gothic abbey, replacing the previous Romanesque building, was built over a series of crypts and includes the Salle des Hôtes, the Guest Room, and Salle des Chevaliers, the Knights' Room. Above these is the church, supported by two earlier vaults and with a figure of St Michael adorning the top of its steeple. At the same level there are the long and narrow refectory and the cloisters, which have the slender columns typical of the Norman style of Gothic architecture.

A small town grew up below the abbey and was fortified, due to the position of the island between Normandy and Brittany. The fortifications were strengthened during the Hundred Years War, really a series of wars fought by successive English kings, who claimed the French throne, beginning with Edward III in 1337 and including the Battle of Agincourt. The English besieged the island in 1423 but were unable to capture it and left behind two bombards, heavy siege cannons, which remain near the outer wall of the defences and are known as Les Michelettes.

After the Reformation of the Catholic Church in the 16th century the abbey began to fall into disuse and the last few monks remaining were forced to leave when the abbey was dissolved during the French Revolution. It was converted into a prison and, initially, held opponents of the revolution, but, when the monarchy was restored, it was used to confine republican political activists. Auguste Blanqui, a revolutionary socialist who took part in a number of armed insurrections, was held there during the reign of King Louis-Philippe (1830–1848) and was released after the revolution of 1848. A campaign, supported by Victor Hugo, to close the prison succeeded and the abbey was returned to the Church by Napoleon III in 1863. It was declared a national monument in 1874 and restoration work began, some of which, particularly the building of the causeway, had the unintended result of increasing the level of siltation in the bay that has become such a problem today. On the positive side, the salt marshes that have grown up on the mudflats provide grazing for sheep and the resulting agneau de pré-salé, or salt marsh lamb, has become a local speciality on the menu of the many fine restaurants in the area.

FACT FILE

COORDINATES
48°38'08" N, 1°30'40" W

LOCATION
Normandy, France

FORMATION
Granitic outgrowth approaching 3,150ft (960m) in circumference that reaches 302 ft (92m) above sea level

VISITORS
3,200,000 each year

MOUNT EVEREST

The mountain ranges of the Himalayas stretch from Pakistan and Afghanistan in the west across India, Nepal, Tibet, China and Bhutan, forming a huge crescent of mountains that separate the Indian subcontinent from the Tibetan Plateau. The tectonic plate on which the subcontinent sits has been moving northwards for millions of years and is colliding with the Eurasian plate, forcing the rocks at the edge of the Indian plate upwards. This process is continuing and the Himalayas get fractionally higher every year, including Mount Everest, the top of the world, which stands on the border between Tibet and Nepal and, at 29,028ft (8,848m), is the highest mountain in the world.

In 1802 the British army surveyor Colonel William Lampton began the enormous task of mapping British territories on the Indian subcontinent, which became known as the Great Trigonometrical Survey, by establishing a baseline in Madras, now Chennai, in the south of India. George Everest, also an army officer, was appointed as Lampton's assistant in 1818, taking over the survey in 1823 after Lampton had died and becoming the Surveyor-General of India in 1830. He retired and returned to England in 1843 and Andrew Waugh took over the survey. By the late 1840s it had reached the borders of Nepal, which were closed at that time, and observers measured the high mountains from Indian territory. By the time the trigonometrical calculations had been done, Radhanath Sikdar, the leader of the team of observers, knew that the mountain they had called Peak XV was the highest peak in the Himalayas, which made it the highest in the world. Everest had, where possible, always used local names for the features he surveyed and was not particularly impressed when he was told that Waugh had named the mountain after him, although Waugh claimed he could not ascertain a local name for it. In 1865 the name Mount Everest was officially adopted and, as both Tibet and Nepal were closed to foreigners at the time, perhaps it is possible to forgive Waugh for not having heard the Tibetan name of Chomolungma, which means Mother of the Universe, because, surely, had he known it, this is what we would all be calling Mount Everest now.

Tibet remained closed to travellers, but maintained cordial relations with the British Government and, in the early 1920s allowed a number of British expeditions to Everest. In 1924, on the third of these expeditions, George Mallory and Andrew Irving made an attempt on the summit of the mountain that has since entered mountaineering folklore and is still discussed to this day. They set out in early June to follow what is known as the North Col route and, as photographs from the time show, they were wearing an assortment of tweed jackets and woolly jumpers, the standard equipment for alpine climbers of the day. They were last seen high on the mountain and, as one of the expedition members put it, were 'going strongly for the top' before being enveloped in cloud. They did not return and the mystery of whether they made it to the top or not remains. In 1999 Mallory's body was found on the mountain, but there was no way of telling for certain if he had died while coming down having got to the summit. It is thought that Irving would have taken a camera with him and, should it ever be recovered and it

be possible to develop the film, it may provide definitive proof.

Tibet was closed again after the Second World War and remained so until the 1980s. All subsequent expeditions had to approach the mountain from the Nepal side, including, in 1953, the British expedition led by John Hunt. This expedition was better organised than those before it and set up a series of camps high up on the mountain. The first attempt on the summit, by Charles Evans and John Bourdillon, got to within 300ft (95m) when they had to turn back due to bad weather and exhaustion. The second attempt was by Edmund Hillary and Tenzing Norgay and, at 11.30 on 29 May, they succeeded in standing on the summit of the world. News of the success reached Britain a few days later, on the morning of the coronation of Elizabeth II.

Since then there have been many successful climbs, notably by the Italian Reinhold Messner, who was the first person to climb the mountain solo, without oxygen or support. Every year there are numerous expeditions setting out to climb the mountain and there are stories of how, to fulfil personal ambition, climbers have left people who are in distress to die while they make their own attempt on the summit. What they think they are achieving by behaving in this manner is open to question.

FACT FILE

COORDINATES
27°59'17" N, 86°55'31" E

LOCATION
Himalaya, Nepal and China

ALTERNATIVE NAMES
Qomolangma or Sagarmatha or Chomolungma

HEIGHT
29,028ft (8,848m)

FIRST IDENTIFIED AS WORLD'S HIGHEST PEAK
1852, Radhanath Sikdar

MOUNT FUJI

FACT FILE

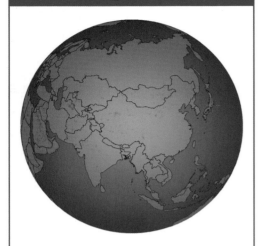

COORDINATES
35°21'29" N, 138°43'52" E

LOCATION
Chubu region, Honshu, Japan

ELEVATION
12,388 ft(3,776m)

LAST ERUPTION
1707

One of the most recognisable scenes in Japan is that of Mount Fuji, of the snow-capped mountain rising in the distance with water features and forests in the foreground. It is often described as a symbol of Japan itself and is as familiar and emblematic as the rising sun, cherry blossom and the samurai sword. For thousands of years it has been an object of veneration and it is sacred in the Shinto religion, for which it is a place of pilgrimage and the site of a shrine. Some of the best known images of it are the woodblock prints, known as ukigo-e, meaning 'the floating world', by Kataushika Hokusai (1760–1849) and called *36 Views of Mount Fuji*. These show Fuji from a variety of places and distances and in changing seasons and weather conditions. *The Great Wave of Kanagawa*, from 1832, was the first in the series and one of the most famous. It shows a huge wave about to crash over two boats with Mount Fuji in the background.

The islands of Japan stand on the junction of three tectonic plates, within a zone of high seismic activity around the edge of the Pacific Ocean known as the Ring of Fire. On Honshu, sometimes called the Japanese mainland and its largest island, earthquakes are frequent occurrences and there were large ones in 1995, in Kobe, and in 2004, in the Chuetsu area of Niigata Prefecture, in the west of the island. The Great Kanto Earthquake hit Tokyo in 1923 and virtually flattened the city. It has been estimated to have measured at least 7.9 and it killed more than 100,000 people. Volcanic activity is not as common, but the presence of the huge volcanic cone of Mount Fuji, which is about 100 miles (160km) south-west of Tokyo, from where it is visible on days when it is not shrouded in cloud, is a very obvious sign of the extent of the activity in the past. Fuji-san, as it is often called, is the highest mountain in Japan, at 12,388ft (3,716m), and it towers over the surrounding area.

It is a stratovolcano, a common type of volcano formed in what geologists call subduction zones, where one tectonic plate is subsumed under another. Water from the Earth's crust seeps down into mantel rock and has the effect of lowering the rock's melting point, causing it to rise and form a magma chamber under the site of the volcano. Pressure builds up as the magma and its associated gases accumulate, which, when a critical level has been reached, are released with a sudden explosive eruption. Over the course of successive eruptions the conical shape of the volcano develops, as layers of lava and ash build up. The characteristic cone shape occurs because the lava produced by these volcanoes is highly viscous and, on erupting, cools before it can spread out over a wide area.

Four separate volcanoes have developed on the site of Mount Fuji, one on top of the other, over a period of several hundred thousand years. The latest, or 'New Fuji' as vulcanologists call it, began to form about 10,000 years ago, with major eruptions occurring every few hundred years. Extensive lava flows from the summit and from side vents have blocked water drainage to the north of the volcano, forming the lakes known as the Fuji Five Lakes which, together with the mountain, make up the Fuji-Hakone-Izu National Park. The last major eruption occurred in 1707 and created a large new crater on the side of Mount Fuji and it entirely consisted of volcanic ash, which fell as far away as Tokyo. Since then the volcano has murmured on several occasions and plumes of steam have risen out of the crater, but there have been no eruptions. There is currently considered to be a moderate risk of an eruption and Japan's Meteorological Agency has set up a series of seismographs and other monitoring equipment on it to give as much warning as possible, and a disaster management plan has been developed to be implemented if and when it happens.

There is a proverb in Japan along the lines of 'A wise man climbs Fuji once and a fool climbs it twice' and, during July and August, when the facilities on the mountain are open, there are a large number of, no doubt, wise men and fools doing just that. The traditional way to climb it is to set out in the afternoon, spend the night in one of the many huts situated along the route and, in the early morning, to get to the top in time to catch the rising sun. This, like miso soup and the bullet train, is a truly Japanese experience.

MOUNT KILIMANJARO

Near the southern end of the East African Rift Valley there is a cluster of about 20 volcanoes, including the three peaks of Mount Kilimanjaro, Shira, Mawensi and, between them, the youngest and the highest, Kibo. They are in northern Tanzania, on the border with Kenya, and the highest point of Kibo, Uhuru Peak, on the rim of its volcanic crater, is the highest point in Africa at 19,340ft (5,895m). This height also makes it the tallest free-standing mountain in the world, as much of its height rises straight out of the savannah, and, as well as this, it is one of the largest volcanoes on Earth. None of the three peaks is currently active, although there are fumaroles, small holes, in the crater on Kibo, which emit steam and sulphur, and some geologists have suggested the possibility of a major eruption at some point in the not too distant future.

Images of Kilimanjaro almost always concentrate on Kibo, which, although not all that far from the equator, retains its ice cap throughout the year because of its great height. In fact, ascending Kilimanjaro is like taking a trip through almost all of the world's climatic zones. On the lower slopes there are extensive and lush montane rainforests, which contain some of Africa's iconic animals, such as elephant, buffalo and leopard. The forests begin to thin out and give way to bush and scrubland and then into open moor, covered with heathers interspersed with giant senecias and lobelias, which are spiny and cactus-like. Higher still is an alpine desert landscape of bare scree slopes, supporting little life other than some hardy mosses and lichens and, finally, above this, there are glaciers and snow fields on the slopes immediately below the summit.

The ice cap and the glaciers flowing down from it have attracted attention in recent years because they are said to provide an illustration of the extent to which climate change has affected the world's ice sheets. The glaciers have been retreating on Kilimanjaro for many years and the ice cap almost disappeared in 2005. Ice cores taken on the mountain have shown that the ice cap has been there continuously for the past 11,000 years, but has been retreating since the 19th century and, at the rate it is going now, will have disappeared completely in about 20 years. An alternative explanation has suggested that East Africa has experienced a drier climate since the 1880s, leading to less snow on the top of Kilimanjaro, but this only accounts for the glacier retreat up until the 1970s, since when the climate not become wetter again. The increasing rate would seem to be a response to climate change, although, with numerous other examples of glaciers melting from all around the world, Kilimanjaro is only one example among many. The implications of the loss of the ice caps are serious for the people who rely on the glacier-fed rivers flowing from Kilimanjaro for their water supply during the summer months.

The Chagga people who live on the lower slopes of Kilimanjaro are not overly reliant on glacier run-off for the type of farming they practise. They use a system of terracing on the slopes of the mountain and grow trees to hold the soil together. Under the trees they plant cash crops of coffee, which is sold in European and American markets, and they also grow bananas, maize, beans and garden vegetables. They fertilise these fields with manure from their animals and have developed an extensive system of irrigation to use the large amounts of rain that fall on the mountain, although this may have to change if the region becomes drier as a result of climate change. The economy of the Chagga also benefits from the number of tourists visiting Kilimanjaro, traditionally by acting as guides on the mountain and selling produce to the many local hotels, but, increasingly, by running their own businesses to take advantage of the money coming into the area themselves.

The first European to report on Kilimanjaro was a Swiss missionary, Johannes Rebmann, who made a series of trips to northern Tanzania in the 1840s. At the Royal Geographical Society in London his reports of a snow-capped mountain in East Africa were not believed. In 1926 another missionary, Pastor Richard Reusch, climbed the mountain and found the frozen carcass of a leopard at the rim of the crater, which, some years later, would inspire Ernest Hemingway to write one of his best known stories *The Snows of Kilimanjaro*, about a dying writer reflecting back on his life. In 20 years' time, if the climate scientists have got it right and the summer snows of Kilimanjaro have become a thing of the past, it will be a sad story indeed.

FACT FILE

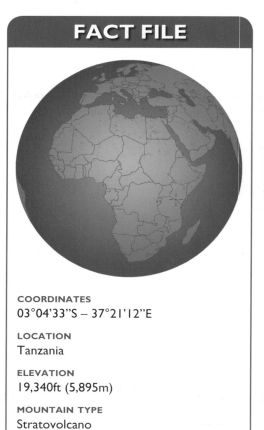

COORDINATES
03°04'33"S – 37°21'12"E

LOCATION
Tanzania

ELEVATION
19,340ft (5,895m)

MOUNTAIN TYPE
Stratovolcano

MOUNT RUSHMORE

The Needles, in the Black Hills of South Dakota, are huge pillars of eroded granite and it was here, in 1923, that Doane Robinson, a local historian, first proposed the idea of carving monumental statues of famous people. He had been inspired by Stone Mountain in Georgia, where the images of Confederate generals were being cut into the rock, and his original idea was to sculpt people from the history of the West, like General George Armstrong Custer, Buffalo Bill or Lewis and Clark, to attract tourists to the Black Hills. Gutzon Borglum, a sculptor who had been a student of August Rodin and had been involved in the Stone Mountain work, was invited to come to the Black Hills to consider the project.

Objections were raised from the start, from people who thought it would ruin the natural landscape and from Native Americans, who considered it to be a sacred site, and permission and funding by the State Government was denied. After inspecting the Needles, Borglum, who thought the rock there was too brittle for sculpting, decided to move the project to Mount Rushmore and suggested sculptures of great American presidents instead of Western celebrities. He chose Mount Rushmore because of its more prominent position and south-easterly aspect as well as for its granite structure, which was harder and more suitable for carving. Permission was obtained, but it was not until 1927, after President Coolidge visited the Black Hills and was persuaded to support the plans, that funding was obtained. Coolidge had insisted on balance in the sculptures, leading to the choice of George Washington, Thomas Jefferson, Theodore Roosevelt, who had been a friend of Borglum's and had died eight years previously, and Abraham Lincoln as the subjects of the sculptures.

The work began in October 1927 and Borglum, who had developed techniques of working in rock on a large scale at Stone Mountain, used dynamite to clear most of the rock from around the proposed sculptures. Many local people were employed in the work, including miners who were experienced in the use of explosives and they developed their skills to such a degree as to be able to blast the rock away to within 4in (10cm) of the intended finished surface. The huge amount of scree on the lower slopes of Mount Rushmore is the remains of the 450,000 tons of rock the dynamiters removed and, after they had finished, the work of carving the rock down to the finished sculptures began. The proportions of each figure had been worked out from scale models and transferred to the rock surface and, to remove the last few inches of rock, holes were drilled to the exact depths required, a process known as honeycombing. The rock was then chipped away with chisels and the surface finished with pneumatic drills with specially designed bits, leaving it smooth.

The original plans included the torsos of the presidents down to the waist, but, in 1941, Borglum died and although his son took over the project, the impetus and funding both dried up and

the sculptures were left as they are today. The original intention of attracting tourists has certainly succeeded, with something like three million people visiting Mount Rushmore every year. The National Park Service, who have managed the site since 1933, see it as a symbol of America, representing freedom and democracy for all people, but, while the Park Service are putting forward a view shared by many, there remain some dissenting voices, particularly in the Native American community. A brief look at the history of the area in the 19th century illustrates why.

In 1868 the Treaty of Fort Laramie was signed between the United States and the Lakota, one of the seven tribes of the Great Sioux Nation, which guaranteed the ownership of the Black Hills to them. Some years later, in 1874, General Custer led an expedition into the area and, later, announced the discovery of gold, leading to the Black Hills Gold Rush. Thousands of prospectors poured into Lakota territory and their presence there prompted an armed response. In the spring of 1876 the 7th Cavalry, led by Custer, was dispatched to the Black Hills to return the Lakota to reservations. Subsequent events led to the Battle of the Little Big Horn, where the 7th Cavalry were defeated and Custer killed. More army units were sent and the Lakota beaten, resulting in a new treaty in which they ceded large areas of the Black Hills to the government, legalising the presence of the prospectors. To this day the Lakota think of the Six Grandfathers, as they call Mount Rushmore, as being sacred and, while it is hard to see the land being given back, attitudes are at least changing to include their history at the monument as well as that of the rest of America.

FACT FILE

COORDINATES
43°52'44"N – 103°27'35"W

LOCATION
South Dakota, USA

CONSTRUCTION
1927–1941

MOUNT VESUVIUS – POMPEII

Cape Miseno, on the northern edge of the Bay of Naples, sheltered the Roman naval base of Portus Julius, of which almost nothing remains today. The Roman writer Pliny the Younger, who was 18 at the time, was on the cape on the afternoon of 24 August AD 79 and witnessed the eruption of Mount Vesuvius on the other side of the bay, which engulfed the surrounding area, obliterating the towns of Pompeii and Herculaneum. His uncle, Pliny the Elder, already a famous author and the commander of the Roman fleet, was also there and crossed the bay in a galley in an attempt to rescue people caught up in the eruption. He died in the attempt, being overcome by poisonous gases or, possibly, suffering a heart attack from the shock of what he saw.

Pliny the Younger wrote first-hand accounts of that day, describing a volcanic cloud shooting straight up into the air and what we would now call a pyroclastic flow covering the ground and continuing on into the bay. The last gasp of it reached him and,

with almost all its force expended, deposited a fine layer of ash on his feet. At the time, he explains, minor earth tremors were a common occurrence in the region, as they are today around Naples, and were ignored, which was why people were caught by surprise by the eruption and, once it had begun, it all happened too quickly for them to escape.

The pyroclastic flow, surging down the side of the volcano in an avalanche of hot gases, ash, pumice and rock, hit Herculaneum first, killing everybody in its path instantly and burying them under 20ft (8m) of debris. Excavations have found the bodies of more than 200 people who had congregated at the port, vainly hoping to escape the eruption, clutching their valuables and huddled together. In Pompeii people were killed by the collapsing roofs of their houses or, if they were out in the open, by asphyxiation from the ash and noxious gases. It is impossible to say now how many people were killed, but estimates run into the tens of thousands. The catastrophe was so complete that neither

town was ever reoccupied, although tunnels were dug down to them by Roman looters, looking for anything of value in the buried houses.

After the two towns were rediscovered in the mid-18th century, and were excavated initially with the same motives as those of the Roman looters, they were found to have been preserved in much the same state as they were in on that day in 79 AD, offering an extraordinarily detailed look at everyday life in the Roman world. Pompeii was not as deeply buried as Herculaneum and has been more extensively excavated. The original streets, paved with hexagonal stones, are still there, as are many of the houses, which have been damaged by the volcanic material raining down on them but are otherwise intact. People-shaped spaces have been found in the rock that formed from the volcanic ash and plaster casts have been made of these voids where the people of Pompeii died. It was a city, it has been estimated, of 20,000 people and, as well as the houses, there are gardens, shops, bakeries,

bars and all the other places the people of Pompeii would have used in the course of their daily lives. The public buildings, the forum, the theatres, the temples and bathhouses, have all been uncovered, and their tools, cooking pots and wine jars have also been found. There is graffiti on the walls and, in the houses, beautiful frescoes showing scenes of everyday life: of people and their families, of heroes and goddesses, and some of a more pornographic nature. Seeing all this, an obviously busy and vibrant city so utterly devastated, can be an emotionally draining experience.

For some years now the excavations at Pompeii have been almost completely halted, with about two-thirds of the city having been uncovered. Major problems with the preservation of what has already been dug out of the rock have had to be addressed before going any further. The city, when covered with rock, was protected from the weather, but now it has been exposed the buildings have begun to deteriorate. The problem has been exacerbated by some of the methods used in previous excavations as well as by the high levels of visitors to the site and, on occasion, by theft and vandalism. Estimates of the costs of the preservation required to maintain the site in its present condition are astronomical and it would make no sense to continue until solutions to this crisis have been found. Any further excavations will have to be done by future generations, to ensure that more is not lost than is being found.

FACT FILE

COORDINATES
40°49' N, 14°26' E

LOCATION
Pompeii, Italy

ELEVATION
4,202ft (1,281m) as of 1944

MOUNTAIN TYPE
Stratovolcano

LAST ERUPTION
1944

NEUSCHWANSTEIN

erched on the top of a rocky outcrop, overlooking a lake and surrounded by mountains and forests, Neuschwanstein looks like the embodiment of a medieval castle out of a fairy tale. But things are not entirely as they seem, because it was built in the late 19th century to fulfil the fantasies of King Ludwig II of Bavaria, for whom there were to be no happy endings.

Ludwig had spent part of his childhood in southern Bavaria, not far from the Austrian border, at Schloss Hohenschwangau, which translates to the Castle of the High Swan Country and was the summer residence of his father, King Maximilian II of Bavaria. A real medieval castle had stood on the site and had fallen into ruins when Maximilian built his own in the neogothic style. It had been decorated with scenes from medieval legend, including that of Lohengrin, the Knight of the Swan, and it is not hard to imagine Ludwig identifying with this romantic tale of medieval chivalry. In 1850 Richard Wagner adapted the story for an opera and Ludwig, who was 15 when he first saw it, was deeply moved, the beginning of a lifelong association with the composer.

On 10 March 1864 Maximilian died and Ludwig, as the elder of his two sons, succeeded to the throne at the age of 18. One of his first actions was to invite Wagner to his court and, when Wagner arrived, Ludwig paid off his debts and offered him a salary and a house in Munich. Bavaria was then a constitutional monarchy, with Ludwig's signature required on any government legislation before it passed into law. It was a time of great political turmoil and complex manoeuvrings and Ludwig appears to have been entirely out of his depth. The Prime Minister of Prussia, Otto von Bismark, was attempting to establish a unified Germany from the then loose confederation of states, with the King of Prussia at its head, and, to this end, provoked a short-lived war with Austria in 1866. Bavaria had sided with Austria and, at the ensuing peace settlement, was forced to accept an accommodation with Prussia and the newly created North German Confederation which, effectively, ended Ludwig's constitutional power. A few years later the start of the Franco-Prussian War compelled Bavaria to join with the confederation which, along with the annexation of Alsace-Lorraine which would become a contributing factor to the outbreak of the First World War, resulted in the formation of the German Empire. Bismark had achieved his aim and, although Ludwig remained King, Bavaria was no longer independent.

As the power of Ludwig's position declined, he began to withdraw from public life, becoming more interested in the arts and, in particular, Wagner's operas. His personal life had become complicated, with a broken engagement and a number of infatuations with male members of his household and young army officers, and he began to spend much of his time in Bavaria. His behaviour, which had always been eccentric, became more erratic, raising questions about his sanity. In hindsight it is easy to suggest that his actions were a retreat from reality into a fairy tale world, in which he was absolute monarch and his every word was obeyed, with the castle of Neuschwanstein, inspired by Wagner's operas and designed by the set designer Christian Jank, at the centre of his fantasy kingdom.

The site he chose for it was very close to Hohenschwangau and the plans were on a much grander scale, perhaps Ludwig's attempt to outdo a distant and domineering father. Work began in 1869 and would continue until after his death in 1886, when his body and that of his doctor were found in a lake in mysterious and unexplained circumstances. The structure of the building had mostly been completed by then, but only 14 of the 67 rooms had been decorated. Of those that were finished, there was an elaborate throne room and a private theatre, where Ludwig could have Wagner's operas staged while remaining apart from the increasingly distant outside world. The walls were decorated with tapestries and scenes from the operas and, during his life, Ludwig sponsored many of Wagner's works and paid for the building of the Bayreuth Opera House, where the annual Wagner festival continues to be held. His extravagant building projects, including the Linderhof Palace and Falkenstein, an even more elaborate castle which was never built, as well as Neuschwanstein, almost bankrupted him and were probably one of the contributing causes of his downfall.

History has not been kind to Ludwig, labelling him as a fantasist and as 'Mad King Ludwig'. In Germany he is also known as the 'Märchenkönig', the Fairy Tale King, which is less unkind and probably nearer the truth. He comes across as a sad and lonely man, who escaped a misunderstanding world into a castle in the air.

FACT FILE

COORDINATES
47°33'16" N, 10°44'10" E

LOCATION
Near Hohenschwangau, Germany

STYLE
19th-century neo-romantic

NIAGARA FALLS

Towards the end of the last Ice Age, something like 12,000 years ago, retreating glaciers gouged out what would become the Great Lakes and caused the formation of the Niagara River, which runs between Lake Erie and Lake Ontario. The course of the river has changed a number of times since its formation, settling into the present one about 5,000 years ago. This flows over the Niagara Escarpment and, because the river is split into channels by Goat Island, the water forms three waterfalls, the Horseshoe, or Canadian, Falls, the American Falls and the smaller Bridal Veil Falls, which are collectively known as the Niagara Falls. Immediately below the falls themselves, the river turns at an abrupt right angle, forming the Whirlpool, and continues on through the Whirlpool rapids. Both the falls and the rapids are the largest such features in North America and, although the falls themselves are not particularly high, at about 170ft (52m), they are very wide. The largest, the Horseshoe Falls, are 2,600ft (790m) wide and get their name from their shape, where

the rock of the escarpment has eroded to form a semicircular drop.

The name is an adaptation of the original Native American name of Onguiaahra, which means 'Thunder of Water' and refers, of course, to the huge noise of such a large volume of water crashing over the falls. The water itself is famously blue-green in colour, a feature remarked upon by Charles Dickens when he visited in 1842, and is caused by its high mineral content, gained from the eroding properties of its turbulence. This erosion was causing the falls to retreat by about 4ft (1.2m) a year until, at the start of the 20th century, water began to be diverted away from the falls to power hydroelectric generating plants. The amount of water diverted has increased over the years, particularly at night, and this, together with preventative engineering measures, has reduced the erosion considerably. The edges of the falls have been strengthened and weirs built to redirect the most destructive currents. In 1969 the Niagara River was directed away from the American Falls

for several months, by an earth dam constructed across the mouth of the channel leading to it, while faults in the rock were stabilised. These faults had previously led to a huge rock fall from the face of the falls, forming the large pile of scree that can be seen at the base of the falls today. Luna Island, the small piece of ground separating the American Falls from the Bridal Veil Falls, has been off-limits to the public for years because it is thought to be unstable as a result of cracking in the rock and it could collapse at any time.

The border between New York State and Ontario runs along the middle of the river, splitting the falls between America and Canada, and the twin cities of Niagara Falls have grow up on either side. There are three bridges linking the two cities, both of which have grown on the back of the huge tourist industries associated with the falls and the power generated from them, which is used in the industries of the area. Although always a popular place with tourists because of its great natural beauty, the falls began to attract more and

more people as the level of rail traffic increased in the late 19th century. The New York Central Railroad began promoting the falls as a destination for honeymooning couples, starting a romantic tradition that continues today.

A tradition of daredevils has also developed at the falls, although, given the number of people who have been killed in various stunts, calling them idiots rather than daredevils might be more appropriate. The first person known to have survived going over the falls is Sam Patch, who jumped from the top as a stunt in 1829. Not very many people had come to watch him, so he decided to do it again with better publicity. Choosing a Friday the 13th for the attempt, he did not survive the second fall. Charles Blondin, the French tightrope walker, crossed the falls in 1859, starting a rush of people doing the same and competing to outdo each other by being blindfolded or by pushing a wheelbarrow. The first person to go over the falls in a barrel was Annie Taylor in 1901, who survived and became famous briefly, although she recommended that nobody else should try it. Several people, not listening to her advice, have been killed attempting to recreate her feat and it is now illegal to go over the falls in anything or to jump off them. This has, of course, not stopped everybody, as, it seems, there are always a few who are intent on removing themselves from the gene pool.

HURRICANE DECK

NOTRE DAME

Victor Hugo wrote *The Hunchback of Notre Dame*, or, in the original French, *Notre Dame de Paris*, very much with the cathedral in mind. He conceived the building as one of the main characters of the novel, along with Quasimodo and Esmerelda, saying 'Let us inspire in the nation, if it is possible, a love for our national architecture'. The novel became enormously popular and rekindled interest in the cathedral itself, which, by the time of the book's publication in 1831, was in a state of dilapidation and was being considered for demolition by the city planners. The building had been neglected for many years and, during the French Revolution, had, in accordance with its Enlightenment ideals, been turned into a Temple of Reason and then, under Maximilian Robespierre, was used for the Cult of the Supreme Being. A great deal of damage was done to the interior, with many of the contents either broken or stolen, and it had ended up being used as a food storage warehouse.

A campaign began to raise funds to restore the cathedral, rather than to knock it down, and in 1845 work began under the supervision of the architect Eugene Viollet-le-Duc, who, due to his restoration work and espousal of the style, would go on to become one of the central figures in the Gothic Revival of the mid-19th century. He was responsible, among other things, for the *flèche*, the tall slender central spire of the cathedral, and for renovating both the Gallery of the Kings above the three portals of the main entrance and many of the chimeras, the grotesque statues, decorating the edges of the roof. He also provided a new reliquary for the Crown of Thorns, which is thought to have come to Paris originally as a gift from the Emperor Justinian of Constantinople in the 6th century.

The cathedral stands on the Île de la Cité, one of the two islands in the River Seine in central Paris, and the site of the original founding of the city. A Gallo-Roman temple dedicated to Jupiter had stood where the cathedral now stands, but had been replaced by a church by the 6th century and then by the first cathedral, which was built in the 10th century. The present cathedral was commissioned by the Bishop of Paris, Maurice du Sully, in 1160, during the reign of King Louis VII, and building work began in 1163 with Pope Alexander III laying the first foundation stone. The most distinctive feature, the Western Façade, was begun before the nave had been fully finished and progressed in a number of stages, under various different master masons (the idea of an architect had not begun at this time). This can be seen from the distinct levels of the façade, rising up from the three portals to the Rose Window and on to the towers. The unique square shape of the towers is, in fact, a result of them not being fully completed to their originally intended height. The exterior in general is a classic example of Gothic architecture, including the flying buttresses, which were considered to be no more than part of the building process when the cathedral was first built, but give it an impressive appearance and also allow for the high vaulted ceilings inside.

Perhaps the most notable features of the interior are the two large stained-glass windows, the West Rose Window and the North Rose Window, both of which survived the 17th-century Reformation of the Roman Catholic Church, when many such features were removed from Gothic churches in France. The west window is earlier than the north, which dates from 1250 and is in the High Gothic style. The main difference is that the north window sits flush in the wall rather than being recessed, but both windows show typical Gothic designs. They are of a naturalistic nature, which sets them apart from the earlier more formal Romanesque styles, and they depict scenes from the New Testament, including Christ and the Virgin Mary. There is also a notable sculpture of Mary, known as the Virgin of Paris, which has been described as one of the most decorated sculptures in all of the Catholic Church. It dates from the early 14th century, a period of prosperity in France, and was paid for by wealthy local merchants.

After almost 800 years of use Notre Dame de Paris, the Cathedral of Our Lady of Paris, continues to be used as a Roman Catholic place of worship, where Masses and Confessions are heard daily, as well as welcoming visitors, of many different faiths, from all around the world. In more words from Victor Hugo, about Quasimodo, 'And the cathedral was not only company for him, it was the universe; more, it was Nature itself.'

FACT FILE

COORDINATES
48°51'11" N, 2°20'59" E

LOCATION
Paris, France

TOTAL HEIGHT
3,212ft (979m)

HEIGHT OF WESTERN TOWERS
226ft (69m)

PANAMA CANAL

The Isthmus of Panama is a relatively narrow strip of land, about 50 miles (80km) wide, which connects North and South America. The idea of a canal across it had been advocated for many years because of the obvious advantages of avoiding the long and dangerous shipping passage around Cape Horn that was required to transfer from the Atlantic to the Pacific. After the success of the Suez Canal, opened in 1869, the French, who had built it, took on the proposal of building the Panama Canal, beginning in 1880. Their plan involved a sea-level canal all the way across the isthmus but ran into engineering problems almost immediately. These were compounded by the tropical conditions, which resulted in high incidences of disease among the workers, particularly malaria and yellow fever. No accurate records were kept, but it has been estimated that more than 20,000 people died during the work and, by 1893, the French abandoned the canal.

Theodore Roosevelt, who became US President in 1901, recognised the strategic and commercial advantages of the canal, but failed to obtain permission from the Colombian Government, who controlled the territory at the time, to take over the work. In a highly controversial move, the US backed a Panamanian independence movement, which had been unsuccessful in the past, by sending a warship to the area to deter the Colombians from interfering. Panama declared its independence on 3 November 1903 and, almost immediately, the Americans, without consulting them, reached agreement with the French company who owned a controlling interest in the canal to take it over. Under the terms of the agreement the US bought the shares and assets of the French company and, as the Panamanians had no choice but to agree to it or lose US support for their independence, the US also gained rights to a canal zone extending for five miles on either side of it, excluding the cities of Panama City and Colon.

Work began in 1904 and the Americans paid much greater attention to the health of their workers than the French had, particularly by initiating a programme to eradicate mosquitoes, the carriers of both malaria and yellow fever. Even so, more than 5,000 people died during the ten-year construction period, leading to the total cost in human life of the canal being considerably greater than 25,000 people. The Americans also made much more sensible engineering decisions, including building dams to create artificial lakes and the inclusion of locks, but, even so, it was an enormous engineering challenge. From its opening, in 1914, the canal was a huge success, cutting, for example, the journey time by sea from New York to San Francisco by more than half.

The sovereignty of the Canal Zone became a constant source of conflict between the US and Panama, not least because no Panamanian had signed the original agreement. In 1964 students attempted to fly a Panamanian flag in the Canal Zone and, after it was ripped down, rioting broke out. In the ensuing chaos, 22 Panamanians and four US soldiers were killed and the incident is now marked in Panama as Martyrs' Day, a national holiday. It led to the start of negotiations between the two countries over sovereignty, leading to the Torrijos-Carter Treaty of 1977. This treaty, signed by US President Jimmy Carter and Omar Torrijos, who had come to power in Panama in a military coup in 1968, began the process of handing the canal over to the Panamanians, first as a jointly administered territory and then, at 12 p.m. on 31 December 1999, giving Panama full sovereignty. It also guaranteed the right of the US to defend the canal from any threat to its neutrality, in terms of it being open to ships of all nations. Evidence has come to light since of a Panamanian contingency plan to sabotage the canal had the treaty not been ratified. The existence of this plan has been confirmed by the notorious General Manuel Noriega, who came to power in Panama after Torrijos was killed in a mysterious plane crash and is now serving a sentence in a US prison for drug trafficking after he was taken prisoner in the 1989 US invasion of Panama.

The Panama Canal Authority was formed after the handover and it awarded the management contract for the canal and the two ports at either end to the Hong Kong-based conglomerate Huchinson Whampoa. Critics in the US have suggested the company's chief executive, Li Ka Shing, has links to the Chinese Government, but no evidence for this has been produced. Business has been booming at the canal and there are now plans to enlarge it, from the current maximum tonnage of 65,000, the so-called Panamax, to accommodate the much larger container ships common today.

FACT FILE

COORDINATES
9°04'48" N, 79°40'48" W

LOCATION
Panama

DEATHS IN CONSTRUCTION
27,500

CONSTRUCTION
First attempt led by the French began in 1880. Under the United States the canal was finished in 1914

PANTHEON

The Pantheon in Rome is the most complete Roman building that remains today and is, in its use of concrete to build the dome, which is still, at 142ft (43m), the largest of its type in the world, a supreme example of architectural skill and the application of geometry to the design of a building. The architect is unknown, although it is often said, without any supporting evidence, to have been Apollodorus of Damascus, and it dates from about AD 125, during the reign of Emperor Hadrian. It was built to replace a previous temple built by Agrippa in about 25 BC, which had burnt down, and it was, as the name suggests, a temple dedicated to all the Roman gods of the seven planets. To this end there are seven niches built into its walls, which would have contained shrines to these gods.

Hadrian is known to have been an admirer of Greek architecture and this comes through in the structure of the Pantheon. The entrance is a great portico of Corinthian columns, each made from a single piece of Egyptian granite. This leads into the main part of the building, a huge cylindrical rotunda with a hemispherical dome on top of it. The geometry of this is such that the diameter of the floor of the rotunda is the same as the vertical distance from the floor to the centre of the dome. The height of the cylinder formed by the rotunda is also the same as the height of the dome, which, if it were to continue down to form a complete sphere, would fit perfectly into the rotunda. On the outside of the building, the walls of the rotunda continue above the rim of the dome, making the dome's exterior aspect look quite shallow. The walls of the rotunda, which are more than 20ft (6.5m) thick, are made of brick-faced concrete and are the only support for the 5,000 tons of the dome. This huge weight is carried from the oculus, its central opening, down by barrel vaulting and this, together with the internal design of the dome, which is of concrete coffers, transfers the weight down vertically through the walls. The dome does not exert a great lateral force, as most large domes do, because of the inherent strength of the cast concrete, so the building does not need to be reinforced with buttresses.

The low tensile strength of modern concrete means that, had it been used in the dome without being reinforced, it would not have been able to support its own weight. Although the concrete mix used in the Pantheon is not known, Roman concrete was generally made from volcanic ash, pumice, lime, small pieces of rock and water, which is not substantially different from modern concrete, so the strength must have come from the care with which it was made and applied. It must have been mixed to an exact consistency and then used very carefully, probably being cast over wooden scaffolding, so that it dried out in such a way as to minimise the number of air bubbles in it, which is what causes the weaknesses in concrete. The fact that it has stood so long, (almost 1900 years) is a tribute to the skill of the Roman builders who erected it as much as to the architects, whoever they may have been.

Not a great deal is known about what the Romans actually did in the Pantheon, other than honouring their gods. The coffers originally contained bronze ornaments depicting the stars and these, together with the open oculus, suggest the dome was a symbol of the Roman cosmos. In can also be seen, from its monumental scale, as a statement of Roman dominion over the known world, represented as being everything under the sky, including the formerly dominant civilisations of the Egyptians and the Greeks. After the Roman period, in AD 609, it was given to Pope Boniface IV by the Byzantine Emperor Phocus and was re-consecrated as a Christian church. This is the main reason why it has survived relatively intact until today, as many Roman temples were destroyed or allowed to fall into disrepair at around this time. The interior is the only part to have been substantially altered, having lost most of its marble cladding and bronze ornamentation.

The Pantheon has been a huge influence on architects since the Renaissance, including Filippo Brunelleschi, who spent several years studying it before going on to build the Duomo in Florence. It was also a favourite of Michelangelo's, who said it looked as if it had been built by an angel rather than a man, a fitting tribute from one of the greatest artists of the Renaissance to an unknown genius of the Roman era.

FACT FILE

COORDINATES
41°53'55" N, 12°28'36" E

LOCATION
Rome, Italy

MEANING OF NAME
Temple of the Gods

DOME DIAMETER
30ft (9.1m)

CONSTRUCTION
AD 125

PARTHENON

The Golden Age of Athens came in the 5th century BC. The political leader of Athens for much of this period was Pericles, who ruled from 461 BC to 429 BC, and was a great patron of the arts. The philosophers Socrates and Plato, the dramatists Sophocles and Euripides and the historians Herodotus and Thucydides were all in Athens at this time and they, together with a host of others, led a cultural flourishing unequalled in world history. Pericles also initiated a period of building work in Athens, including what is considered by many to be the finest achievement in all of Greek art and architecture, the Parthenon, which, from its prominent position on the Acropolis, the sacred rock of Athens, overlooks the entire city.

After the Persian invasion of the Greek mainland had been repulsed in 479 BC, Athens became the dominate force in the Delian League, an association of Greek city-states originally based on equality, which, from then on, gradually became an Athenian Empire. The treasury of the league had been kept on the island of Delos, but was moved to Athens in 454 BC and some of the money, intended to be used for the defence of the league, was used by Pericles to finance his ambitious building plans. Work began on the Parthenon in 447 BC and continued until about 432 BC, but the purpose of the building is now not fully known. It was certainly a temple to Athena, but was also used as a treasury for the empire and for rich Athenians. It was also a monument to the recent military victory over Persia and has been described as a symbol of the dominance of Athens over the rest of the Greek world. It is, of course, entirely possible that Pericles intended it to fulfil all of these functions and, perhaps, for it to be a statement of his own personal achievements as well.

The Parthenon was built under the supervision of Phidias, who was regarded as one of the greatest classical sculptors, and designed by the architects Iktinos and Kallikrates. It is Doric in style, characterised by the fluted columns which stand directly on the stylobate, the paved floor, rather than on a base, as they do in the later Ionic and Corinthian styles. The architects designed the stylobate and columns to counteract an optical illusion created by parallel rows of columns, which makes them look as if they curve inwards. This is overcome by the stylobate being curved and the columns, which taper in towards the top, being arranged so they curve outwards slightly, to give the impression of a straight line. It was built of Pentelic marble in a rectangle, 8 columns wide by 17 long, and there was a cella, an enclosed inner chamber, containing the monumental statue of Athena Parthones in gold and ivory, which, unfortunately, has since been destroyed. This is considered to have been Phidias' greatest work and is said to have stood 38ft (12m) tall.

The upper parts of the exterior of the building were decorated with metopes, a series of marble panels which ran around the entire building, and there were also Ionic friezes around the top of the cella. Some of these, and some statuary from the pediments, are now in the British Museum in London and are popularly known as the Elgin Marbles, although the museum prefers to call them the Sculptures of the Parthenon. Their presence in the museum has been the subject of intense debate since the majority of them were removed from the Parthenon by Lord Elgin while he was the ambassador to the Ottoman Empire at the beginning of the 18th century. The Parthenon had survived relatively intact until 1687, when, while Athens was under siege by the Venetians, it was hit by a shell. The Ottomans, who had captured Athens themselves in 1456, had fortified the Acropolis and were using the Parthenon as a power store for their guns. In the ensuing explosion extensive damage was done to the building and its sculpture. It was in this ruined state when Lord Elgin was given permission by the Ottoman Sultan to remove sculptures from it. He took almost everything he could find and, according to the Greeks, did further damage while he was doing so.

The Greek Government has made repeated requests to the British Museum for the return of the marbles, all of which have been refused. A variety of reasons have been given by the museum. If they give the marbles back to Greece they will be asked by for the return of almost everything else. It is hard to get away from the fact that the Greeks, while not being legally entitled to the marbles, hold the moral high ground in this argument.

FACT FILE

COORDINATES
37°58'17" N, 23°43'36" E

LOCATION
Athens, Greece

CONSTRUCTION
5th century BC

NUMBER OF PILLARS
46 outer pillars, 19 inner pillars

PEARL HARBOR

• Alan and I stayed in O'ahu, Hawaii in July 2005. Unfortunately we didn't go to Pearl Harbour as we were too late for the trip.

The Us Navy has had a base at Pearl Harbor, on the Hawaiian island of Oaha, since 1887. It was originally leased from the Kingdom of Hawaii, in a reciprocal agreement that allowed Hawaiian sugar to be imported into the US with no duty, until Hawaii was annexed in 1898, going on to become a full state in 1959. The intention was to give the US a presence in the Pacific and, by 1941, Pearl Harbor had become the base of the US Navy's Pacific Fleet.

At 7.55 a.m. on 7 December 1941 the Japanese attacked Pearl Harbor and the US forces stationed on Oaha with no warning and no declaration of war. A Japanese naval task force had been assembled 200 miles north of the island, including six aircraft carriers, and the attack, by 350 planes in two waves, took the Americans completely by surprise. Five battleships, three destroyers and three cruisers were either sunk or badly damaged and 2,403 people were killed, with 1,178 wounded. The following day President Franklin D. Roosevelt addressed Congress, saying it was 'a date which will lie in infamy' and calling for a declaration of war, which would follow immediately afterwards. The Japanese had already invaded British Malaya and attacked Hong Kong, and attacks on the Philippines and Thailand would follow in the next few days. On 11 December, Germany and Italy, under the terms of the Tripartite Pact between the two countries and Japan, declared war on America, which, having remained neutral up until these events, was now in the Second World War on all fronts.

Within days of the attack rumours began to circulate concerning how much Roosevelt had known about it in advance, but had done nothing to prevent it as it gave him an excuse to enter the war, an action not considered to have any great support with the American people at the time. This rumour has, over the years, grown into full-blown conspiracy theories, some of which accuse Roosevelt of treason, while others implicate Churchill and Stalin as conspirators. It is hard to know now what is based on fact and what is wild speculation, but most serious commentators on the events of Pearl Harbor come down on the side of it being a series of monumental mistakes, rather than a conspiracy, which led to any prior knowledge the Americans might have had of the attack being ignored, closely followed by attempts of those involved to cover up their mistakes.

Relations between America and Japan had been deteriorating for some years before the attack, particularly after the escalation of the war between Japan and China in 1937. Previously, America had been Japan's major supplier of natural resources, particularly oil, of which it had none itself, and this became one of the driving forces behind its expansionist policies, along with ideas of racial superiority it held in common with Nazi Germany. By 1939 America, although officially neutral, was supplying Britain, Russia and China with arms and oil, under the terms of the Lend-Lease Agreement, and this increased after Japan signed the Tripartite Pact in 1940. Japan was aiming to consolidate its position of dominance in South East Asia by capturing natural resources held by other countries in the region, but knew that, by doing this, it would provoke a war with the US. By destroying the Pacific Fleet, as it hoped to do at Pearl Harbor, Japan was hoping to give itself time to invade Malaya, Burma and the Philippines before America recovered sufficiently to mount a response, thereby securing the resources it needed.

The Americans had developed a plan to enter the war in Europe by 1943, when, it considered, its military would be completely ready. It was entirely focused on this and, although information existed to suggest Japan was planning an attack, acquired through the deciphering of Japanese coded messages, which the Americans could do quicker than the Japanese themselves, the information gathered was either ignored or not fully understood. The Americans did not believe, or perhaps did not want to believe, that the Japanese would mount an attack against them on such a scale and, despite the signs, when it came, were caught completely off guard. The attack was initially a great success for Japan and, as they had hoped, it gave them time to invade a large part of South East Asia. Six months later the tide of the war would be turned permanently against them with the American victory at the Battle of Midway. Once provoked, the power of the American military, combined with the British and the other Allies, was always going to be decisive and, almost four years after Pearl Harbor and after atomic bombs had been dropped on Hiroshima and Nagasaki, Japan surrendered, on 14 August 1945.

FACT FILE

COORDINATES
21°21'43" N, 157°57'13" W

LOCATION
O'ahu, Hawaii

ATTACK ON PEARL HARBOR
7 December 1941

PETRA

The Wadi Araba is part of the Great Rift Valley and runs between Israel and Jordan, from the southern end of the Dead Sea to the Gulf of Aqaba. The area it cuts through is arid and very hot and, moving east into Jordan, the land rises into mountains cut with deep ravines. The Nabataeans lived here from about 600 BC, displacing the previous occupants, the Edomites, and they established their capital city at Petra. Not a great deal is known about the origins of the Nabataeans, but they spoke Aramaic and they controlled the trade routes through their territory. They travelled by caravan between oases, trading in silk, frankincense, myrrh and spices across a wide area of what is now Jordan, Egypt, Israel, Yemen and Saudi Arabia and getting as far north as Syria. To enable them to live in this arid and inhospitable place, they developed a complicated system of storing water, from a spring near Petra that continued to run all year round, and by capturing rain from the very occasional storms, using dams and cisterns they had dug into the rock.

The position of Petra, which is in a wadi surrounded on all sides by rock faces with only one main entrance, which is through a narrow ravine called the Siq, made it easy to defend. Attempts were made to capture the city, by the Seleucid Empire, the Roman Emperor Pompey and Herod the Great, who were all attempting to gain control of the lucrative trade routes, but none of them was successful. Most of the buildings in the city date from the Hellenistic period from about 100 BC to AD 106, and during this period the Nabataeans began to mint coins, which have left a record of the names of their kings who are, presumably, buried in the elaborate tombs. The later ones are Aretas IV Philopatris, from AD 9 to AD 40, Malichus II, from AD 40 to AD 70, who reigned along with his sister, Shaqilath, who also appears to have been his wife, and Rabbel II Sotor, who ruled from AD 70 to AD 106. The Romans finally took over the city in AD 106, during the reign of Emperor Trajan, and it became known as the province of Arabia Petrea.

The city continued to flourish under Roman rule and the building, particularly of the tombs high up on the rock faces on the sides of the wadi, continued for about another 100 years then stopped, along with the minting of coins. The reasons for this are not clear, but it could have been due to a decline in the population of the city as the trade routes moved away, with the overland routes going to Syria and more goods going by sea, or the city may have been attacked by another group who disrupted life to the extent of trade no longer being possible. In AD 393 an earthquake destroyed many of the buildings and disrupted the water system and, from then on, the city was only sporadically occupied. It was not until 1812 that it was first recorded by a European, the Swiss traveller and Orientalist Johann Ludwig Bernhardt, although it remained almost inaccessible until much more recent times.

Approaching Petra now, through the narrow rock walls of the Siq, the first building that comes into view is the most famous and elaborate one in the city. It is known as Al Khazneh, which is Arabic for the Treasury, although it was actually either a temple or a tomb. The façade has been carved into the sandstone face of a cliff and is in the Hellenistic style, dating it to about 100 BC. There is a portico of Corinthian columns which rise into a decorative architrave and on to another level of smaller columns. This highly impressive façade leads into a square undecorated room, a theme repeated in other tombs situated higher up on the rock faces. Further into the city is an enormous amphitheatre, with seating for 8,000 people, which is also cut into the rock and then the wadi opens out into what was the main street of Roman Petra. It is paved with cut stone and lined with columns and there is a market place and a public fountain. There is another temple at the far end, originally dedicated to the main god of the Nabataeans, Dushara, then later rededicated to one of the Roman gods. The largest building, known as the Monastery, is yet another temple and it has been carved out of rock in a similar style to Al Khazneh.

Standing in the midst of these incredible buildings, cut into the rock face in what must have been searing heat, it is difficult to imagine what possessed the Nabataeans to embark on such a remarkable undertaking. Although comparatively little is known about these people, they have left their mark in their rock-carved temples, which have lasted more than 2,000 years.

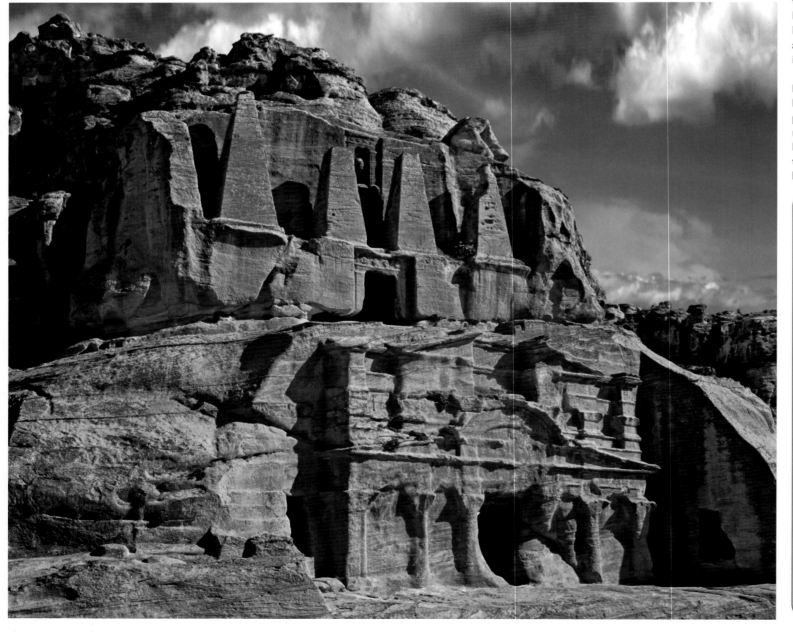

FACT FILE

COORDINATES
30°19'43" N, 35°26'31" E

LOCATION
Situated between the Red Sea and the Dead Sea, Jordan

FIRST NON-INDIGENOUS SIGHTING
1812, Swiss explorer Johann Ludwig Burckhardt

PETRONAS TWIN TOWERS

From the 1970s to the mid-1990s Malaysia experienced a period of unprecedented economic growth. Although it is not thought of as one of the original Asian tiger economies, which were South Korea, Hong Kong, Taiwan and Singapore, Malaysia went through a similar process of transformation, from an economy dependent on its primary industries, particularly mining and farming, to one of export-driven manufacturing. With large overseas investments, Malaysian industries grew rapidly and the government initiated a programme of financial liberalisation and investment in education. It also formed Petronas, a state-owned oil and gas company, to manage and add value to the country's energy resources, and it quickly became the largest company in Malaysia with far and away the highest turnover. It now contributes, through taxes and dividends, about 25% of the total revenue collected by the Malaysian Treasury.

In 1981 the Malaysian Government began the development of Kuala Lumpur's emerging business district, the Golden Triangle, and in 1991, held an international competition to find the design for a building to be both the centrepiece of the Kuala Lumpur City Centre complex and a signature building for the corporate headquarters of Petronas. They were also looking for a landmark building to symbolise the transformation of Malaysia as a whole and one which would gain worldwide attention. The Argentinian–American architect César Pelli won the competition with his design of what would become the Petronas Twin Towers. The design employed the latest advances in the technology of constructing tall buildings while, at the same time, used locally sourced materials to keep the costs down. It also combined cutting-edge design with elements of the architecture and decorative arts of Malaysia, which are predominantly Islamic. The floor plan of both towers, for example, forms an eight-pointed star out of two interlocking squares, a traditional geometric pattern in Malaysian Islam.

The construction project began in 1993 and would take slightly over three years to complete. The site of the towers meant that they required extremely deep foundations, because of the depth of the bedrock and, with the main structure being built of reinforced concrete, because the towers would be considerably heavier than the more usual steel-framed structure of tall buildings. Each tower was built by a different contractor, so that the structures could be cross-checked against each other and to foster a sense of competition between the two companies. A monitoring programme, employing global positioning technology, was developed to maintain the exact verticality of both buildings, both to ensure that the aesthetic quality of each was being maintained and so that the high-speed lifts would be able to function properly once the buildings had been finished. The outer shell of the towers, which, together with their tapering shape, gives them such a distinctive look, is of stainless steel and glass.

The essential structure of each tower consisted of cylindrical concrete columns at the inner corners of the star-shaped floor design, forming what César Pelli described as the 'soft core' of the buildings, and these were then linked with concrete beams. This simple structure allowed for a greater area of usable space within than a steel frame would have done and, although heavy, concrete is much more sway-resistant. This design also allowed for a square-shaped central core to contain the service facilities of the buildings, including the lifts. At the 41st and 42nd floor a double-decked skybridge was constructed to connect the two towers, a highly complex engineering feat because of the independent sway of each tower. The solution to this was to construct an inverted V-shaped arch to support the skybridge at the middle. This would accommodate the movements of each tower while remaining the same distance away from them. Pelli described the towers with a bridge between them as forming a space which was 'a doorway to the infinite', an idea he got from Eastern philosophy with a bit of postmodernism thrown in.

The towers, each with 88 floors, opened in 1998 and, at 1,483ft (452m) high, including the antennae, were declared the world's tallest buildings. There was a certain amount of controversy at the time because the Sears Tower in Chicago, the previous tallest building, had higher occupied floors and this caused the Council for Tall Buildings and Urban Habitat to define their categories more clearly. The Petronas Twin Towers, under the amended rules, kept the title, until they were beaten in 2004 by the Taipei 101 Tower which, surprisingly enough, is in Taipei and is 101 floors high. To soften this blow slightly the towers were given the 2004 Aga Khan Award for Architecture, with the jury of the awards saying in their citation: 'The building has become an icon that expresses the sophistication of contemporary Malaysian society and builds on the country's rich traditions to shape a world city'.

FACT FILE

COORDINATES
3°09'28" N, 101°42'42" E

LOCATION
Kuala Lumpur, Malaysia

CONSTRUCTION
1995–1998

HEIGHT
1,483ft (452m) top of antenna/spire

ARCHITECT
César Pelli

PONT DU GARD

The Roman city of Nemausus, now Nimes, in the South of France, grew up on the Via Domitia, the road running between Italy and Spain which also gave the Romans military and commercial access to their provinces in Gaul. It had been established shortly after Julius Caesar's conquest of Gaul, in 52 BC, and had become an important Roman city by the time of Emperor Augustus, from 27 BC to AD 14, when it is thought it had a population of around 60,000. The Roman buildings still there, including the Maison Carrée, a remarkably well-preserved Roman temple, and the huge amphitheatre, show the high status of the city at that time. At some point in the 1st century AD, the population must have begun to outgrow the available water supply, as, during the middle part of the century, an aqueduct was constructed to bring water to it from the springs near Uzes, a distance of about 30 miles (50km). With typically Roman flare, the aqueduct was built with a drop of only 56ft (17m) over its entire length and crossed one of the main obstacles between Uzes and Nimes, the valley of the River Gardon, with the Pont du Gard, which remains almost completely intact to this day and is a hugely impressive feat of engineering.

To maintain the gradient of the aqueduct the bridge had to rise about 150ft (50m) above the river and this height was achieved with three tiers of arches, giving it the appearance of one bridge having been built on top of another. In the construction of the six arches of the lower tier,

attention must have been paid to the course of the river and to the likelihood of it flooding. The arches are high enough to allow flood water through them, rather than to batter against the side of the bridge, and the piers of the arches which face into the current are concave, reducing their resistance to the abrasive action of the flowing water. The top tier has much smaller arches than the previous two and shows the classical proportions of Roman architecture, which is such a common feature of Roman buildings it is almost as if they were incapable of building anything without sticking to these rules. There are 35 arches remaining of the original 47 and this tier, which contained the actual aqueduct and so had to have a watertight channel, shows the most attention to detail in its construction. The channel itself is built of small square ashlars, dressed stones, with a lining of flat stone slabs, cut to fit together almost perfectly.

Although it is beautifully designed, the Pont du Gard was built as a functional aqueduct, with no extraneous ornamentation other than its use of classical proportion. It also looks as if the builders were working to a tight budget, as it is mostly built of large stones, some weighing six tons, which were quarried very near to the site. Mortar, a relatively expensive commodity at the time, has only been used in the top tier, around the masonry of the channel, with the rest of the stones being held together with iron clamps. During the building process wooden scaffolding would have

been erected around the bridge and the masonry lifted into place using a block and tackle system of ropes and pulleys. The blocks of stone protruding from the bridge on which the construction gear would have stood are still there, rather than being chiselled away as they would have been in a more prestigious building. The signs of the wooden frames over which the arches would have been built are also still there, in the form of ridges around the edges of the arches. This could be described as leaving the bridge looking rather roughshod and it shows how low the priority of the final appearance of it actually was. The Pont du Gard was built to be used, not to be looked at.

From its inception in the Middle Ages Les Compagnons du Tour de France, an organisation of craftsmen and artisans still going today, which has nothing to do with the cycle race, sent apprentices on a trip around France to work under masters of their trade and to study examples of fine workmanship. Aspiring masons were dispatched to the Pont du Gard to study the quality of the Roman work with the idea, presumably, that, as it has now stood for almost 2,000 years, its builders knew a thing or two about masonry. The extent to which these French students were inspired by their Roman forebears is open to question, but they must have been impressed by the position of the bridge in the beautiful Languedoc countryside, where some of the best wines in France continue to be made.

FACT FILE

COORDINATES
43°56'50" N, 4°32'08" E

LOCATION
Near Usèz, South of France

HEIGHT
150ft (50m)

NUMBER OF ARCHES
Lower level: 6
Middle level: 11
Upper level: 35

POTALA PALACE

The Potala Palace was the winter residence of the Dalai Lamas of Tibet and stands on Marpo Ri, the Red Mountain, in the Lhasa Valley. It looks out over the River Kyi-chu and what was once the Shol, a walled enclave of old Lhasa, now almost entirely swallowed up by the increasing sprawl of the city. The fifth Dalai Lama began the building work on the present palace in 1645 on the site of previous palaces going back to the 7th century, when Songsten Gampo, the second Emperor of Tibet, chose the site because, according to Buddhist mythology, it was the dwelling place of the Bodhisattva Avilokiteshvara, who is said to be reincarnated in the Dalai Lama. The name of Potala is thought to derive from the name of the mystical Mount Potalaka in the south of India, also associated with the Bodhisattva.

The complex is made up of more than 1,000 rooms, comprising the Potrang Kopo, the White Palace, and its ancillary buildings and, in the centre and rising above the other buildings, the Potrang Marpo, or the Red Palace. The White Palace was where the Dalai Lama and his staff lived and, as he was the Tibetan Head of State, it also contained the seat of government and was where any state ceremonies were held. The Deyangshar, a yellow-painted courtyard, separates the Red Palace from the rest of the buildings as it is the spiritual centre, dedicated to religious study and Buddhist prayer. It contains a warren of halls and chapels, and in its libraries there are the Buddhist scriptures, the Kangyur and the Tengyur. Two small chapels, the Phakpa Lhakhang and the Chogyal Drubphuk, are the oldest surviving parts of the building, dating to the 7th century, and these are the most sacred areas. The Phapka Lhakhang contains the Arya Lokeshvara, a statue venerated by Tibetan Buddhists and an object of pilgrimage, and below this chapel, is the Dharma Cave, where Songsten Gampo is believed to have studied Buddhism. The stupa containing the mummified body of the fifth Dalai Lama is in another chapel. It is made from sandalwood and is entirely coated in solid gold and encrusted with semi-precious stones. The stupas of the preceding Dalai Lamas are also in chapels within the building, including that of 13th Dalai Lama, Thubten Gyasto. Before he died in 1933 he predicted that, if Tibet were not protected, the Dalai Lamai and the Tibetan way of life would come to an end.

The 14th, and current, Dalai Lama, Tenzin Gyatso, was recognised as the new incarnation in 1937, when he was two years old. He began his monastic education at the age of six and, at 11, met the German explorer Heinrich Harrer, who would become his unofficial tutor on the world outside Tibet. At the age of 15, in 1950, he became the Tibetan Head of State and within months the Chinese army invaded. In the following year he was presented with little choice other than to sign the Seventeen Point Agreement for the Peaceful Liberation of Tibet presented to him by the Chinese, which confirmed China's right of sovereignty in Tibet. After a period of respecting the traditional government, the Chinese began a programme of repression and introduced reforms which were highly unpopular. In 1959 a Tibetan resistance movement began, supported by the CIA, who provided training, but it was easily crushed by the Chinese and the Dalai Lama, thinking his life was in danger, left Tibet with his followers for exile in Dharamsala in northern India, on the other side of the Himalayas.

The Dalai Lama set up a government in exile in India, which, almost 50 years later, continues to claim it is the legitimate government of Tibet and that the invasion by China was illegal. In the 1960s the Chinese began a campaign of repression against Buddhism, destroying many monasteries and killing Buddhist monks. Positions on both sides have softened since then, with the Dalai Lama saying recently he would accept Tibet as an autonomous state within China, much as Hong Kong is, and the Chinese are pursuing more tolerant policies which allow some religious freedoms. The Dalai Lama, who is now in his seventies, has asked the Chinese for permission to visit Tibet, but no agreement has been reached as yet. Both sides are aware that, as the Dalai Lama gets older, the issue of the next incarnation could have serious consequences. For the exiles, the loss of their spiritual leader could lead to their movement falling apart and, for China, finding a new Dalai Lama could provoke civil unrest if they try to do so without involving the present one. While the prospect of the Dalai Lama returning to the Potala Palace is as remote as ever, the more accommodating attitudes of both sides could eventually lead to some sort of compromise solution.

FACT FILE

COORDINATES
29°39'35" N, 91°07'01" E

LOCATION
Red Mountain, Lhasa Valley, Tibet, China

AREA
5sq mi (13sq km)

ALTITUDE
12,100ft (3,700m)

ROOMS
1,000

PYRAMIDS

The Necropolis of Giza is a complex of ancient monuments on the outskirts of Cairo. The three large pyramids in the complex are thought to be the tombs of Khufu, Khafre and Menkuare, pharaohs of the Fourth Dynasty in the Old Kingdom of Egypt, making them about 4,500 years old, and they are, arguably, the most recognisable landmarks in the world. There are thousands of other pyramids, including many more in Egypt, but if anyone refers to 'the Pyramids' without specifying which ones they are talking about, they mean the Great Pyramids of Giza. And, as if that were not enough, the Sphinx is also situated right next to them, along with smaller pyramids, tombs, cemeteries and a host of other ancient remains.

The great familiarity of the pyramids can sometimes get in the way of an appreciation of them, including such apparently straightforward considerations of where they are, how big they are and what they were built for. Photographs always show them set against an ocean of sand, this being their most photogenic aspect, but they are not really marooned in the Western Desert. The urban sprawl of Cairo spreads out to the edge of the necropolis and there are roads, shops and modern buildings right next to them. It is also impossible to get an impression of their size from photographs, which make it look as if the central Khafre Pyramid is the largest of the three when in fact it is the Khufu Pyramid, or Great Pyramid as it is usually known is considerably bigger. The square base of the Great Pyramid covers an area of

about 12 acres (5ha) and each of its sides is 756ft (230m) long. It is slightly shorter now than it was when it was first built, because what is left of the pyramidion, its capstone, lies in pieces at its base, but it is still 455ft (138m) high and was the tallest building in the world for 4,000 years, until it was overtaken by the spire of Lincoln Cathedral in the 14th century. Something like 2.5 million blocks of stone were used in its construction and, with the average block weighing 2.5 tons, its total weight is of the order of 6.25 million tons. This, by any standards at all, is a big building.

What is actually known about the pyramids is, for the most part, a great deal less than is often stated in many accounts of them. There is no direct evidence of exactly who built them, the pharaohs ascribed to them being mentioned in secondary texts of a much later date, and there is also no consensus on the dates given as to when they were built. The dating techniques used to try and settle the question, such as carbon dating, have thrown up a wide number of possibilities, few of which coincide with the known dates of the lives of the three pharaohs in question. Details of the methods of construction are almost all based on reconstructions of how we think this might have been achieved, not on any direct evidence, and the fact that these buildings are thought to have been constructed in the Bronze Age, with the limited technology then available, which hardly seems possible at all, is generally glossed over entirely.

The pyramids were definitely used as tombs. Sarcophagi have been found in the chambers within

them, but whether the burial of pharaohs was their main function or they were built for another purpose entirely is, again, not known for certain. What can be said is that their specific location is not random, with the corners of each being orientated almost exactly to the points of the compass, and there is also a complex geometrical relationship between their positions relative to each other. The passageways and chambers within them are specifically orientated and the air shafts, narrow shafts through the pyramids from the chambers to points on the exterior surfaces, are thought to be orientated towards particular stars. The amount of work involved in creating these features within the pyramids would have been enormous, so, it is assumed, they must have important functions, but, like so much else to do with the pyramids, these are not known.

With real evidence so thin on the ground and speculative interpretations presented as though they were literal truths, it is hardly surprising to find so many alternative theories occupying the grey areas. From lost Atlantean civilisations to visiting extraterrestrials, from fantasy to plain crazy, they are all there and all based on the selective use of the existing evidence, exploiting our apparent need for explanations. And yet, despite all this speculation and theorising, the truth remains out of reach. The pyramids are a paradox, of the familiar and the mysterious, the known and the unknown, and perhaps it would be better to accept them as such.

FACT FILE

COORDINATES
29°58'33" N, 31°07'51" E

LOCATION
Cairo, Egypt

DIMENSIONS
Khafre's Pyramid: Height: 471ft (143.5m), Length: 705ft (215m), Slope: 53°10'. Khufu's Pyramid: Height: 455.2ft (138.8m), Length: 758ft (231m), Slope: 51°50'40". Menkuare's Pyramid: Height: 215ft (65.5m), Length: 344ft (105m), Slope: 51°20'25"

RAFFLES HOTEL

The story of a tiger being shot under the billiard table of Raffles Hotel in Singapore is, in the great tradition of bar-room tales, a bit of an exaggeration, but it is not so far from the truth either. The story makes it sound as if hunting tigers in the hotel, for which, presumably, tropical suits and pith helmets would have been the correct dress, was a regular occurrence, only remarkable on this occasion for interrupting a game of billiards. It is quite easy to imagine the colonial governor pointing out to the hunters, as the carcass of the tiger was being dragged away and before taking his next shot, that black ties were required in the billiards room at all times. In what is probably as close to the real story as it is going to get, another version says a tiger which had escaped from captivity nearby had hidden under the part of the hotel containing the billiard table and was shot, but this hardly conjures up romantic images of colonial life in one of the bastions of the empire. Singapore gained independence more than 40 years ago, but a certain ideal, of colonial elegance and grandeur, is still attached to the hotel, even though this ideal is probably as much of an exaggeration as the tiger story itself.

The name of Sir Stamford Raffles, along with such other figures as Clive of India and Cecil Rhodes, is one of those associated with the expansion of the British Empire. He joined the East India Company, an empire itself within the empire which had presided over the formation of the British Raj, and was sent out to Penang, now part of Malaysia, in 1805. Due to his ability and, more than likely, because he had learned the Malay language, he rose rapidly in the company's ranks and was appointed as the Governor of Java after its annexation from the Dutch in 1811. Towards the end of the Napoleonic Wars, in 1814, the Anglo-Dutch Treaty returned Java to the Dutch and Raffles returned to England under something of a cloud because of the financial failure of the colony under his governorship. He returned to the Far East a few years later, initially to the colonial backwater of Bengkulu in Sumatra, and in an effort to restore his name and because of the likelihood of Bengkulu also being ceded back to the Dutch, began to look for an alternative trading post. He chose an island in the Raiu Archipelago at the tip of the Malay Peninsula and, in 1819, signed a treaty with the Sultan of Johor allowing him to develop it as a free trade port. He named it Singapore after the original Malay name of Singapura, which means Lion City, but did not spend a great deal of time there, as he was still the Governor of Bengkulu. He returned to England in 1824 and died there of a stroke a few years later at the age of 45.

Trade in the area boomed and the city grew rapidly, becoming a British Crown Colony in 1867, giving it the same status as such colonies as Hong Kong and Gibraltar, which were administered directly by Britain, as opposed to the nominally independent status of dominions and protectorates. In 1887 four Armenian brothers, Martin, Tigran, Aviet and Arshak Sarkies, who had come to the Far East from Isfahan in Iran and had already established two hotels in Penang, branched out by converting a large colonial bungalow in Singapore into a hotel. They named it after the founder of the city and it became an immediate success. With Singapore's location, between India and China, and status as a free port, travellers were constantly coming through and there was also great demand from the large expatriate community for a stylish venue for entertaining. Raffles Hotel enlarged quickly, with the present building, with its characteristic colonial style, being put up by 1899.

The early years of the 20th century were the heyday of the hotel, with the invention of the Singapore sling in its cocktail bar and stories of tigers under the billiard table. In keeping with much of the British Empire at the time, the local people were not allowed in, a situation that did not change until the 1930s. During the Second World War Singapore was occupied by the Japanese, who, so the story goes, on first entering the hotel, found the remaining guest dancing a last waltz. After the war it reflected the faded glory of the empire for many years, until it was renovated in 1989. These days it is owned by an international investment company and is thought of as one of the best hotels in the world, perhaps now becoming a symbol of the economic success of post-colonial Singapore.

FACT FILE

COORDINATES
1°17'41" N, 103°51'16" E

LOCATION
Singapore

FOUNDERS
Arshak, Aviet, Martin and Tigran Sarkies

COCKTAILS
Singapore sling – invented by bartender Ngiam Tong Boon in 1910 at the Raffles Hotel

RIVER GANGES

In the Hindu religion the goddess Ganga, who is the personification of the river of the same name, which is known as the Ganges in the West, came down to earth to cleanse the souls of people so they could ascend into heaven free from sin. Accordingly, the Ganges is sacred to Hindus, who believe that bathing in its water will result in forgiveness, and they scatter the ashes of the dead in it because immersion in its waters will facilitate the transport of their souls to heaven. Many Hindus keep a vial of Ganges water in their homes and will try to make a pilgrimage to the river at least once in their lifetime. There are many holy cities and sacred sites along its banks and religious festivals also take place there. The Kumbla Mela, in which many millions of Hindus gather on the banks to follow the bathing rituals, is thought to be the largest gathering of people anywhere in the world.

The source of the Ganges is high in the Indian Himalayas at the base of the Gangotri Glacier. This place is known as Goumuka, literally the cow's mouth, which it is supposed to resemble, and the melting ice from the glacier forms the Bhagirathi River. Numerous other rivers and streams coming down off the high peaks of the Himalayas flow into it and, after its confluence with the Alakanada River at the town of Devprayag, it becomes known as the Ganges. It emerges from the mountains at the holy city of Haridwar, one of the seven most holy places in Hinduism, and begins to flow in a south-easterly direction across the plain of North India. A dam diverts some of its water into the Ganges Canal, for use in agricultural irrigation and to connect it to the Yamuna River, on the banks of which Delhi and Agra stand. The two rivers merge at Allahabad where, according to Hindu belief, the mythical Sarasvati River also joins them. From here it flows east to Varanasi in Uttar Pradesh, another of the most holy places in Hinduism and one of the oldest cities in the world. It is sometimes known as the City of Temples because there are so many, including, on the banks of the river, the Kashi Vishwanath Temple, which is dedicated to the god Shiva and is a place of great religious significance.

The river meanders through the Rajmahal Hills of West Bengal, emerging to flow southwards towards Bangladesh and beginning to split into the channels of its delta. Through Bangladesh, where it is joined by the Brahmaputra and its main channel is known as the Padma River, it becomes the largest delta in the world as it flows out into the Bay of Bengal in the Indian Ocean. The delta stretches along the coast from its western edge near the Indian city of Calcutta, now known as Kolkata, for 220 miles (350km) across the coast of Bangladesh. The alluvial soils of the delta are very fertile, supporting a rich agriculture based on rice, tea and jute. It is made up of many waterways, swamps and lakes and is very low lying, making it prone to flooding, a feature expected to increase with the rising sea levels associated with climate change, making Bangladesh one of the most vulnerable countries in the world to rising global temperatures, compounded by its high and densely packed population. Where the channels of the delta run out into the Bay of Bengal there is a huge expanse of mudflats and mangrove forests known as the Sundarbans. This area has become infamous as the last place on earth where man-eating tigers still exist and they are responsible for the deaths of more than 100 people every year, leading to a complex problem of balancing the conservation of a critically endangered species with the protection of local people from them.

The main problem facing the Ganges is the amount of pollution finding its way into it. Industries along its banks use it as a waste disposal facility, particularly leather-making, which uses chromium and other chemicals and then dumps them in the river. The sheer number of people living near the river, along its 1,500-mile (2,500km) course, contributes to the pollution, as water treatment facilities are often non-existent and raw sewage flows directly into it. Even the Hindu tradition of scattering ashes into the water has caused serious problems, with partially decayed bodies finding their way into the river. Considering the Ganges is sacred, it would appear that, in the past, the Indian authorities have not given the environmental issues of the river as much attention as they could have, although attitudes have been changing in more recent years. The sacred river would surely, given the opportunity, be able to cleanse itself as well as those who bathe in its waters.

FACT FILE

COORDINATES
30°59' N, 78°55' E (Source)
22°05' N, 90°50' E (Mouth)

LOCATION
Northern India and Bangladesh

LENGTH
1,557mi (2,510km)

BASIN AREA
400,000sq mi (1,000,000sq km)

ROCK OF GIBRALTAR

The death of the Spanish King Charles II in 1700 without an heir prompted the War of the Spanish Succession, fought between, on one side, Spain and France, who supported Philippe duc d'Angou's claim to the throne, and, on the other, the Holy Roman Empire, whose Emperor Leopold I made a rival claim. The English and the Dutch, along with a number of other European countries, sided with Leopold, principally to check French expansionism by preventing the union of the French and Spanish crowns. In 1704 the English, under the naval commander Sir George Rooke, captured Gibraltar from the Spanish, but it would be another ten years before the war came to a final resolution. In 1713 Great Britain, which had come into existence in 1707 with the union of England and Scotland, signed the Treaty of Utrecht with France and Spain, recognising Philippe as the King of Spain provided he renounce the rights of his descendant to the throne. One of the other settlements agreed under the treaty was that Spain ceded Gibraltar to Britain in perpetuity and, 300

years later, it remains a UK Overseas Territory despite numerous requests by the Spanish for the return of its sovereignty. One of the main points of dispute is how much of Gibraltar was actually ceded by the Spanish in 1713, as the treaty did not include specific descriptions or maps of the exact area in question.

The Isthmus of Gibraltar projects out into the Mediterranean Sea from the Iberian Peninsula just east of Tarifa, the most southerly point of Spain. The Rock of Gibraltar itself is a huge limestone headland, rising to 1,396ft (426m) at the end of the isthmus, from where it overlooks the Straits of Gibraltar, the eight mile (13km) wide body of water at the entrance to the Mediterranean which separates Europe from Africa. The Rock, as it is often known, and Monte Hacho in Cueta, a Spanish enclave in Morocco, together make up the Pillars of Hercules and are both important strategic locations, from where the entry of ships to the Mediterranean can be controlled. Consequently, the Rock became a major British military base,

and a large naval presence is maintained there to this day, which has responsibility for the security of the British Gibraltar Territorial Waters, and there are facilities for the berthing of the UK's nuclear submarine fleet. There is also believed to be a secret listening post based on the Rock, to intercept signals and for other intelligence-gathering purposes.

The saying 'as solid as the Rock of Gibraltar' is used to describe a person who can be relied upon time and again in difficult circumstances and comes from the perceived ability of the defenders of the fortress on the Rock to resist attack, as happened on numerous occasions during the 18th century. The Great Siege of Gibraltar, which lasted for more than three years, began in 1779, when the British garrison was attacked by the French and Spanish. Despite being a large force, they could not dislodge the British, who had built a series of underground fortifications which made them all but impregnable. These fortifications were continued after the siege was lifted and became particularly important again

during the Second World War, when the civilian residents were evacuated and the Rock became an important staging post for the supply of the Allied military in North Africa and Malta.

The upper area of the Rock is a nature reserve and is home to what are probably its most famous residents, the Gibraltar apes, which, despite the name, are actually Barbary macaques. There are several troops of them, with a total population of about 300, and they are the only free-living monkeys in Europe and one of Gibraltar's main tourist attractions. A legend has grown up around them suggesting that while they remain on the Rock it will continue to be under British rule, a story taken seriously enough by Winston Churchill during the Second World War for him to order their numbers to be replenished with wild macaques from Morocco when they began to decline. Some of them had become so used to human interaction, particularly at the tourist spot known as the Ape's Den, that they were beginning to be a nuisance and it is now an offence to feed them. Opinion is divided about how they got onto the Rock in the first place, with one possibility being that they were brought over from North Africa by the Moors, who occupied southern Spain and Portugal from 711 to 1492. The Moors named it Gibr al-Tariq, the Rock of Tariq, after Tariq ibn-Ziyad, who led the first Moorish incursion into Spain from North Africa, landing on the Rock which, just about, still bears his name.

FACT FILE

COORDINATES
36°08'43" N, 05°20'35" W

LOCATION
Gibraltar, Straight of Gibralter, Iberian Peninsula

HEIGHT
1,396ft (426m)

FORMATION
African tectonic plate colliding with Europe

SAGRADA FAMILIA

There can be no other architect in the world whose name is associated with a particular city in quite the same way as Antoni Gaudi's has come to be with Barcelona. This has not happened because he was responsible for the design of large parts of the city or for its overall layout, as, say, Baron Haussmann was in Paris, or because he was the favoured architect of the ruling elite, as Albert Speer was in Nazi Germany; it is because of his sheer brilliance and the individuality of his work. In his lifetime he completed only a handful of buildings, such as the Palau Guiell and the Casa Mila, better known as La Pedrera, the Quarry, because it looks as if it has been sculpted out of solid rock, but, while they are all very different from each other, they form a body of work that could not possibly be attributed to anyone else. Many architects have been influenced by him, and some could even be described as being imitators of his style, but he remains unmistakable and unsurpassed. His last building, the Sagrada Familia, or, to give its full title in English, the Expiratory

Temple of the Holy Family, is a synthesis of his philosophy on architecture, combining his views on art, the natural world and Catalan culture with his intense belief in the Roman Catholic faith.

Gaudi was born in Reus, a small rural town to the south of Barcelona, in 1852 into a family who were involved in the metal-working trade. From an early age he began to study the natural world, becoming fascinated by the structures he found there and these, along with the rural buildings of the Catalan countryside, which appeared to have grown out of the ground organically themselves, would influence his work for the rest of his life. He became a student of architecture in Barcelona, famously doing badly at the academic parts of the discipline, but he graduated nonetheless in 1878. Within a year he had been employed by Eusebi Guiell, a rich industrialist and devout Catholic, who would become his patron, allowing him to develop his own style and unconventional ways which did not rely on working out designs on paper. He used weighted lengths of string, which he would suspend

from a frame to form an inverted version of the design he was interested in, allowing gravity to form the shapes and arches he wanted naturally. His architecture is characterised by these natural shapes, although the lack of straight lines did not always make his buildings popular during his lifetime.

In 1884 he began work on the Sagrada Familia, designing the church with 18 towers, one for each of the 12 Apostles and 4 Evangelists, one for the Virgin Mary and the largest and central one for Jesus. For the last 15 years of his life he stopped all secular work and devoted himself exclusively to it, going to the extreme of living within the precincts of the building for long periods of time. On 8 June 1926, when he was 74, he was hit by a tram in a Barcelona street. He was not recognised immediately, because of the shabby clothes he was wearing, and was sent to a public hospital for the poor, from which he refused to be moved after his family had found him, and he died there two days later with his masterpiece far from finished.

Work continued on the church until the start of the Spanish Civil War in 1936, during which part of the unfinished building and Gaudi's models and workshop were destroyed, making life difficult for the architects who took up the work again in the 1940s. It has been estimated that, using the building techniques available in the early 20th century, it would have taken 200 years to finish the work completely. At the moment the most recognisable parts of the building are the four towers of the North Façade, which, typically of Gaudi, are hyperboloid in shape. They were well advanced by the time of his death, although many of the numerous sculptures have been added since, some controversially so because they do not conform to Gaudi's original plans. They give the façade an incredibly rich ornamental look with their depictions of scenes from the Nativity and many different examples of Christian symbolism. Two further façades, known as the Glory and the Passion, are under way and work has speeded up quite considerably in more recent times. The introduction of computer-aided design, which has been particularly beneficial for the cutting of the huge number of individually shaped stone blocks required for the unusual shapes of the building, has led to the hope of it being finished in time for the centenary of Gaudi's death in 2026, which will be a fitting memorial to an extraordinary man.

FACT FILE

COORDINATES
41°24'13" N, 2°10'28" E

LOCATION
Barcelona, Catalonia, Spain

ORIGINAL ARCHITECT
Antoni Gaudi

LATER ARCHITECTS
Domènech Sugranyes, Francesc Quintana, Isidre Puig Boada, Lluís Bonet i Gari, Francesc Cardoner, Jordi Bonet i Armengol

SAHARA DESERT

The word Sahara comes from the Arabic name for the region, As-Ahra Al-Kubra, which means the Great Desert, and it is indeed the largest desert in the world, stretching from the Atlantic Ocean in the west for about 3,000 miles (4,800km) across North Africa to the Red Sea in the east. To the north it begins at the Mediterranean Sea and in the Atlas Mountains of Morocco and goes south for about 1,200 miles (1,900km) to the Sahel, another word taken from Arabic, which means border land and denotes the semi-arid savannah region between the desert and the tropical region of Central Africa. The area covered by the Sahara is about 3.5 million square miles (9 million km²), about the size of the contiguous United States of America. It is divided into regions, with the western part being known as the Maghreb and the eastern region being made up of the Libyan, Nubian and Eastern Deserts. The climate is one of the harshest in the world and could, perhaps, best be described as being very hot and very dry. There are places in the centre of the Sahara where it has not rained for 50 years and where the temperature can rise above 50 °C (120 °F) during the day and fall below freezing at night.

The Sahara is often thought of as being a great expanse of sand, but, while there are large areas of sand, including the huge dune systems known as the erg, the most extensive desert type is the hamadas, a plateau of denuded rock. There is also the reg, a desert of coarse gravel and stones, the wadis, which are dried-up river valleys, and areas of salt flats. In the centre of the Sahara there are some mountain ranges, where the climate is somewhat milder and there is relatively more rain. Mount Koussi in Northern Chad is its highest point, rising to over 11,000ft (3,400m), and it is so remote and in such an inhospitable area that, although it is known to be a volcano, it is not known when it last erupted.

The climate of the Sahara has changed between wet and dry a number of times in the past. The present dry phase began about 5,000 years ago, and before this there was a wet period lasting something like 6,000 years. Neolithic rock carvings have been found in the Tassili N'Ajjer Mountains of Algeria which show animals associated with a much wetter climate, including crocodiles, and the name itself translates to the Plateau of Rivers. The processes behind these cycles of wet and dry periods are not well understood, but they are thought to be associated with complex changes in the world's climate brought on by the end of the Ice Ages and the shifting patterns of monsoon rains, which, during the current dry period, do not progress further north from the tropics than the Sahel. The large aquifers underlying some areas of the desert must have accumulated during these wet periods, with water percolating down into the underlying sandstone bedrock, and it is water from these that forms oases, where the water-table is quite close to the surface or where there is a depression in the land.

The population, outside of the few cities like Cairo and Nouakchott, the capital of Mauritania, is very sparse, although there is a great diversity in ethnic background and in the languages spoken by the few people who do live there. One of the well-known nomadic peoples of the Sahara, who live by pastoralism and by trading, are the Tuareg, who have become as famous in the West for their music, a version of their traditional music influenced by rock and blues, as they are in the desert for their blue turbans and independence. In the 10th century they established Timbuktu as a trading centre for gold, slaves, ivory and salt, because of its position at the edge of the Sahara and on a number of trans-Saharan trading routes. The city became very wealthy, until, from about the 17th century, Europeans established routes for trade by sea, limiting the need for the trek across the desert by caravan. These days Timbuktu is known mainly in the West through its name alone, although it has recently twinned with the town of Hay-on-Wye, on the border between England and Wales.

The wildlife of the Sahara, given the harshness of the environment, is more diverse and abundant than might be expected. Unfortunately one of the most beautiful of the large antelopes that used to be found in the region, the scimitar-horned oryx, has been hunted to the edge of extinction in the wild, with the remote possibility of small numbers still living in Niger and Chad.

FACT FILE

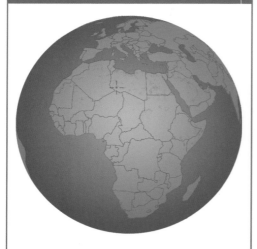

COORDINATES
24°29' N, 12°06' E

LOCATION
North Africa

AREA
3,500,000sq mi (9,000,000sq km)

TEMPERATURE RANGE
Daytime: 136 °F (58 °C)
Night: 22 °F (-6 °C)

AVERAGE ELEVATION
1,300–1,600ft (400-500m)

SAMARKAND

By the time Timur the Lame, sometimes known as Tamberlane, made Samarkand his capital, in 1370, it was already an old city. It had been an important centre on the Silk Road, the 5,000 mile (8,000km) long trading route between China and the Mediterranean, since at least the 8th century BC and had, in the past, been a large and prosperous city. Control of Samarkand, giving control of the Silk Road, had changed hands any number of times, between Persians, Turks and Arabs, before becoming the capital of the Khwarezmian Empire at some point in the 11th century. In 1220 Genghis Khan and his Mongol army invaded the empire and besieged the city, sacking it and killing almost everybody there. What was left became part of the Mongol Empire and it began to build up again. After Genghis's death in 1227 his empire gradually began to splinter apart and, with the death of his grandson Kublai Khan in 1294, generally regarded as the last of the Great Khans who ruled over the entire empire, it fractured into four parts. One of these, the Chagatai Khanate, had been originally established by one of Genghis's sons, but, by Timur's day, although it was still ruled by a descendant, it had split further into Transoxiana and Mughahstan.

Timur was a descendant of the Mongol invaders and had been born in Transoxiana, not far from Samarkand. His father, who had converted to Islam, may have been a high ranking military leader, although this is not known for certain, and Timur, who claimed to be related to Genghis himself by marriage, became prominent through military achievement and by forming alliances with those already in power. By the time he established his capital in Samarkand, he was in control of Transoxiana, although he never claimed the title of khan, and he used the city as a base to establish his own empire, following in the footsteps of Genghis. For the next 35 years, until he died on a military campaign against the Ming dynasty in China, who had ousted the Mongol Yangs, he built up his empire, until it stretched from India to Turkey. Somewhat at odds with his reputation as a brutal conqueror, he was also a great patron of the arts and he brought the most talented builders and craftsmen from around his empire to Samarkand, allowing them the artistic freedom to construct beautiful buildings in his city.

The dynasty he founded, the Timurids, continued the work he had started on the city, but the empire he had established would also gradually decline, much as Genghis's had, until it was conquered by the Uzbeks in 1506. One of Timur's direct descendants, Babur, would go on to found the Mughal dynasty in India in the 16th century, which continued to be ruled by a descendant of Timur's until it was dissolved by the British Empire in 1857. Samarkand came under Russian control in 1868, becoming part of the Soviet Union until Uzbekistan declared independence in 1991, with Tashkent as its capital.

The architecture of the Timurids in Samarkand has been described as the pinnacle of Islamic art in Central Asia. It drew heavily on the traditions of the Seljuq Turks and Persians, both of whom had controlled the region at different times in the past, and the buildings remaining today show

these influences as well as exhibiting the particular characteristics developed by the Timurids themselves. They all demonstrate some degree of axial symmetry and have façades decorated with geometric patterns, often with turquoise and blue tiling. There are many domes, although these are of different shapes and sizes, and the interiors are also usually tiled and are further decorated with paintings and stucco relief. Many of these features were carried into the Mughal Empire and some of them can be seen in the greatest of all Mughal buildings, the Taj Mahal.

The Gur-i-Amir was built by Timur in Samarkand in 1403 as a mausoleum for his grandson and heir Muhammad Sultan, who had died on one of Timur's campaigns. It has a huge azure dome, one of the most distinctive architectural features of the city, and would become Timur's own mausoleum and that of the future Timurids. The *madrasa* of the Registan in the centre of the city were built at different times and now occupy three sides of a huge square. The oldest, from 1420, was built by Ulugh Beg, another of Timur's grandsons, who became a famous astronomer and also built an observatory. Of the other buildings the oldest and one of the most beautiful is the Shah-i-Zinda, said to have been built over the grave of a cousin of the Prophet Muhammad, and one of the largest is the Bibi-Khanym Mosque, which had fallen into ruin and has now been entirely rebuilt.

FACT FILE

COORDINATES
39°39'17" N, 66°58'32" E

LOCATION
Province of Samarkand, Uzbekistan

POPULATION
412,000

FOUNDED
circa 700 BC

SERENGETI

To the east of Lake Victoria the volcanic soils of the Central African Plateau stretch over northern Tanzania and south-western Kenya and support an area of savannah, of open grassland, deciduous woodland and dense thicket, called the Serengeti. The name is derived from the Maasai word for the place where they live and means the endless plain. It spans about 300 miles (800km) from north to south and, by African standards, does not cover a huge area, but it is what many people from outside the continent would see as typically African, with its dusty brown grassland and scattered acacia trees shimmering in a heat haze caused by the equatorial sun. But it is, perhaps, the animals here that are most evocative of Africa, and the Serengeti is the scene of one of the most spectacular sights in the natural world, or anywhere else for that matter, the mass migration of wildebeest. More than a million of them, along with hundreds of thousands of zebra and antelope, follow the seasonal variations in rainfall and set a

pattern to the year with their rhythmic behaviour, the heartbeat of the Serengeti, which is followed by almost everything else. Monsoon rain comes to the open grassland in the north-west, around the Ngorogoro crater, late in the year and the great herds head towards it, crossing obstacles like the Mara River, where huge Nile crocodiles lay in wait for them, and they arrive there just as the lush newly grown grass is at its best. All of the females in the herd calve within a few weeks of each other, in late December and January, and the calves get to their feet within minutes of being born and start to run. The dry season begins in late May and, as the grass turns brown and begins to die off, they start to move west, towards Lake Victoria, gradually turning to the north and the Maasai Mara, where it all started from and where they will stay until the cycle begins all over again.

The wildebeest may provide the heartbeat of the Serengeti and its greatest spectacle, but it is the lions who provide the glamour. The Serengeti and

Maasai Mara National Parks, which are essentially one big park on either side of the border between Tanzania and Kenya, are some of the best places in the world to see lions in the wild. The prides spend their days stretched out in the shade of an acacia or on a kopje, a rocky outcrop, occasionally stirring to swish the flies away with their tails. In the cool of the evening the females may go hunting communally, the males very rarely joining them, and they somehow manage to coordinate their movements and know what each other is doing. Lions lack the endurance to chase their prey over long distances and give the impression of that being too much like hard work anyway, and they hunt by stalking, getting as close as they can before launching themselves in ambush, or by chasing prey towards another member of the pride. And king of the beasts they may be, but they are not above stealing kills made by hyenas or the increasingly rare hunting dogs, if they think they can get away with it. The other big cats in the Serengeti adopt

different approaches, with the smaller and more delicate-looking cheetahs using bursts of incredible speed to catch their prey and the solitary leopards waiting for hours in woodland, camouflaged so they fade into the background, until some unfortunate animal gets too close.

All the rest of them are here to; elephant, rhinoceros, hippopotamus, giraffe, buffalo and a whole array of other species. It is one of the last areas of the world where such a collection of large animals still roam wild and, while their numbers have been badly affected by poaching and habitat loss, many of them continue in relatively large populations. The exception is the critically endangered black rhino, still poached for its horn and, despite enormous efforts by park rangers and conservationists, still extremely rare and on the brink of extinction.

The Oldupai Gorge, which is on the border between the Serengeti National Park and the Ngorogoro Conservation Area, has been excavated for more than 50 years, beginning with Louis and Mary Leakey. Remains of early hominids and of their camps, tools and even their footprints have been found, including those of *Australopithecus boisei*, known as nutcracker man, *Homo habalis* and *Homo erectus*. These are thought to be some of our direct ancestors and the finds in the gorge have led to a much better understanding of human evolution and to the theory that human beings originated in Africa and spread out throughout the rest of the world from there.

FACT FILE

COORDINATES
2°32'52" S, 36°47'44" E

LOCATION
Tanzania and Kenya

AREA
23,166mi² (60,000km²)

MEANING OF NAME
Endless plains

SOMME BATTLEFIELD

The River Somme flows through Picardy in the north-west of France, heading towards the English Channel. To the north of the river, around the small rural town of Albert, the countryside is typical of the whole region. There are huge fields of wheat and sugar beet, creating rectangles in the gently undulating ground, and there are hardly any hedges and just a few small stands of trees. These days, not many of the fields are speckled red by the poppies for which the region was once famous. The only unusual features here, in the regular lines created by modern farming methods, are the war memorials and cemeteries interspersed between the fields. Some of the cemeteries contain no more than a handful of war graves, but in others the rows of headstones disappear off into the distance as if they will never come to an end. Because it is here, in this rural backwater of France, a few miles to the west of Albert and on a 25 mile long front on either side of the river, that one of the biggest and bloodiest battles of the First World War was fought. The Battle of the Somme, beginning on 1 July 1916 and continuing until the middle of November, by which time the front lines had moved little more than five miles, resulted in the deaths of 310,486 men, with half a million more wounded. For those nations involved, Britain, France, Australia, Canada, New Zealand, Newfoundland and South Africa on one side and the German Empire on the other, after the monstrous anger of the guns had become silent, the world had changed into a different place.

By 1916 the war on the Western Front had become a stalemate, with machine guns dominating the trenches and preventing either side from gaining any real advantage over the other. Tactics had been reduced to trying to inflict as many casualties as possible on the enemy in a war of attrition, both sides attempting to wear the other one down until the last man standing would win. General Sir Douglas Haig, the commander of the British forces, and the French commander, General Joseph Joffre, had agreed a strategy for a combined attack on the German army at the Somme in an effort to achieve a decisive breakthrough, but the Germans attacked the French at Verdun first in February. The battle developed into a bloodbath and the aims of the Somme increased to include diverting German resources away from it.

The battle began with a continuous five-day artillery bombardment and then, at 7.30 a.m. on 1 July, the combined Allied infantries attacked across the entire length of the front, and what followed was the greatest military disaster in British history. German machine gunners, who had sheltered in deep bunkers during the shelling, opened up on the Allied soldiers, decimating them as they advanced across no man's land, having been told to expect minimal resistance. In the chaos that followed, and with communications all but non-existent, more waves of infantry advanced straight into the machine-gun fire. By the end of the day the British had suffered 57,470 casualties, with 19,240 killed.

Some divisions had been all but annihilated, with casualty rates of over 90 per cent.

It is hardly possible to comprehend now, more than 90 years later, but even so it still has the capacity to shock and, however often the story gets repeated, as it does every anniversary and on Remembrance Days, familiarity on this one occasion does not lessen the impact. The war would continue for another two years, until the eventual Allied victory in 1918, and the debate on the significance of the Somme, both on the war and on the countries involved, continues to this day. Some military historians think the German armies were so weakened by the Somme and Verdun that an Allied victory became inevitable, particularly after the Americans joined the war in 1917. Whether this is true or not, it cannot possibly have been worth it.

The ground the battle was fought over now looks much the same as any farmland does, with, in a few places, some stretches of the trenches and the craters of shell bursts preserved. Occasionally the remains of one of the soldiers listed as missing are found and, if the remains can be identified, the soldier is given a funeral with full military honours. His name can then be removed from the Memorial to the Missing of the Somme at Thiepval, one less in the 72,000 names listed there. In recent years the last few surviving soldiers of the First World War, who are now well past 100 years old, have been interviewed and they have, without exception, spoken with great eloquence of their memories of that terrible war. They will not be with us very much longer and, when the last living link is broken, we must continue to remember them, and their fallen comrades, for their courage and dignity. That way we will not forget the horror and futility of war.

FACT FILE

COORDINATES
49°58'16" N, 2°17'32" E

LOCATION
Picardie region, France

OCCURRENCE
1 July, 1916

ST PAUL'S CATHEDRAL

On the night of 29 December 1940, at the height of the London Blitz, the Luftwaffe mounted one of its most destructive air raids, fire-bombing the City of London and the surrounding area. That night the *Daily Mail* photographer Herbert Mason took what would become one of the most famous photographs of the entire war from the roof of the newspaper's headquarters in Fleet Street. It showed the dome of St Paul's Cathedral illuminated by fire and wreathed in thick black smoke, but still standing, as if the building itself was defying Hitler. Winston Churchill was very aware of the importance to the morale of the country of such national monuments, and that night had ordered fire fighting resources to be concentrated around it, knowing the greatest danger to it was from fire. The cathedral had already survived a direct hit from a huge time-delayed bomb a few months earlier, which, had it gone off, would have totally destroyed the building, but it had been defused in time by the Royal Engineers. Over the course of The Blitz it would be hit a few more times, but, despite being damaged, it remained a symbol of the indomitable spirit of the nation.

It was not the first time the cathedral had been associated with fire, having been built on the site of the previous 11th-century Norman cathedral, which had been destroyed in the Great Fire of London in 1666. The fire had started in a bakery, owned by Thomas Farrier, in Pudding Lane, within the walls of the City of London, where the buildings were tightly packed together and built from wood with thatched roofs. As the fire began to take hold, efforts to control it were crucially delayed by the Mayor of London, who refused to give permission for buildings to be pulled down to create a fire-break, and, as the fire grew, the flames were fanned further by a strong east wind. The cathedral was being renovated at the time and wooden scaffolding stood around it, which went up like tinder when the fire reached it, spreading it to the wooden rafters and causing an inferno. The diarist John Evelyn, who watched the progress of the fire from Southwark, on the other side of the River Thames, wrote of stones flying from the building like grenades, of molten lead from the roof flowing in the streets and of 'the very pavements glowing with fiery redness, so as no horse, nor man, was able to tread on them'.

In the aftermath of the fire King Charles II, who had only been restored to the throne six years earlier on the death of Oliver Cromwell and was deeply concerned about the effect of the fire on public order, encouraged plans to be submitted for the rebuilding of the destroyed area and Sir Christopher Wren was one of many who drew up designs. The area was rebuilt by the owners of the land on the same plan as the pre-fire streets before any of these schemes had started, although the new buildings were in brick and stone rather than wood, but Wren's design for a new cathedral was accepted. The plans were heavily criticised by the clergy because of their daring and modernity, and Wren revised them a number of times until a compromise, known as the Warrant Design, which had a small dome with a steeple on top of it, was reached. The king gave Wren permission to make ornamental changes to this design if he felt they were necessary and, during the course of the building work, he used this permission to change virtually everything. In fact the finished building bears almost no resemblance to the original designs and the great dome, inspired by St Peter's Basilica in Rome, itself highly influenced by the 2nd-century Roman Pantheon, was to become its crowning glory.

The last stone of the building was laid in 1708, although work on it would continue for a few more years. Wren died in 1723, after, according to his son, catching a cold during a winter visit to the cathedral, and he was interred in its crypt, under a simple black marble flagstone. There is a Latin inscription on a nearby plaque and it reads '*Lector, si monumentum requiris, circumspice*', meaning 'Reader, if you seek his monument, look around you'. For the 300th anniversary of the cathedral in 2008 an extensive programme of restoration has been undertaken, the most obvious signs of which has been the cleaning work carried out on both the inside and outside of the building. The original cream-coloured Portland stone has emerged from centuries of accumulated grime and the cathedral now looks as magnificent as it must have done when it was first built. There could be no better tribute than that.

FACT FILE

COORDINATES
51°30'50" N, 0°05'52" W

LOCATION
Ludgate Hill, London, United Kingdom

ARCHITECT
Christopher Wren

CONSTRUCTION
1675–1710

STATUE OF LIBERTY

From 1892 to 1954 Ellis Island, at the mouth of the Hudson River in New York Harbor, was the main entry point for immigrants into the United States, with something like 12 million people passing through its immigration stations. For all of these people, as their ships were approaching New York, one of the first things they would have been able to see was the Statue of Liberty. With many of them coming to America to escape tyranny and persecution or with the hope of rising out of poverty, the first sight of this shining beacon, a symbol of the land of freedom and opportunity, must have been a truly uplifting experience.

The Statue of Liberty Enlightening the World, to give its full title, stands on Bedloe's Island in New York Harbor, less than a mile (1.6km) from Ellis Island, although it is now more usually called Liberty Island. The statue is of a colossal size, standing 151ft (46m) high, with the pedestal and foundation adding a further 154ft (47m), and it depicts the Lady of Liberty, who faces out towards the Atlantic Ocean. She is made of pure copper and stands up straight with her right arm raised, holding a gold-plated torch in her hand to greet people as they arrive in America and to light their path. In her left hand she holds a stone tablet, the Declaration of Independence, telling people, in Thomas Jefferson's words, that 'all men are born equal'. At her feet there are a set of broken shackles and, on her head, a seven-pointed crown, representing the seven seas and showing that she welcomes people from all parts of the world.

The statue was a gift from the people of France, the money for it being raised by public donation, and the idea was originally conceived in 1865 as a way of marking the centennial of the Declaration of Independence, which would fall on 4 July 1876. At that time France was ruled by Napoleon III, who had established the Second Empire by staging a *coup d'état*, and the idea of acknowledging the formation of a republic in America was intended to be something of a rallying call at home as well. The implementation of the idea got off to a slow start, with fund-raising being a particular problem, and, by 1876, the plans were all in place but nothing had actually been built. In France the sculptor Frédéric Auguste Bartholdi, who had been involved right from the beginning, had some influential people helping him. Gustave Eiffel was responsible for the internal metal structure, although, as would later be the case with the Eiffel Tower, much of the actual work was done by the structural engineer Maurice Koechlin, and the architect Eugene Viollet-le-Duc was involved with the metal working of the statue itself. The Americans had agreed to build the pedestal, but lack of funds had also proved a problem and it was not finished until 1886. Finally everything was ready and the statue, which had been shipped over from France in sections, was re-assembled on its pedestal.

There was more to the relationship between France and America than the shared ideals of republicanism. The French had been actively involved in the American Revolutionary War and they had a great influence on its outcome. After the Americans had beaten the British at the Battle

of Saratoga in 1777, the French became convinced that the revolutionaries would win. They signed the Treaty of Alliance with the Americans the following year, the two agreeing to help each other in the event of attack by the British. The Spanish and the Dutch came into the war on the republican side after that and the broadening of the conflict outside of America, and including a naval war in which, up until then, the British had held a vast numerical superiority, was one of the deciding factors of the war. The decisive battle came at Yorktown, Virginia, in 1781, where the British army, under General Cornwallis, came under siege from a combined American and French force, under General George Washington and the Comte de Rochambeau. The French navy prevented the resupply of the town and Cornwallis was forced to surrender. This led directly to negotiations between Britain and America and, in September 1783, to the Treaty of Paris, in which Britain recognised the United States and agreed to remove all its troops from American soil. The French, meanwhile, had run up huge debts during the war and the impact of these on the economy would be one of the factors leading to the French Revolution of 1789. The idea of republicanism had existed in France for many years before then, but the success of the American revolutionaries must surely have influenced the French to follow suit.

STONEHENGE

During the Late Neolithic and Early Bronze Age, a period of about 4,000 years, from 5,000 BC to 1,000 BC, a large number of stone monuments, or megaliths, were erected along the Atlantic seaboard of western Europe, stretching from the Orkney Islands down to southern Portugal. Structures showing some striking similarities were also put up in the South of France and on some Mediterranean islands, notably Malta and Sardinia, leading to suggestions of a maritime culture, perhaps connected by trade routes along the coast, who either spread out over the whole area themselves or exerted an influence over the already existing cultures. Well-known examples of these megaliths are the lines of standing stones at Carnac in Brittany, the chambered passage tomb at Newgrange near the Boyne River in Ireland and, in Wiltshire, in the west of England, the complex of stone circles and avenues of Avebury. But, without a shadow of a doubt, the most famous of them all is on Salisbury Plain, also in Wiltshire, and it is, of course, Stonehenge.

There are a large number of ancient sites on Salisbury Plain and a particular concentration of them around Stonehenge. At Durrington Walls, a few miles away, there was a similar circle, made of wood rather than stone, and recent excavations have uncovered a Neolithic village nearby of about 100 houses. There are also a large number of burial tombs, or barrows, around Stonehenge itself and an avenue, sometimes called a processional way, of ditches linking it to the River Avon. These features, taken together, have been called by some archaeologists a ritual landscape and they have attempted to explain the purpose of Stonehenge within this context. They propose that the ritual landscape was used to transfer people who had died from the world of the living, represented by the wood of the Durrington Walls circle, via the processional way and including the liminal zone of the river, where transitions between the two realms would have taken place, to the dead world of stone and, once they had arrived there, bodies would then have been buried in the barrows. The village, thought not to have been occupied all year round, would have been used while people were attending these funeral rituals and also for seasonal festivals, such as the winter and summer solstices, when great feasts were held.

One way of looking at Stonehenge itself is to consider it as a series of concentric circles, not all of which still exist, although they have left archaeological remains. The number of different building phases, over a period of several thousand years, makes it difficult to be certain of the dating of the different parts, but the main work was done during the 3rd millennium BC. The outer ring is of ditches and earth banks and, immediately within this, there is a ring of post holes that would have contained standing wooden poles. Two more rings of pits, called the X and Y holes, are immediately outside Stonehenge itself, a circle of 30 shaped stones, 13ft (4m) high, not all of which remain upright, with an interlocking ring of lintel stones on top of them. Within these there are smaller standing stones, known as the bluestones, which came from the Preseli Hills of North Wales, a distance of 150 miles (250km). At the centre are the largest of the standing stones, forming five trilithons, each made up of two standing stones with a lintel stone on top of them. They are arranged into a horseshoe shape and there is a single stone, known as the altar stone, within this open circle.

The alignment of the stones shows that the people who erected them had a detailed knowledge of astronomy and, in particular, of the movements of the sun and the moon, as they have been arranged with the positions of the winter and summer solstices in mind. They also knew about lunar standstills, a phenomenon of the moon occurring every 18.6 years when the moon reaches it maximum declination and appears, over a period of only two weeks, to move from high in the sky to low on the horizon. A recent theory suggests Stonehenge was associated with the moon and Durrington Walls with the sun. At the time of their construction, society was going through a period of enormous change, from a hunting and gathering way of life to farming. This shift was accompanied by a change in religious practices, from the old ways of worshipping the moon of the hunter to a new religion based on the sun of the farmer, but this change did not come without cost and the monuments were built to try to ameliorate these difficulties by showing that the moon had not been abandoned. This is, of course, like all theories to do with Stonehenge, based entirely on speculation, but, in its favour, at least it is reasonably sensible speculation.

SUEZ CANAL

The idea of connecting the Mediterranean and the Red Sea has had a long history, possibly going back as far as the Egyptian pharaohs, almost 4,000 years ago, and certainly to Darius I of Persia, who controlled Egypt in the 6th century BC. In more recent times, the prospect of a trade route from Europe to India and the Far East, cutting out the sea voyage around Africa, was a very attractive proposition and, potentially, a very lucrative one. Egypt was part of the Ottoman Empire when, in 1854, the French diplomat and engineer Ferdinand de Lessop obtained a concession from its Viceroy, Said Pasha, authorising him to form a company to build a canal from Port Said, on Egypt's Mediterranean coast, to Port Tawfiq on the Gulf of Suez, a branch of the Red Sea.

The Suez Canal Company, with shares split between private French investors and the Egyptian Government, was formed in 1858 and plans for the canal were drawn up by the Austrian engineer Alois Negrelli. The excavation work took 11 years and was carried out by Egyptian forced labourers, a common occurrence in large colonial building projects at that time. No records were kept, but, it would be safe to assume, many thousands of people were killed during the progress of the work. The British had opposed the building of the canal in the first place, mainly because the concession had gone to the French, and did their best to disrupt the work. Despite this, and some technical problems, which caused the project to cost almost twice its original estimate, the canal opened in 1869 and was immediately very busy, as it continues to be today. During the early 1870s the Egyptian Government, in the face of a mounting financial crisis, sold its shares in the canal to Britain, but the money raised did not solve the crisis and the British and French, now joint owners of the canal, assumed control of the government as well. A mounting nationalist movement in Egypt persuaded the British to send troops to the country to protect their investments and, from 1882, Egypt, although still part of the Ottoman Empire, effectively became a British colony.

At the outbreak of the First World War, with Britain fighting the Ottomans, Egypt was declared a British Protectorate and the nominal Ottoman ruler was replaced by another member of his family, who was considered to be friendly to the British. After the war a full-blown nationalist rebellion began and was brutally suppressed, but was followed by Britain granting Egypt independence. A constitutional monarchy was formed, with Ahmed Fuad, an Ottoman of Albanian descent, installed by the British as King Fuad I, although the nationalists, who, with some justification, regarded Fuad as a British puppet, were not much mollified. King Farouk succeeded his father in 1936 and, in the same year, signed the Anglo-Egyptian Treaty, which required the withdrawal of all British troops from the country except at the Suez Canal.

In the years after the Second World War, when Egypt had been an important base for Allied operations in North Africa and the Mediterranean, the nationalist movement and anti-British feeling began to grow again. In 1952 a group of army officers, including Lieutenant Colonel Gamal Abdel Nasser, overthrew the king, whom they blamed for the disastrous outcome of the 1948 Arab–Israeli War as well as for his pro-British sympathies. Nasser became the President of Egypt in 1954 and, in 1956, after the British and Americans had reneged on an agreement to finance the building of the Aswan High Dam, possibly because of Nasser's contact with China, he nationalised the canal, intending to use the money raised from tolls to pay for the dam and prompting what came to be known as the Suez Crisis.

The British still had a 44 per cent interest in the canal and the Prime Minister, Anthony Eden, citing Egyptian expansionism and comparing Nasser to Hitler, decided on military force to take back control. In conjunction with the French, a secret meeting was held with Israel and a conspiracy was agreed between them. The plan called for Israel to deliberately provoke the Egyptians by invading the Sinai and moving up to the banks of the canal. This would give the British and French an excuse to intervene and demand the withdrawal of both sides from the canal, even though the Egyptians had not started the trouble. They would then argue that the canal should remain under their control because of its importance to international trade. From a military point of view, the plan worked perfectly, but it turned into a political disaster when the Americans did not support the invasion and demanded a ceasefire. This, along with condemnation from around the world, forced the British and French to withdraw and Eden to resign.

FACT FILE

COORDINATES
30°42'18" N, 32°20'39" E

LOCATION
Egypt, connecting the Red and Mediterranean seas

CONSTRUCTION
1859–1869

SIZE
101mi (163km) long, 984ft (300m) wide

SYDNEY OPERA HOUSE

There is an old joke about Australia which goes something like this:

Q: What is the difference between Australia and a pot of natural yoghurt?

A: A pot of yoghurt has got more culture in it.

It would be ridiculous to suggest that the Sydney Opera House was built in response to an old joke, but it does serve to illustrate the perception of the Australia of the 1950s as being something of a cultural backwater. Many Australian artists and writers certainly appear to have thought so, as there was a constant exodus from the country, heading for the bright lights of New York or London. Australia was still a young country then, having gained independence from Britain in 1900, but not really having shaken off its colonial ties until after the Second World War. Culture was imported from abroad and there was very little going back in the other direction. The idea of an opera house was first put forward by Eugene Goossens, the English conductor who was the Director of the New South Wales Conservatorium of Music in the early 1950s, but did not have a venue of sufficient size to stage large operatic productions. He suggested building it on Bennelong Point in place of the disused Fort Macquarrie Tram Depot and although Joseph Cahill, the NSW State Premier at the time, had never been to the opera, he supported the idea.

Bennelong Point projects out into Sydney Harbour immediately to the east of Sydney Harbour Bridge and Circular Quay. The Conservatorium is in the Royal Botanic Gardens, which sweep around Farmers Cove and right up to Bennelong Point, so it is not hard to work out why Goossens favoured the site, but it is also one of the most spectacular locations in Sydney. In 1955 the New South Wales Government held a competition to find an architect for the opera house and it was won by Jørn Utzon, from Denmark. His submissions to the competition had consisted of little more than some preliminary drawings and had been rescued from the reject pile by the Finnish-American architect Eero Saarinen, who was on the selection panel and is best known for the Gateway Arch in St Louis. If Utzon was surprised to have won, having never previously worked outside Denmark, he did not show it, but now he had to convert his thoughts on paper into an actual building.

The main problem Utzon faced was with the roof and, in particular, with the parabolic shape of its shells, as he called them. They looked fantastic, but the way they had been designed meant they would not have been structurally sound and would have been almost impossible to build. The structural engineer for the project was the Anglo-Danish Ove Arup, generally considered now to have been one of the foremost engineers of his time, and his particular speciality was in precast concrete, the principal building material of the roof. The two of them spent thousands of hours over a period of three years struggling with the problem, using computer-aided design for the first time on such a large project, and eventually they came up with a solution. There are several different stories about exactly who cracked it, but the idea, in the end, was a relatively simple and elegant one, with the sections of the shell being made from a sphere. Perhaps the best way of considering this is to think of the sections as being like triangular pieces cut out of the peel of an orange. This shape solved the problems of construction and could also be made relatively easily in precast concrete. Utzon has never been particularly forthcoming when asked about his inspiration for the final shape, saying, 'In the hot sun of the day it will be a beautiful white shimmering thing'. They have been variously described as being like the spinnaker sails of yachts in the harbour or of upended shells on a New South Wales beach. In straightforward language more typical in Australia, they have also been said to resemble a bunch of nuns in a scrum.

Utzon may have thought his troubles were over, but if he did he was very wrong. By the mid-1960s the government had changed in New South Wales and the new administration were much less sympathetic towards him and to the huge time and budget overruns the project had incurred. In 1966, with relationships between all parties irrevocably broken, Utzon resigned and work to finish the building, which by then mostly involved the interiors, was taken up by a team of Australian architects. It opened in 1973 and was an immediate sensation, and although the interiors have been refurbished since with Utzon's approval, they have never really matched the spectacular look of the building itself.

FACT FILE

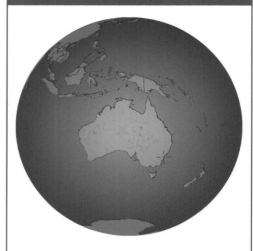

COORDINATES
33°51'24" S, 151°12'55" E

LOCATION
Sydney, New South Wales, Australia

CONSTRUCTION
1973

ARCHITECT
Jørn Utzon

DIMENSIONS
605ft (183m) long, 388ft (120m) wide

TABLE MOUNTAIN

Before the Suez Canal was opened in 1859 the main route from Europe to India, the Far East and Australia was round the Cape of Good Hope, the south-westerly tip of the African continent. It is not actually the most southerly point, which is Cape Agulas to the east, but it marked the dividing line between the Atlantic and the Indian oceans to sailors and became an important landmark for those making the trip, who referred to it simply as the Cape. It also shelters Table Bay, where the Dutch established a supply depot for their ships heading out to the Dutch East Indies, now Indonesia, in 1652, which would become Cape Town. The town sits in what is known as the city bowl, a natural amphitheatre formed by the horseshoe of mountains around it, including Signal Hill, Lion's Head, Devil's Peak and, by far the best known and most distinctive, Table Mountain.

The name is, of course, a descriptive one, as the mountain's sheer cliffs rise up to a level plateau, which is about 2 miles (3km) across. It is a very old geological feature, having been uplifted from below the sea about 280 million years ago, and the main body of it is made up of sandstone which sits on a bed of granite. The process by which it was uplifted is known as isotacy, or emerging relief, and is caused by upward pressure exerted by the movement of tectonic plates. Although the rock, known as Table Mountain sandstone, is actually very hard, it has been subjected to erosion for a very long time and this has resulted in the craggy features of its cliffs

and the flat top. The highest part of the plateau, at its eastern edge and marked by a beacon from the trigonometrical survey, stands at 3,563ft (1,086m) above sea level.

The whole area of the mountain, including the part known as the Black Table at the rear, falls within the Table Mountain National Park. The plateau has an incredibly high floral biodiversity, amongst the highest in the world, and it forms part of the Cape Floristic Region World Heritage Site. The main type of vegetation found is known as the fynbos, an Afrikaans word meaning fine bush, which refers to a common feature among many of the shrubs here of having thin pointed leaves. The species richness of this type of vegetation can be illustrated by the fact that there are 1,470 species of plants on the plateau of Table Mountain alone, more than there are in the entire United Kingdom, and a very high number of them do not occur anywhere else. It is made up predominantly of shrubs, particularly the large broad-leaved proteas and lower-growing heathers, and there are also the reed-like restios, a family of plants almost exclusively occuring in the fynbos, and a huge number of flowering plants, most of which grow from bulbs. There are, for example, 96 different types of gladioli alone. The fynbos relies on fire, a common occurrence in the dry summer months, to maintain it. Where it grows near to houses, where the fires are extinguished soon after they begin, it becomes moribund and a few species will gradually begin to dominate at the

expense of its diversity. The plants of the fynbos are adapted to fire and some of them actually need to be burnt before they can spread their seeds. The proteas exhibit a phenomenon known as serotiny, where the seeds produced by the flowers of the plant are retained in resistant structures until they are released by fire. This is the reason why they are often used in displays of dried flowers, as they can persist in this state for long periods of time.

Table Mountain is a popular tourist destination from Cape Town and there is a cable car for those who do not fancy the arduous walk. The view is often spoilt by cloud coming down over the plateau and it sometimes appears to spill over the edge of the mountain in a feature known locally as the table cloth. On clear days the views over Cape Town, Table Bay and the Cape of Good Hope are spectacular and, about six miles (10km) out into Table Bay, there is also Robben Island, a reminder of South Africa's recent troubled past. The notorius prison on the island is where political prisoners of the apartheid system were kept, including Nelson Mandela and Walter Sisulu. They were both released in 1990, Mandela having served 27 years and Sisulu 26, and shortly afterwards they were elected as president and vice-president of the African National Congress, positions they would fill in the Government of South Africa itself in 1994, after the ANC won the first multi-racial elections of the post-apartheid era.

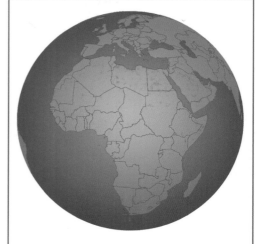

TAJ MAHAL

Not a great deal is known about Arjumand Banu Begum who, on marrying Prince Khurram, the son of the Mughal Emperor Jahangir, in 1612 became known to his court as Mumtaz Mahal, the beloved ornament of the palace. In 1628 Khurram, in a move typical of the Mughal dynasty, deposed Jahanghir and became emperor himself, being known from then on as Shah Jahan. Mumtaz is said by poets to have been a woman of great beauty and virtue, although they would say such things about the emperor's wife, and she became his constant companion and adviser as he travelled around his empire and conducted military campaigns. But, three years after Shah Jahan had succeeded his father and at the age of only 31, Mumtaz died during the birth of their fourteenth child. Shah Jahan is said to have been inconsolable, withdrawing into secluded mourning and emerging with his hair having turned white and his features having become those of an old man, although he was not 40 years old by then. To fulfil a deathbed promise to his adored wife and, perhaps, to console himself, he commissioned the building of the Taj Mahal as her mausoleum, her last wish being for a monument to symbolise their love.

The Mughal Empire had been established about 100 years previously by Babur, a Timurid prince from Central Asia who was descended from both Timur the Lame and Genghis Khan. Babur, who was a follower of Islam, had invaded Hindustan, defeating the Sultan of Delhi in 1526 and establishing an empire encompassing most of the Indian subcontinent. He is said to have missed the buildings and gardens of Afghanistan and tried to recreate them, beginning a tradition of Islamic architecture that would be continued by his successors. By the time of Shah Jahan, the empire had become fabulously wealthy and he commissioned many extravagant buildings, almost bankrupting himself in the process.

The Taj Mahal, the Crown Palace, stands on the banks of the Yaruma River in Agra, the capital of the Mughal Empire and the site of many other Mughal buildings. It is the pinnacle of Mughal architecture and its design is influenced by the Timurids and Persians and by earlier Mughal tombs, particularly those of Humayun, the second emperor, in Delhi and of Itmaid-Ud-Duala, who was the Mumtaz's grandfather, although the Taj is built entirely of white marble rather than of red sandstone, as the older buildings were. The main tomb is set in a traditional Islamic garden, a Charbaoh, with formally laid out water features, and is flanked by a mosque and a guest house. It is symmetrically designed around a central axis and stands on a square podium, which has a minaret on each of its four corners. There are arched doorways, iwans, on each of the tomb's four sides and this square rises into the onion-shaped central dome. On each of the corners of the building itself, around the dome, there are four smaller domed kiosks, known as chattri, adding balance to the design. The surfaces are covered with traditional Islamic decoration: swirling calligraphy of passages from the Qur'án, repeating geometric patterns, motifs of plants and arabesques of intertwining leaves and vines.

The interior of the tomb is fittingly dark and sombre, with what light there is filtering through marble grills, which have been placed over the windows. It is the shape of an octagon, of two overlapping squares, and all the surfaces have been decorated with inlaid semi-precious stones; there is jade from China, turquoise from Tibet and lapis lazuli from Afghanistan. At its centre is Mumtaz's cenotaph, a richly inlaid marble casket, and next to it, in the only visible asymmetric feature of the building, there is the slightly larger cenotaph of Shah Jahan. As it is against Islamic tradition to have elaborate graves, the two actual tombs lie next to each other in the crypt below.

In 1658 Shah Jahan fell ill and a power struggle developed between his four sons to succeed him. He favoured his eldest son, Dara Shikoh, but Ahrangzeb, his third son, won both the military and political battles. On arriving victoriously in Agra, Ahrangzeb declared himself emperor and refused to see his father, confining him to the Citadel of Agra, from where he could see the Taj. He lived for eight more years, dying at the age of 76, in 1666, and his body was placed in the Taj rather than in a specially built mausoleum, as all previous emperors had been. It is impossible to know now if this was an act of spite by the son he had not supported as his heir or if it was his choice to spoil the symmetry of his greatest building so that he could rejoin his wife, who had died so many years before him.

FACT FILE

COORDINATES
27°10'30" N, 78°02'32" E

LOCATION
Agra, India

CONSTRUCTION
1632–1648

DOME DIMENSIONS
60ft (18m) diameter, 80ft (24m) high

HEIGHT
180ft (55m)

THE GREAT TEMPLE OF TENOCHTITLAN

The Spanish Conquistadors, under the leadership of Hernan Cortes and in alliance with Native American enemies of the Aztecs, besieged the Aztec capital of Tenochtitlan in the spring of 1521. They captured the city in August and raised it to the ground, putting an end to the Aztec Empire that had flourished for the previous two hundred years and had extended over most of the area that is now Mexico. The Spanish founded Mexico City on top of the ruins. It was not until 1978 that the remains of the Great Temple were found, when workman came across a huge carved stone portraying the Aztec moon goddess Coyolxauqui. Archaeologists began excavating the area and gradually uncovered what was left of the temple after if was destroyed by the Spanish.

Tenochtitlan was founded on an island in Lake Texcoco in 1325. A prophecy had told that a site for their city would be shown to them. It could be found where they saw an eagle perched on a cactus with a snake in its mouth, an image that now adorns the Mexican flag. The city grew rapidly as the Aztec Empire flourished and artificial islands were created to allow the city to expand further. Causeways linked the island to the mainland, aqueducts were constructed to bring fresh water into the city, as the lake water was brackish, and a series of canals allowed transport through the city by canoe. At the height of the Empire there were 200,000 inhabitants in the city. At its centre, there was a walled ritual precinct containing public and ceremonial buildings, including, on the spot where the prophecy had been fulfilled, the Great Temple – the largest and most important building in the city.

The temple took the form of a symbolic representation of the Hill of Coatepec where, according to Aztec myth, Huitzilopochtli the god of the sun and of war was born. From its first incarnation in 1390, it was rebuilt a total of seven times and enlarged on eleven occasions. At the time of the Spanish conquest it consisted of a platform on which a wide pyramid, composed of four sloped tiers with a passage between each level, was built. It was about 190ft (60m) high and had two stairways leading up to the top, where there were two shrines, one dedicated to Tlaloc, the rain god, who was also associated with agriculture and fertility, and the other to Huitzilopochtli. At the base of the steps there were carved stone snake heads and at the top of each stairway were large stone blocks on either side of the steps, known as balustrades. The entire building was originally covered with stucco reliefs and painted. Archaeologists have found one of the platforms which led up to the pyramid and on it there is a stucco relief of a tzompantli, a wooden rack used to display the skulls of sacrificial victims.

Sacrifice appears to have played an important part in the Aztec religion. There is no agreement about the extent to which it was practised, estimates range from just one or two to a quarter of a million sacrifices a year. In one of the Aztec codices, which were books made up mostly of pictures, a figure of 84,400 is given for the number of sacrifices that took place during the four day reconsecration of Great Temple in 1487, after the building had been enlarged. This may be a wild exaggeration, however there is no doubt that sacrifices really did take place and that, in Tenoctitlan, they were conducted by priests at the top of the Great Temple. Victims were prisoners taken in war and, it has been suggested, wars may have actually been fought for no other purpose than for the taking of prisoners for sacrificial purposes. This practice, it is thought, led to the Aztec's having many enemies, some of whom were prepared to join with the Spanish to fight against the Aztecs during the conquest, although sacrifice after capture in battle appears to have been regarded, at least by some of the victims, as a great honour.

Since it's rediscovery in 1978, a museum (Museo del Templo Mayor) has been built next to the site of the Great Temple, which is near the Metropolitan Cathedral in Zocalo. It houses some of the World's finest collections of Aztec artefacts, all of which were discovered during the excavation of the Great Temple and its surroundings. It is also possible to walk around the archaeological site and to stand at the base of the platform leading up to the temple, where Aztec people of the city of Tenochtitlan would have stood 500 years previously.

TERRACOTTA ARMY

In the 3rd century BC the country of China began to emerge out of the seven feudal states then occupying the region, who themselves had developed by annexing their neighbouring fiefdoms. The State of Qin, which had a superior army and more resources than any other, began to take them over, culminating in an epic battle with the Chu State in 223 BC. With the Qin victory the few other independent states left, the Han and Qi, quickly acquiesced and, in 221 BC, King Zheng of Qin was declared the Emperor of China, changing his name to Shi Huangdi, usually translated as the First Emperor. This was the beginning of Imperial China, which lasted in one form or another and with a number of changes in ruling dynasty, for more than 2,000 years, until 1912 and the creation of the Republic of China. After the fall of the Qin Dynasty, the First Emperor became known as Qin Shi Huangdi, as he is still known today. He is generally thought of as being a tyrant who brutally repressed his people, killing anyone who opposed him and forcing labourers to work on his vast building projects, including a Great Wall, a precursor of the one built by the Ming Dynasty in the 16th century, and his huge mausoleum, which took 38 years to complete and involved an enormous number of workers.

In 1974 farmers drilling a well for water to irrigate their fields near the site of the mausoleum, known as Mount Lishan and not far from the city of Xi'an in central China, found the remains of some buried terracotta figures of soldiers. Excavations began shortly afterwards and, as more and more of this Terracotta Army, as it soon became known, was found, it became apparent that a major archaeological discovery had been made. Excavation continues to this day and it has been estimated that there are more than 8,000 figures buried, together with something like 100 horses and chariots, and they vary in condition from being almost complete to almost entirely destroyed. The soldiers of this army were arranged by rank in what is assumed to have been battle formation and they stand in pits, four of which had been dug, although only three of these were filled with the figures before work stopped. They are life-sized, except the height of the upper ranks has been exaggerated slightly, with generals, for instance, standing at 6ft 6" (2m), and the uniforms and hairstyles reflect each figure's rank. They were vividly painted and the faces lacquered, but the paint has not survived, and each one has an individually moulded face thought to have been modelled on the features of an actual soldier. They were given real armour and weapons but, unfortunately, none of these remain, having either been looted or the metal having corroded away. The process by which they were made is thought to have been similar to how terracotta drainage pipes were made at the time. Parts of the figures were massproduced and fired together in what amounts to a factory nearby, and then each figure was assembled from its parts and erected in its correct place.

The remains of wooden structures surrounding and covering the army have been found and there is evidence of it burning down. The Han Dynasty historian Sima Qian, writting in the 2nd century BC, about 80 years after the events, tells of Xiang Yu, a Chu general, who was one of the leaders of the rebellion that brought down the Qin Dynasty a few years after Qin Shi Huangdi died. According to Sima Qian, Xiang Yu raided the mausoleum, looting the tomb and setting fire to the wooden structures there, including, presumably, those surrounding the army. Many of the terracotta figures would have been crushed as the roof fell in and many more, no doubt, have crumbled away over the proceeding 2,000 years, but even so a significant number have survived and more have been reconstructed from their remaining fragments.

During his life Qin Shi Huangdi made many enemies, no doubt because of his tyrannical ways, and he was subjected to numerous assassination attempts. He is said to have become deeply paranoid over threats to his life and obsessed with death and the possibility of eternal life. Having become convinced that mercury held the secret, he began to take pills containing the toxic heavy metal and died as a result. He was interred in his mausoleum with all manner of treasures from his empire and Sima Qian writes of there being flowing streams of mercury and rooms with gem-encrusted ceilings. He does not mention the Terracotta Army, which may have been completely buried by that time, but perhaps it had been assembled around this paranoid emperor's tomb to protect him as he moved from this world into the next.

FACT FILE

COORDINATES
34°23'06" N, 109°16'23" E

LOCATION
Shaanxi, China

NUMBER OF STATUE FIGURES
8,099

TIANANMEN SQUARE

The Tiananmen, or the Gate of the Heavenly Peace, is the public entrance to the Forbidden City, the former palace of the emperors of China in central Beijing. The gate stands on the north side of Tiananmen Square, which is the largest urban feature of its kind in the world and a place of great symbolic significance to the Chinese people because a number of key historical events have occurred there. It came to prominence in the West in 1989 after a series of pro-democracy demonstrations that were being held there were forcibly broken up by the Chinese army, under orders from the government, leading to many deaths and the condemnation of their actions around the world.

The square is an open space, with no seating or other public amenities, broken only by flagpoles and lamp-posts and by two large monuments, the Mausoleum of Mao Zedong and the Monument to the People's Heroes, an obelisk commemorating the people who died during the formation of the People's Republic of China. Before it became a square, the area had contained buildings connected with the Forbidden City and a number of the legations of foreign governments, including those of Britain and America. During the Boxer Rebellion, an uprising against the influence of foreign powers in China beginning in 1899, the compound containing the legations came under siege by the rebels. A military force, formed by an international alliance, entered Beijing and relieved the compound. In the fighting many of the buildings in the area were destroyed or badly damaged and it was subsequently cleared, creating the first open space there.

The Boxer Rebellion may have been put down, but civil unrest continued, leading to a revolution and the establishment of the Republic of China, which was declared by Sun Yat-sen in 1912, but was immediately beset by discord and infighting. Civil unrest and rebellion persisted for many decades until, in 1949, the Chinese Communist Party defeated Ciang Kai-shek's Kuomintang, the republican forces, and the People's Liberation Army entered Beijing. On 1 October 1949, Mao made a speech from the top of the Tiananmen to a huge crowd who had assembled in the square, declaring the foundation of the People's Republic of China and famously saying, 'The Chinese people have stood up'.

Mao died in 1976 and after the arrest of the Gang of Four, who were perceived as the real power in the country in Mao's declining years, a period of economic reform began under Deng Xiaoping. Political reform was much slower in coming, unlike in the Soviet Union under Mikhail Gorbachev, and sporadic student demonstrations began, mostly centred on Tiananmen Square. In April 1989 Hu Yaobang, who had been a reformer in the government, died and a demonstration of support was held for him in the square. The demonstration grew, particularly after Deng condemned it, with the protesters now demanding democracy and freedom of the media. A hunger strike began in May, by which time the students had been joined by many other people and the protests had spread to other parts of China, leading the government to order a crackdown to break it up. The army entered Beijing and, on the night of 3 October, used its infantry and armoured personnel carriers, backed up with tanks, to assault the unarmed

protesters in the square. Western journalists who were there reported indiscriminate gunfire and, by the morning, the square and the surrounding streets had been cleared and many people had been killed. The Chinese Government now say 186 people died that night, while the Chinese Red Cross puts the figure at 2,600, but the real number is likely to be considerably higher.

News footage shot on the morning of 4 October, of a man standing in front of a line of tanks as they were leaving the square, was shown around the world and has become one of the defining images of the late 20th century. In the footage the man is standing still as the first tank approaches him and it comes to a stop a few feet from him, with the three following tanks stopping in a line behind it. He appears to be remonstrating with the tank and waves the jacket he is carrying at it. The tank driver attempts to go round him, but he moves across in front of it again and it lurches to a stop, the driver, unlike the soldiers the night before, clearly unwilling to kill an unarmed man. The stand-off continues for a few seconds and then the film stops. There are a number of conflicting reports concerning his identity and what happened to him afterwards, but his extraordinary actions remain a symbol for the terrible massacre unleashed by the Chinese Government on its own people that night, which continues to be a stain on its reputation to this day.

FACT FILE

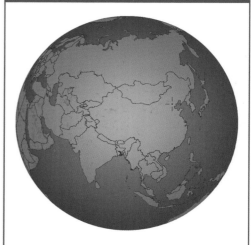

COORDINATES
39°54'12" N, 116°23'30" E

LOCATION
Beijing, China

SIZE
2,887ft (880m) south to north and 1,640ft (500m) east to west, area: 4,736,120ft² (440,000m²)

HISTORICAL EVENTS
4 June 1989 – Massacre in Tiananmen Square

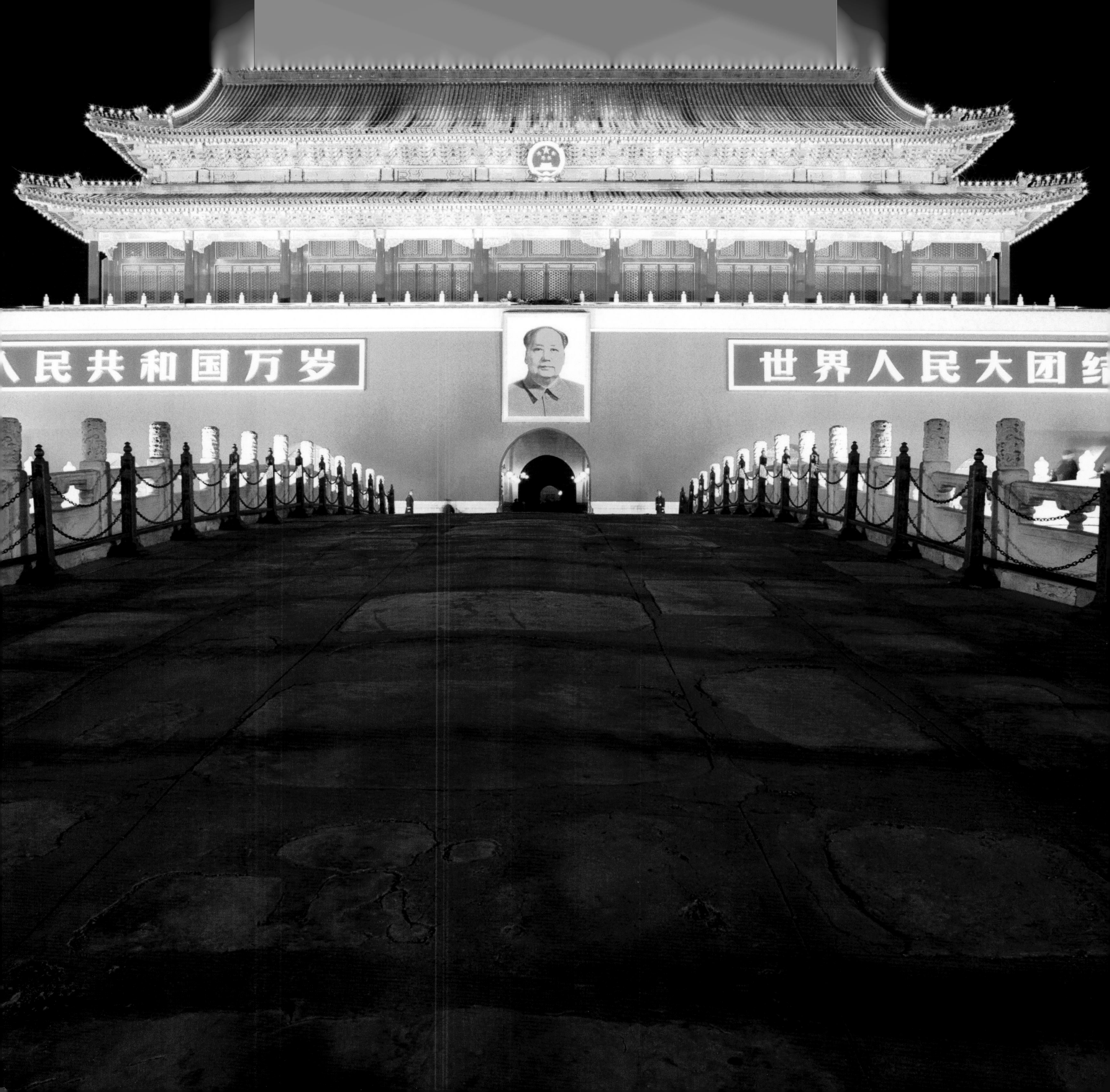
人民共和国万岁
世界人民大团结

TORII GATE – ITSUKUSHIMA SHRINE

The philosopher Hayashi Razan is said to have been the first person to list the Three Views of Japan in 1643 and they are still thought by many Japanese people to be the most beautiful places in the country. The Amanohashidate, the Bridge of Heaven, is a thin strip of land connecting one side of Miyazu Bay with the other, and Matsushima is the name of a group of 260 small pine-covered islands in a bay, so beautiful they inspired a haiku poem that simply repeats their name because the poet was lost for words on seeing them. The other one is the island of Itsukushima, sometimes known as Miyajima, the Shrine Island, and it is here, according to some people, that the standards of beauty for the whole of Japan are set, against which any other view can be evaluated. With the combination of three elements, of the man-made, in the form of its Shinto shrine in the centre, the sea in the foreground and the mountains in the background, it approaches the ultimate expression of what is considered to be beautiful by combining human creativity with the natural world.

The island is in the Seto Inland Sea, not far off the south-western coast of Honshu, the main island of Japan, and has been an object of veneration in the Shinto religion since ancient times. In Shintoism, nature in all its forms is held to be sacred and natural features are said to have spirits within them,

known as Kami, the Shinto gods, so, by being close to nature, a person becomes close to the gods. The place of worship, the public shrine, can hold any number of Kami, in whatever form they may take, and these can be petitioned by worshippers for the fulfilment of wishes, such as for a long and happy life or for the gift of a child. There are many thousands of shrines all over Japan and one of their most distinctive features is the entrance gate, the Torii, which separates the material world from the spiritual one, into which people step as they go into a shrine.

The origins of the Itsukushima Shrine are said to go back to the 6th century, although the shrine in its current form dates to 1168. The main buildings are constructed of wood and stand on piers over a small bay and, due to their position over water, tend to decay quite quickly and have been replaced on a number of occasions, although the replacement buildings have always taken the same form. The shrine was commissioned by the

most powerful political leader of the late Heian period, Taira no Kiyomri, who also introduced the first Samurai-dominated government to Japan. The complex of buildings, of which there are more than 50 altogether, are in the style of aristocratic residences of that time, called the Shinden style of architecture, and it is the same as the style used for the Imperial Palace in Kyoto. The main sanctuary of the shrine, the Honden, is open-sided and has vermilion-painted beams holding up a highly decorated roof of cypress bark, common features in many of the buildings. Both the structure, said to resemble a succession of folding screens, and the colour are intended to emphasise the contrast between the buildings, the green forests on the mountains and the blue of the sea. In front of it there is a broad wooden stage, the Hirabutai, and in the middle of this there is a smaller high stage, the Takubuti. These are used for performances of the traditional style of Japanese dance called Buguku. To one side, and also built over the sea,

is a traditional Japanese theatre where the classical Noh form of drama is staged.

The most widely known and photographed feature of the shrine is its Torii, the design of which dates to the same period as the Honden but, for similar reasons, the structure has been replaced a number of times, most recently in 1875. It stands about 50ft (16m) high and is built in the Yotsu-Ashi style, which refers to the fact that it has supporting legs as well as main ones. It has the two cross-beams typical of all entrance gates and is also painted vermilion. Perhaps its best known feature is that, when seen while the tide is in, it has the appearance of floating on the water rather than standing in it. When the tide goes out it stands on mudflats and can be reached on foot from the shore, and it is common practice for visitors to insert coins into cracks in its wood and make a wish.

FACT FILE

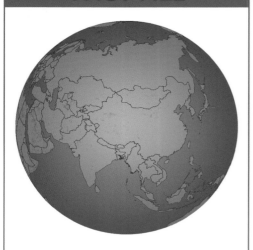

COORDINATES
34°17'51" N, 132°19'06" E

LOCATION
Itsukushima Island, Hiroshima Prefecture (city of) Hatsukaichi, Japan

CONSTRUCTION
1875 (A gate has existed on the site since 1168)

HEIGHT
50ft (16m)

MATERIAL
Camphor wood

TOWER BRIDGE

There has always been a certain amount of confusion concerning the name of Tower Bridge. For one thing, the name comes from its position on the River Thames, right next to the Tower of London, not from the fact that it has two 213ft (65m) towers, which were clad in Cornish granite and Portland stone to protect the steel structure and hydraulic mechanism within them. It is sometimes mistakenly called London Bridge, presumably because it is such a recognisable London landmark, whereas the actual London Bridge, the next one upstream to it, is relatively inconspicuous. There is something of an urban myth saying that the American who bought the old London Bridge in the 1960s at an auction, did so thinking he was buying Tower Bridge and got a nasty surprise when, as far as he was concerned, the wrong bridge turned up in America. The man in question, Robert McCulloch, who had bought the bridge as a feature for the planned town of Lake Havasu City, Arizona, which he was developing at the time, was in London to make the winning bid and was an extremely successful businessman, so it seems unlikely he could have been that much of a fool.

The distinctive design of the bridge was actually the solution to the specific problem of how to increase the road traffic crossing the river in the east of the city without blocking the passage of tall ships to the wharves on the Upper Pool of the Thames, one of the busiest and most important parts of the Port of London and the furthest point of the river accessible to those ships. In the middle decades of the 19th century Britain was experiencing the height of the Industrial Revolution and London was at the centre of the British Empire. It was a booming city and the East End, the home of the workers who were making the boom happen, was expanding rapidly. London Bridge was the only crossing point of the Thames in the east of the city and the roads leading on to it were becoming terrible bottlenecks. In true Victorian fashion, a committee was formed to find the solution, which came in the shape of the bridge designed by the architect Horace John and his assistant John Wolfe-Barry. With an unshakeable confidence in the technology and engineering skills available at that time, they proposed to build a double-leaf bascule bridge, which, when it was built, would be the largest one of its type in the world by a considerable distance. The design involved the central span of the bridge splitting in the middle and its two leaves being raised to allow ships through, with the two piers holding the leaves standing in the river and being connected to the banks with suspension spans.

Bascule is the French word for a balance or a see-saw, which both work on the same principle, of a weight being moved by another weight on the other side of a pivot and, in Tower Bridge, there are weights in each of the piers to counterbalance the 1,000 ton weight of each of its leaves. The force required to raise them was originally supplied by water being pumped up into the towers under pressure by steam engines and stored in accumulators, so, when the bridge needed to be raised, the energy could be released instantly and, rather than having to wait while the water was pumped up the towers, the leaves could be raised in a few minutes by hydraulic pressure.

When the bridge opened in 1894, after an eight-year construction period, it was being raised to allow ships through something like 50 times a day. Over the years there have been a number of changes, with the steam engines being replaced with electric ones and the water-based hydraulic system with a modern one using oil, but the major change has been on the river itself. The Port of London, once the busiest port in the world, declined throughout the latter half of the 20th century as container ships took over the freight business and were mostly too large for the Thames. The docks and wharves fell into disuse and lay idle for many years, until an extensive programme of redevelopment began in the 1970s, when they converted into leisure facilities. The warehouses on the wharves are now commercial spaces and residential accommodation or have been knocked down and the land developed, as has been the case in London Docklands. The bridge itself remains in working order, but is used much less frequently, and the walkways towards the top of the towers, which were closed in 1911 after they had become notorious as places to pick up prostitutes, are now open again and are a popular tourist attraction. The river and the bridge have, in their individual ways, both adapted to suit these modern times.

FACT FILE

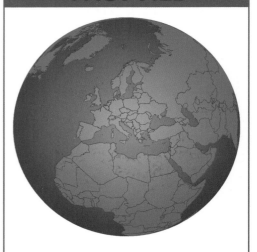

COORDINATES
51°30'20" N, 0°04'32" W

LOCATION
Thames river, London, United Kingdom

ARCHITECT
Horace Jones

CONSTRUCTION
1886–1894

ULURU – AYERS ROCK

Uluru/Ayers Rock, which is, as of 2002, its official name, is an enormous rock formation, visible from many miles around in an otherwise relatively flat desert, in the Northern Territory of Australia and is about 275 miles (440km) south-west of Alice Springs. It is 1,136ft (346m) high and about 2 miles (3.2km) long. The distance around the base is about 6 miles (9.4km) and it is roughly triangular in shape.

Uluru is the name the Pitjantjatjara people have always known it by and, since they have lived in the area for a very long time (archaeologists suggest people have lived at the site for in excess of 10,000 years), perhaps it is the most appropriate name. It was named Ayers Rock in 1873 in honour of Sir Henry Ayers who was, at that time, the Chief Secretary of South Australia.

In 1985 the Australian Government returned ownership of Uluru to the Pitjantjatjara and the Yankunytjatjara, a closely related group who also live in this area, under condition that it be leased back to the Uluru-Kata Tjuta National Park, who held the title to the land at that time, for 99 years. It is now managed jointly, becoming a model for collaborative land management projects throughout Australia. It is a sacred site for the Anangu (the name the indigenous people of this area prefer to be called, which means 'the people') and has great cultural significance for them. The Anangu belief system is closely intertwined with the landscape in which they live, which, according to these beliefs, was created by mythic ancestors, who moved around the land before people were created and left some of their spirit behind in the landscape features. Uluru contains many sacred sites, including springs, waterholes, caves and particular rock formations. There are also many significant rock paintings, both of ancient and more modern origin, as this form of art continues to be practised by the Anangu.

Geologists have a different way of thinking about Uluru. They say it is a huge sandstone outcrop of a much larger underground rock formation. Softer rock has eroded away from around the rock we see today, which has also weathered and eroded, leaving it scarred with channels, caves and ribs. It is of a dusty red colour because of the oxidation of iron minerals in the rock at the surface, which is grey underneath the rust, and it appears to change colour at different times of day, particularly at sunrise and sunset when it becomes a deep orangey-red and appears to glow, because the changing angle of the sun's rays as they hit the rock causes different wavelengths of light to be reflected from it. The rock is very hard, which prevents any plants from establishing themselves on it, and water, on the occasions when it rains in this desert environment, runs off it in the channels on the surface and collects in pools at the base of the rock. Patches of green vegetation grow around the pools, which are a haven for wildlife and are another feature revered by the Anangu.

Uluru, together with the National Park, is a UNESCO World Heritage Site, the designation recognising it as a place of cultural significance as well as an amazing natural phenomenon. It is one of the most popular tourist destinations in Australia. The Anangu welcome visitors but ask them to respect the entire area as a sacred site. One section of the rock is closed to visitors because it is still used for religious purposes and there are signs at various points requesting visitors not to take photographs of specific sacred features. They also request that people do not climb the rock, as they consider this to be sacreligious, but it is a request, not a demand, as the Anangu prefer to leave such decisions up to the individual. The nearest town where visitors can stay is Yulara, which is 11 miles (17km) away, just outside the park. Tours are organised from there and from Alice Springs as nobody, apart from the Anangu, is allowed to stay in the park overnight. After many years of being ignored in their own land, it is only relatively recently that the Anangu have gained recognition as the rightful custodians of Uluru and any visit can only be enriched by learning about their respect and reverence for the site.

FACT FILE

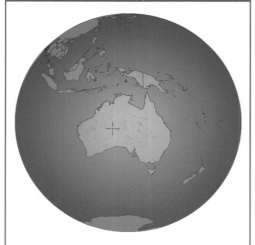

COORDINATES
25°20'41" S, 131°02'09" E

LOCATION
Uluru-Kata Tjuta National Park, Australia

FIRST NON-INDIGENOUS SITING
Ernest Giles – 1872

HEIGHT
1,135ft (346m) height,
5 miles (8km) around the base

VALLEY OF THE KINGS

The Theban Necropolis stands on the west bank of the Nile in Upper Egypt on the opposite side of the river from the ancient city of Thebes and the modern one of Luxor. It is an extensive complex of burial sites which was used throughout the period of the Ancient Egyptian civilisation, but particularly for about 500 years, from the 16th century BC to the 11th century BC, during what is known as the New Kingdom. The pharaohs of this period were buried in tombs cut into the rock walls of the sides of a dry river valley called Wadi Biban el Muluk and known in English as the Valley of the Kings. The pharaohs buried here are amongst the best known of all the pharaohs and include Tutankhamun and Ramesses II.

In what must be the most famous archaeological discovery ever made, the British archaeologist Howard Carter uncovered Tutankhamun's tomb, by far the best preserved tomb of a pharaoh found in the Valley of the Kings. Tutankhamun is not considered to have been a particularly significant pharaoh, reigning from 1333 BC to 1324 BC, coming to the throne at the age of about nine and dying in his late teens of what is now thought to have been gangrene after he had broken his leg badly. On becoming pharaoh his name changed from Tutankhaten to Tutankhamun, from the Living Image of Aten to the Living Image of Amun, reflecting a major religious shift at this period. Although it is not known exactly who his father was, it could have been the previous pharaoh Akenaten, who, it is thought, began the monotheistic worship of the god Aten, which would have meant a huge reduction in the priesthood and appears to have been highly unpopular. During Tutankhamun's reign, this was discontinued in favour of a return to the previous gods, including Amun, and it is thought, as Tutankhamun was so young, this decision would have been taken by his advisers, principal among whom was Ay, who would succeed him as pharaoh.

Tutankhamun was married to Ankhesenamen, who was the daughter of Akenaten and Nefertiti, and so could also have been his sister. Such incestuous relationships were not uncommon among the pharaohs and Ankhesenamen herself had previously been married to her father. The couple are known to have had two children, both stillborn and placed in Tutankhamun's tomb. His lack of standing as a pharaoh, or perhaps his death at an early age, probably accounts for the tomb being relatively small compared to the others in the valley. It consisted of five rooms with only the walls of the burial chamber being painted. The tomb appears to have been forgotten about shortly after it had been sealed, with the tomb of a later pharaoh built right on top of it and its location having not been found by tomb robbers. When Howard Carter entered it he was almost certainly the first person to do so for more than 3,000 years. The sarcophagus he found in the burial chamber contained three coffins, each placed within the next, with the last one being made of solid gold. Tutankhamun's mummy was wearing what has become the most recognisable

artefact of the ancient world, a solid gold mask, showing what is probably an idealised portrait of the young pharaoh and inlaid with semi-precious stones. Next to the burial chamber, Carter found a treasury containing beautiful gilded figures and a chest where Tutankhamun's internal organs, which had been removed during the mummification process, had been placed. The first room Carter came into from the entrance passageway was the antechamber, containing everything Tutankhamun would have needed for the afterlife. There were thrones, chariots, food and a range of other objects, and in the final room, known as the annex, there were more of these astonishing grave goods.

Ramesses II, or Ramesses the Great as he is often known, was a very different pharaoh from Tutankhamun. He was the third king of the 19th Dynasty, ruling from 1279 BC to 1213 BC, and living into his nineties. He had eight wives over the period of his reign, including Nefertari and Isetnfret and several of his daughters, and more than 100 children. He went on military campaigns, including against the Hittites in the Levant, and extended the Egyptian Empire south into Nubia. There are more monuments and statues remaining in Egypt today from his reign than from any other pharaoh, notably the Ramessuem, Abu Simbel and the Tomb of Nefertari, which contains the finest examples of Ancient Egyptian art ever found. Unfortunately his tomb in the Valley of the Kings was comprehensively robbed and, being situated quite low down on the valley wall, badly damaged by the flash floods that occasionally occur there. The treasures the tomb must have held, which would have put those of Tutankhamun in the shade, can only be guessed at now.

VATICAN

The State of the Vatican City, or simply the Vatican as it is often known, is the smallest independent nation in the world, covering an area of just 108 acres (44ha) and with only 558 citizens, and was created in 1929 by the Lateran Treaty, a settlement of the so-called Roman Question. During the early 19th century the independent states on the Italian peninsula began the long process of unification, which would eventually result in the modern state of Italy. One of the main impediments to the unification was the continued existence of the Papal States, the region of central Italy where the popes held temporal power, as the head of the state, as well as holding spiritual and pastoral primacy over the whole of the Roman Catholic Church. The Papal States began to fall to the unifying Italians, including Giuseppe Garibaldi, a military leader and one of the key figures of the unification, and, by 1860, the only part left was Rome and its immediate surrounding area, known as Latium. This was protected by a French garrison, who resisted all attempts to capture the city, until the start of the Franco-Prussian War when it was recalled to France by Napoleon III. Later that year an Italian army entered Rome with only a token resistance offered against them and it was swiftly annexed to Italy. The Italians offered some of the former area of the Latium to Pope Pius IX, including the Leonine City, within which the Vatican stands, but he refused to come to any form of settlement in the belief that by doing so he would have been legitimising the seizure

of the rest of the Papal States. He withdrew to the Vatican, claiming he was a prisoner, and his former residence, the Quirinal Palace, became the residence of the kings of Italy.

The stand-off between the Pope and the Italian Government continued for a further 59 years, with successive popes refusing to become citizens of the Italian State, while it refused to recognise the Vatican as an independent territory. Negotiations eventually began between the government and the Holy See in 1926 and, in 1929, resulted in the Lateran Treaty, signed by King Victor Emmanuel II and Prime Minister Benito Mussolini and, on behalf of the Pope, Cardinal Secretary of State Pietro Gasparri. As well as the creation of the State of the Vatican City, the treaty required the Holy See to maintain neutrality in its international relations and to accept a financial settlement for the loss of the Papal States. To commemorate the treaty, Mussolini commissioned the building of the Via Della Conciliazione, a street to symbolically link the Vatican with the centre of Rome.

The Vatican is separated from Rome by walls and the sides of buildings, except for St Peter's Square, where the border runs along its outer limit but is not marked by a physical barrier. It contains the Apostolic Palace, the official residence of the Pope, and St Peter's Basilica, one of the holiest places in all Christendom because it is held to be on the burial site of St Peter. It is one of the largest churches in the world and it is where the popes are buried, including, in 2005, Pope John Paul II.

The Sistine Chapel is part of the Apostolic Palace and takes its name from Pope Sixtus IV, who was Pontiff from 1471 to 1484. It has the same dimensions as the Temple of Solomon, as set out in the Old Testament, and the interior is decorated with paintings and frescoes by some of the great masters of Renaissance art, including Raphael, Botticelli and Perugino, but it is most renowned for its ceiling. This was painted by Michelangelo from 1508 to 1512, who initially turned down the commission because he considered himself a better sculptor than painter, but accepted after being given a wider degree of artistic freedom by Pope Julius II than was usual in such a setting. After a false start, during which the plaster he was using became mouldy and had to be scraped off, he painted more than 300 figures. The theme of the paintings is the salvation of mankind through the redemption offered by the Saviour. There are scenes from the Old Testament, of the Prophets and of the ancestors of Christ and the Virgin Mary, all leading towards the coming of Christ. There are also figures not taken from the Bible, mostly of naked men, and these depict a more humanist approach, which sees human beings as beautiful in their own right, without reference to God through the Church, although Michelangelo attempts to reconcile these views with the Catholic doctrine of original sin. His success in achieving this aim is open to debate, the position of his ceiling as one of the world's great works of art is not.

FACT FILE

COORDINATES
41°54' N, 12°27' E

LOCATION
Vatican City, Rome, Italy

AREA
0.17sq mi (0.44sq km)

POPULATION
790 (approx.)

INDEPENDENCE
11 February 1929

VENICE

The Venetian lagoon is separated from the northern end of the Adriatic Sea by a series of three long and narrow sandbars, Lido, Pellistrina and Treponti, with inlets between them which allow access to Venice and the other islands in the lagoon. The city of Venice stands on numerous low-lying islands, connected to each other by more than 400 bridges, and the channels between them have been dredged out to form the famous canals. The Grand Canal, the largest of these and the city's main waterway, snakes through the city and is lined by wonderful buildings. They mostly date from the 16th and 17th centuries, when Venice was at its height, and they form one of the greatest architectural vistas in the world. The islands are traditionally said to have first been inhabited by Roman refugees, fleeing from invading Visigoths, in the 5th century and, since then, over their long history, the Venetians have been intimately connected with the sea. Their consummate skill as sailors led to the development of a powerful navy and extensive maritime trade links, and they have had a constant battle against the water to prevent the city from sinking or from being washed away.

Venice has no natural resources and had to rely on its geographical position to develop as a centre for trade, becoming the European end of the Silk Road, the network of trade routes coming from the East. The Republic of Venice grew to dominate the commerce of the Mediterranean and became particularly associated with the spice trade. Marco Polo, generally thought of now as a traveller and explorer, came from a family of wealthy Venetian merchants and his journey took him along the Silk Road in the late 13th century. He was one of the first Westerners to travel its entire length, getting as far as China, where he met Kublai Khan, the ruler of the Mongol Empire and the grandson of Genghis Khan.

Its territories had expanded along the Adriatic coast and into the Mediterranean by the 15th century. Venice was the wealthiest state in Europe and its richest families were building elaborate and beautiful palaces along the Grand Canal in an effort to outdo each other and to show off their fabulous wealth. They built the navy up into one of the most powerful forces in Europe and it was frequently engaged in various wars and alliances, particularly with the other Maritime Republics of Amalfi, Pisa and Genoa. The rich were also great patrons of the arts and, over the next few centuries, its painters, Titian, Tintoretto, Bellini and Canaletto, and composers, Vivaldi and Albinoni, to name a few, would bring it fame as a centre of culture and it became one of the most elegant and refined cities in Europe.

By the 18th century the Ottoman Turks had expanded into the Mediterranean and had captured many of the territories formerly held by Venice. The overland trade routes from the East were declining, with the British and Dutch opening up alternative sea routes around Africa, and the city's wealth declined along with its commerce. The money to pay for the navy began to dry up and, in 1797, Napoleon Bonaparte captured the formerly impregnable city, ending more than 1,000 years of the Republic. It became part of the Kingdom of Lombardy-Venetia, under Austrian rule after Napoleon's defeat in 1814 and then, as a consequence of the Austro-Prussian War in 1866, in which the emerging Kingdom of Italy sided with Prussia, it was finally incorporated into Italy.

The declining fortunes of Venice meant that its old buildings have never been replaced and its decaying grandeur is what makes it so attractive today, as it did for Lord Byron, who lived in the city for a number of years and gave the Bridge of Sighs its name. As well as the Grand Canal there are St Mark's Square, the Rialto Bridge, the Ca' d'Oro, the Doge's Palace and many other beautiful buildings. The total absence of cars from the city is another of its attractions and people get around by walking or on the vaporetti, the waterbuses, unless they are feeling particularly rich or romantic and take a gondola. These days the city is increasingly subjected to flooding, particularly during what the Venetians call the acqua alta, the spring tides, when the water is at its highest and wellington boots become the preferred form of footware. Efforts are constantly being made to protect the city. Freshwater extraction from artesian wells has been stopped because it was causing the city to sink and there are currently controversial plans to build a system of movable barriers that can be raised when the tides are high. The city's close involvement with water is what has led to it becoming so beautiful, but in years to come it could also be the cause of its destruction.

FACT FILE

COORDINATES
45°26'17" N, 12°20'08" E

LOCATION
Grand Canal, Venice, Italy

AREA
159sq mi (412sq km)

POPULATION
271,251 (2004)

VERSAILLES

On the death of Louis XIII, in 1643, his four-year-old son acceded to the throne as Louis XIV, beginning a reign that would last for 72 years. During this time France would become the dominant nation in Europe and Louis XIV would assume the role of an absolute monarch, becoming known as the Sun King. During the period of his minority, his mother, Anne of Austria, held power as Regent, although she delegated this to her chief minister, Cardinal Mazarin. A period of civil war between rival elements of the aristocracy, known as the Fronde, dominated much of the period, and, as Louis approached his majority, he announced he would take control of the government himself. He began to look for a place outside Paris, where he could be away from the influence of his advisers and could establish his own court. After the death of Mazarin in 1661 and on gaining majority shortly afterwards, Louis, much to the surprise of the government and aristocracy, did exactly as he said he would do and, declaring he would be his own Prime Minister, assumed absolute power.

His father had bought a hunting lodge at Versailles, just outside Paris, and begun work to expand it. Louis decided to settle his court there and engaged the architect Louis Le Vau, the landscape designer André Le Notre and the artist Charles Le Brun to oversee the work, which began in 1661. His plan was to move the entire government to his court at Versailles, an ambition it would take almost 20 years to fully realise, so that he could have everything in one place and under his direct control.

When he had finally achieved this, he reduced the aristocracy's influence in the country by requiring them to spend long periods of time at the court. France, for the first time, approximated towards a nation state rather than a collection of feudal powers competing with each other and putting their own regional requirements before those of France. The downside of this was that Louis' lavish lifestyle, innumerable wars and increasingly ambitious building plans almost bankrupted the country, and the establishment of an absolute monarchy, which became increasingly profligate and dissolute, and, at Versailles, increasingly divorced from reality, would be a major factor in the French Revolution, which would begin less than 80 years after Louis' death.

Building work at Versailles continued throughout Louis' life and shows the influences of different people, not always working along the same lines. It would become the largest palace in Europe and modifications continued under Louis XV and Louis XVI, until the latter was forced to return to Paris at the start of the French Revolution in 1789. The revolutionary government ransacked the palace, selling off the furniture and moving the art works to the museum they had established in the Louvre. Versailles fell into disuse and disrepair, only being saved from complete demolition by the short-lived restoration of the monarchy from 1830 to 1848, when King Louis-Philippe provided funds for its maintenance. He established it as a museum in 1837, but serious restoration work would not begin for almost another 100 years. In the 1960s Pierre Verlot, a well-known scholar and writer on

the history of French furniture, began the process of getting the furnishings back from museums and French government buildings, a project that is still going on today. The Royal Apartments are now something like they would have been during the Sun King's reign and are open to the public.

One of the best known rooms in the palace that has also been restored is the Hall of Mirrors. It is a long gallery with something like 400 mirrors covering the entire surface of the walls and a highly decorated ceiling, painted by Le Brun and depicting scenes in which Louis XIV appears in the guises of a Roman emperor and other such historical figures. It was also where the Proclamation of the German Empire was signed, during the siege of Paris towards the end of the Franco-Prussian War, which established King Wilhelm I of Prussia as the emperor of a united Germany. A few days later the French surrendered and an armistice was signed between the two countries, also at Versailles. The Treaty of Frankfurt formally ended the war and, among its settlements, ceded Alsace-Lorraine to Germany, leading to a great deal of resentment in France and becoming one of the contributory factors to the outbreak of the First World War. In an ironic twist of fate, not lost on the French or the Germans, the Treaty of Versailles was also signed in the Hall of Mirrors in 1919, which officially ended the First World War and restored Alsace-Lorraine to France. The terms of this treaty would, in their turn, sow some of the seeds of the Second World War.

FACT FILE

COORDINATES
48°48'16" N, 2°07'18" E

LOCATION
Versailles, France

CONSTRUCTION
1st building campaign: 1664–1668
2nd building campaign: 1669–1672
3rd building campaign: 1678–1684
4th building campaign: 1701–1710

VICTORIA FALLS

The Zambezi, one of the great rivers of Africa, rises in Zambia and flows south towards Namibia and Botswana and then turns east, forming the entire length of the border between Zambia and Zimbabwe before continuing on through Mozambique and emptying into the Indian Ocean. In its upper reaches many other rivers run into it and it becomes very wide, although it remains relatively shallow, and, at about midway along its course, on the border between Zambia and Zimbabwe, it tumbles over a 360ft (120m) precipice into a narrow chasm to form the Victoria Falls, one of the most spectacular sights in the whole of Africa. The river is more than a mile (1.6km) wide at this point and the water drops in a continuous curtain into the chasm, which is only 400ft (120m) wide, creating a huge plume of spray that can be seen for many miles and with a tremendous roar from the falling water, the sound amplified further as it echoes off the opposite rock face of the chasm. Its name in the Mokololo language is Mosi-oa-Tunya, which means the Smoke that Thunders, and it is not hard to known why it was called this by the local people.

The falls have formed over many thousands of years where the river has eroded down into a narrow fault of softer rock running through the hard basalt plateau of this area. It would have originally formed a narrow waterfall of swiftly flowing water many miles downstream from where it is now, which eroded back through the fault leaving a deep zigzagging gorge, through which the river now flows. At the site of the falls, the the fault turns at a ninety degree-angle and the water has, at some point, begun to fall over the wall of the gorge rather than continuing to fall as a narrow waterfall, forming the wide expanse of water that now crashes into the chasm. At the western end of the falls themselves, the water has eroded down into the lip of the precipice, where it is beginning to form a further section of the gorge. The water flows out of the chasm at a single point, which is only about 100ft (30m) wide, and forms a short stretch of the gorge known as the Boiling Point because, when the volume of water passing through it is high during the rainy season, it becomes highly turbulent.

After the Boiling Point the gorge turns sharply to the west and is crossed by the Victoria Falls Bridge, which carries a road and rail link between the towns of Victoria Falls in Zimbabwe and Livingston in Zambia. It was originally built to form a link in an ambitious plan, envisaged by Cecil Rhodes, to develop the Cape to Cairo Railway, which would link a continuous line of British colonies all the way through the length of the African continent by rail. Political and financial problems made this impossible when it was first attempted by Rhodes at the end of the 19th century, but the idea is still alive and may one day be realised, although, of course, it no longer has anything to do with the British Empire.

The falls were named after Queen Victoria in 1855 by David Livingstone, the first European to see them. Livingstone had originally come to Africa in 1841 as a missionary and his stated purpose in life was to bring Christianity, commerce and civilisation to central Africa. The mission where he was working closed in 1852 and he began to explore the Zambezi to find out if it was navigable for commercial traffic, coming across Victoria Falls in the process. On his return to England in 1857 he published a book called *Missionary Travels and Researches in South Africa*, in which he writes of the falls: 'scenes so lovely must have been gazed on by angels in their flight'. The book made his name and he returned to Africa at the head of a large expedition to explore the Zambezi further. The expedition was something of a disaster and the river proved to be unnavigable, due to a series of cataracts and rapids, and Livingstone turned his attention to finding the source of the Nile. He considered he had found its headwaters with the discovery of the Lualaba River, but further exploration by Henry Morton Stanley proved it was actually connected to the Congo not the Nile. Stanley would be a central character in the best known incident in Livingstone's life, which occurred after he had disappeared in Africa and had not been heard from for six years. Stanley was contracted by the *New York Herald* newspaper to find Livingstone and, according to Stanley's journal, on finding him near Lake Tanganyika, he said 'Dr Livingstone, I presume', creating an epigram still in use today.

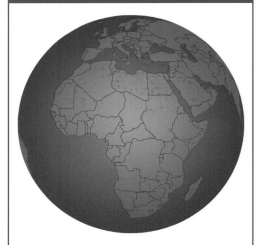

FACT FILE

COORDINATES
17°55'24" S, 25°51'22" E

LOCATION
Zambezi River, Mosi-oa-Tunya National Park, Zambia and Victoria Falls National Park, Zimbabwe

SIZE
360ft (108m) high, 5,577ft (1,700m) wide

HIGHEST RECORDED FLOW RATE
444,965ft³/s (12,600m³/s)

WHITE HOUSE

At the end of the American Revolutionary War, generally known in Britain as the American War of Independence, in 1783, George Washington, the Commander-in-Chief of the victorious American forces, resigned his commission and retired to Mount Vernon, his plantation estate on the banks of the Potomac River in Virginia. A few years later he was persuaded to return to public life because it was felt that the Constitutional Convention needed a prestigious man to be its president, which he duly became. On 17 September 1787 the convention ratified the US Constitution and this, together with the ten amendments of the Bill of Rights and the addition of a further 17 amendments over the years, remains the supreme law of the United States of America. Article Two of the constitution established the requirement for a President of the United States and, in 1789, Washington was elected to the post, the only person to have done so by a unanimous vote of the Electoral College.

To stop a number of states competing with each other to become the home state of a new capital city for the country, the constitution contained a section specifying the creation of a separate federal district, not under the jurisdiction of a particular state. Washington chose the site of the District of Columbia, as it was to be known, on the banks of the Potomac River about seven miles (11km) upstream from Mount Vernon. Many reasons have been given for this choice, and it is as good a place as any for a capital city, but Washington was a farmer, as well as the President, and being close to his estate must have had a bearing on his decision. Land from both sides of the river, formerly parts of the states of Maryland and Virginia, were given to the federal government and plans for the city, which would become Washington D.C., were drawn up. It was built entirely on the north bank of the Potomac and the unused land on the south bank of the river was returned to Virginia,

FACT FILE

COORDINATES
38°53'51" N, 77°02'11" W

LOCATION
1600 Pennsylvania Avenue, Washington D.C. United States of America

CONSTRUCTION
1792–1800

ARCHITECT
James Hoban

including where the city of Alexandria now stands and Arlington County, the location of the Arlington National Cemetery and the Pentagon.

Having established the site of the new capital city, Washington needed an official residence. He held a competition to find a design and chose the one submitted by the Irish architect James Hoban, who had emigrated to America a few years previously. It was based on Leinster House, then the Dublin residence of the Duke of Leinster and,

since 1922, the parliament building of the Republic of Ireland, containing both the upper and lower houses, the Seanad and the Dáil. Washington had the plans revised to make the building larger and construction began with the laying of the first cornerstone on 13 October 1792. Building records kept at the time show that the foundations were dug and built by slaves and much of the rest of the building work was done by Scottish, Irish and Italian immigrants, many of whom were not US citizens at the time. It was built of sandstone and this was rendered with a lime-based plaster, leading to the informal name for the building of the White House, which would later become its official title during Theodore Roosevelt's presidency and has become a metonym for the president's entire administration as well as the name of his residence.

The building has been extended a number of times since George Washington's day and the exterior appearance was changed particularly by the addition of the columned porticoes on both the north and south façades of the building in the 1820s, giving it a much more American look, rather

than having the appearance of being a Georgian country mansion, as previously. Subsequent enlargements have either been underground or have been hidden behind landscape features and, although extensive, have not changed the appearance of the building all that much. The main parts of the complex are formed by three sections, with, in its centre, the Executive Residence, the original part of the building, which contains the rooms where the president actually lives when he is in residence. Other rooms, including the Red Room, the Blue Room and the Green Room, are used for various ceremonial occasions and for entertaining. The West Wing, popularised by the TV show of the same name, is a large extension linked to the residence by a colonnade and it contains the president's own office, the Oval Office, and the offices of his senior staff and the Cabinet Room. On the other side of the building is the East Wing, which was originally built in 1942 to hide the construction of an underground bunker, the Presidential Emergency Operations Centre, and now houses the offices of the First Lady.